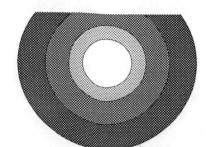

EVERYTHING UNDER THE SUN

EVERYTHING UNDER THE SUN

AN ANTHOLOGY FOR YOUNG TEENS
Edited by Sheryl Prenzlau

TARGUM/FELDHEIM

First published 1993

Copyright © 1993 by Targum Press
ISBN 1-56871-020-8 h.c.
ISBN 1-56871-021-6 s.c.

Phototypeset at Targum Press

Printing plates by Frank, Jerusalem

Published by:
Targum Press Inc.
22700 W. Eleven Mile Rd.
Southfield, Mich. 48034

Distributed by:
Feldheim Publishers
200 Airport Executive Park
Spring Valley, N.Y. 10977

Distributed in Israel by:
Targum Press Ltd.
POB 43170
Jerusalem 91430

Printed in Israel

This book is dedicated in loving memory of
my dear parents

לאה חיה בת הרב יקותיאל רפאל הלוי ע״ה
and
יוסף ברוך בן הרב פסח ע״ה

Leah and Joseph B. Wachsman ע״ה
of Far Rockaway, N.Y.
who always taught me to try my best

Av 5753 / July 1993
Sheryl Wachsman Prenzlau

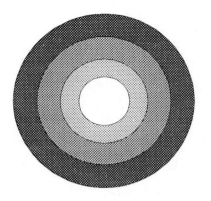

Contents

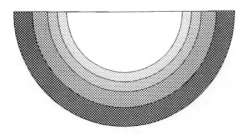

Welcome Aboard

What's your favorite color?

Magenta, perhaps? Royal blue? A warm shade of peach? Or maybe something more basic? Red? Green? Yellow?

You want to know my favorite color?

I'll tell you anyway.

My favorite color is black. And white.

Black print. White paper. The ingredients of a written story. Magic ingredients that can cast a spell, weave a web, transport a body through space and time.

Lately, the written word has been getting something of a bad name. How can the stuff of textbooks and homework compare to glittering computer graphics and realistic, space-age imagery that even makes the right sounds? With a computer, you can relay information and letters instantaneously from one end of the globe to the other. You can fight space invaders (or runaway dinosaurs, or black knights, or any one of a thousand other bad guys) with the press of a button. You can build, destroy, paint, make music, make war.

All you can do with a book is turn the pages.

Right?

Wrong.

There's a lot more to the written word than just —
words. With a good story, you can float on a cloud and look
down at the bustling figures far, far below. You can visit
worlds of the past and future. Maybe best of all, you can see
your very own world through other eyes, other experiences
— and perhaps understand yourself a little bit better.

You may think you are simply holding a four-hundred-
page book (and wow, is it ever heavy!), but not quite. We've
called it an anthology, which means a collection of all sorts
of things. But it's much more. For one thing, it's a time
machine. Don't believe me? Check out the section called
"Long Ago and Far Away." You'll go back centuries in an
instant.

If time travel makes you nervous, you can stay put and
meet some very extraordinary people inside these pages.
There's "Friends and Strangers," a section chock-full of interesting girls and boys. Or "Family Circle," where mothers and
fathers and sisters and brothers figure out how to get along.

One great thing about an anthology is that there's
something in it for every taste and mood. Whether you want
to laugh, cry, think, or learn, you can find something to help
you here in this book. Some of you may want to begin with
the first story and carefully make your way through the book,
piece by piece, word by word. That's fine. Others may prefer
what I call the "butterfly" method of reading: flitting gracefully from one story to the next, sipping the nectar of which-
ever appeals to you. (Yes, I know butterflies don't sip nectar,
but I liked the idea so I rearranged nature a bit. See what
you can do when you're working with words?!)

Whatever way you choose, one thing is certain: You are
beginning a journey into other realms, other times, other

lives. The only tickets you need are your eyes and your mind; the only vehicle you'll use is your imagination.

Have a great trip! And don't forget to write!

Miriam Zakon
Targum Press

GROWING PAINS

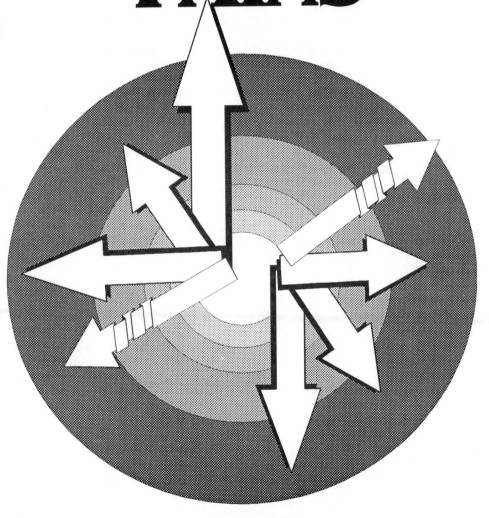

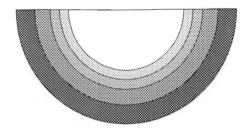

The Game

Zev Spektor

Yitzchok was exasperated. He'd been sure that this month would be the one in which he made the honor roll. But as usual, someone else had received the honor. Life wasn't fair! He'd even told his parents that he was going to be on the honor roll. Now, he'd have to tell them that he was mistaken. How embarrassing! Actually, it was worse than embarrassing. He'd be letting his parents down. Why had he even mentioned the silly honor roll?

The books he was carrying felt heavy in the moist heat of June. He wished he could just drop them right there on the street. English studies were almost over for the year anyway. It was much too hot for schoolbooks. Not that Yitzchok didn't like books; he loved them. But not schoolbooks. Those he could do without.

A muffled ringing startled him. He stopped and turned to see the neighborhood ice cream truck. The driver smiled.

"You don't eat this stuff, do you, kid?"

The author, who is using a pseudonym, studies in a Brooklyn *kollel*. He has also written *The Last Wagon Out* and *Shadows in the Night*.

"Not if it isn't kosher," said Yitzchok, imagining the cold taste of vanilla ice cream as he wiped his sweaty brow.

"Too bad," said the driver as he turned to some children who had appeared near the truck.

Yitzchok resumed his trek home. Life just wasn't fair!

When he got home, his mother asked the dreaded question. "Well, did you get onto the honor roll?" Her eyes looked so proud.

Yitzchok hated himself as he said, "Not this time."

"That's okay, Yitzchok. Maybe next time. As long as you try your best."

He wondered if his mother really meant it, or if she was actually disappointed. "It's not fair," he said. "I was supposed to get on this time. The teacher has something against me."

"Yitzchok, you heard what I told you. All that matters is that you try your best. The honor roll doesn't mean anything."

Yitzchok put his books down on the couch dejectedly. Then, brightening slightly, he remembered about moving. "Well, what happened with the house, Mom? Are we going to move?"

Now it was his mother's turn to look embarrassed. "Abba and I went to speak with the people who are selling the house today. It looks like we'll be staying here in the apartment a little while longer."

"But what about the big room with the desk which you said was going to be for me?"

"I'm sorry, Yitzchok. We wanted the house too, but we just can't afford it right now."

He wanted to argue the point further, but he could see that his mother felt as badly about the house as he did. Wasn't anything about life fair? With tears welling up in his eyes, he fled to the privacy of his room. It was small, but it would have to do for now. Twelve was far too old to be seen crying.

"Don't worry, Yitzchok," his mother called after him. "We'll be moving soon."

About an hour after he'd gone to his room, there was a knock on the door. "Come in," he said. It was his father, holding a small paper bag.

"I have something for you, Yitzchok."

"What is it?"

"Do you know Mr. Zamsky from shul?"

"Yes, he's the one who takes care of the *aliyos*."

"That's right. Last month his father passed away. He'd been going through his father's things and found this. Since he has no children, he thought maybe you'd like to have it."

Yitzchok sat up on his bed. His father opened the bag. "It's a game that Mr. Zamsky's father used to play with in Europe. He got it from his father, so it's quite old."

"A game? I didn't know they had games so long ago."

His father smiled. "Sure they did. Of course, the games then weren't as sophisticated as those of today." He pulled a round object from the bag and then reached in for a little ball.

"Why, it's a puzzle of some sort."

"Yes, you put the ball here, and then you try to roll it into the hole in the middle."

Yitzchok leaned forward to examine the plaything. It looked old, and it was made of wood. It certainly didn't look like a game. He took it in his hands. "What's this?" he asked, noticing Hebrew letters scratched into the wood.

"It says, 'Moshe.' "

"Yes, Abba, it does. Who was Moshe?"

"Mr. Zamsky doesn't know. Perhaps he was the original owner."

"It's interesting. Can I try it?"

"Certainly, Yitzchok. It's yours."

Yitzchok looked at the game. "Did you see this scratch, Abba?"

"Yes, it must have fallen once and chipped."

His father got up. "Yitzchok, Mommy tells me that you were upset about us not buying that house."

Yitzchok shrugged.

"We'll be moving soon, Yitzchok. Just be patient. And about the honor roll, it's not important. You know that. You know you're doing well, don't you?"

"Yes."

"Well, then, who needs the honor roll? Okay?"

"Okay," said Yitzchok, forcing a smile.

"Be down for supper in a few minutes," said his father as he left the room.

To himself, Yitzchok said, "And what about the ice cream truck and everything else? Why is everything so unfair?"

After supper and homework, Yitzchok tried the game and discovered that it was really fun. He tried hard to get the ball into its place at the center, but it wasn't easy. Too soon, it was time to go to sleep. He put the game on the nightstand next to his bed and switched off his bed lamp. Whoever Moshe had been, he must have enjoyed this game, Yitzchok thought as he drifted off. It had been a long and sometimes frustrating day, and Yitzchok was tired. In minutes he was asleep.

*   *   *

...His name was Moshe, and he was sitting on a large, wooden chair in a low-ceilinged, dimly lit room. His mother was pacing back and forth nervously. It wasn't really his mother — it was Moshe's mother, and he was Moshe. His mother glanced at him, and he could see how truly frightened she was. In fact, he himself was terrified.

"When will your father be home?" his mother asked in Yiddish.

Yitzchok didn't understand Yiddish very well, but he seemed to understand it now. "Any second, Mama. He will come any second."

Outside there was the tumult of terror. Men, women, and children were locking doors and windows. People were trying to get off the streets as quickly as they could. He looked at his mother and then down at himself and saw that they were dressed in olden-style clothes.

"He must come home soon. He mustn't be on the street when they come," said his mother, her voice weak from strain.

"Mama, Tatta will be here before they come. He will, I promise you." He could feel the terror in his throat and in his heart. He'd never felt so afraid.

He got up and went to a rough, wooden cupboard. Opening it, he saw the game. It was brand-new. His grandfather had just given it to him yesterday, and he'd chiseled out his name on it. His grandfather was a merchant who traveled far and wide. And he often brought back wonderful souvenirs from the lands he visited. Moshe took the toy and closed the cupboard. He returned to the chair and looked up at his mother. She was now sitting at the table, saying *tehillim*.

He, too, whispered a *kapitel* of *tehillim*, begging Hashem that his father return to the house before the pogrom began. There was no telling what would happen if the wild mob found him on the street.

"Moishele, he isn't coming," said his mother, her face white.

"Maybe he is taking shelter with a neighbor," he suggested.

His mother's face relaxed ever so slightly. "Yes, perhaps you're right." And then she returned to her *tehillim*.

Outside, it was now nearly quiet. The entire Jewish quarter were locked and bolted into their homes. Moshe prayed that his father was safe.

"It's me, Miriam, quickly open the door!"

Moshe's mother rushed to the door. *"Baruch Hashem,* it's him!"

His father entered and quickly shut the door. "The mob is almost here. Have you shuttered all the windows?"

"Yes, Avremel."

"All right then," said Moshe's father, "we will recite *tehillim* together." He took the *tehillim* from the table where his wife had left it and began reciting the ancient words. After each *pasuk*, his wife and son repeated after him.

The mob came with a roar, shrieking, laughing, and smashing. Moshe could smell burning wood. He could hear terrified animals. Worst of all, he could hear the cries of his neighbors as their doors were broken down.

"Will they try to break into here, Avremel?" asked his mother quietly.

"It's not in our hands," said his father, and he continued saying *tehillim*.

The noise of the axe blow nearly knocked Moshe out of his chair. The game dropped from his hand and fell to the hard floor. He saw that it had been scratched on one side. He turned towards the door in time to see the axe brutally chop through it again. His father got behind their big, wooden table and began to push.

"Help me, Moishele! Help me push the table up against the door."

He ran to his father's side and pushed with all his might. Outside, the air was filled with smoke and the sound of demons — demons in human clothing who delighted in breaking down the doors of Jewish homes.

A third hole was smashed in the door, sending wood splinters everywhere. And then, with deafening silence, the axe fell no more. The noise began to diminish.

"The police have decided to stop them for now," said Moshe's father. *"Baruch Hashem,* we were spared."

"But what of the neighbors?" asked Moshe.

*   *   *

"...what of the neighbors?"

Yitzchok sat up in his bed. His room was dark. In the moonlight, he could see the wooden game. The name Moshe faced him, and on the other side was the scratch. His heart pounded. A dream? But it had felt like no other dream he'd ever had. Could a dream possibly be so real?

Relief washed over him as he took in the familiar surroundings of his bedroom. Dream or...what? It had to have been a dream. What else could it have been? Had he somehow viewed a scene in Moshe's life, or had it all been in his imagination? He wasn't sure. One thing, however, was certain. His life was not nearly as unfair as he'd thought it was.

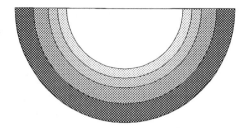

Dare to Dream

Beth Firestone

Maggie sat in the window seat halfway down the stairs, watching the rain fall. The yellow and white checkered cushion was worn from where she'd sat so many times, and the corners were torn from hours of habitual picking. The paint was chipping off the side of the panes. Something about this spot had always calmed her and helped her to think.

For as long as she could remember, this was the spot she came to to sort things out when life got confusing, as it often did, when things just weren't going the way she wanted them to. For as long as she could remember, the faded, white curtains had wiped the tears from her eyes, like a patient, understanding friend, always ready to listen. And for as long as she could remember, Maggie thought today as she watched the rain fall harder and harder against the glass, she'd only had one dream...to be a dancer. And now that

---

"I am the author of *Candles in My Window*. I live in Los Angeles with my husband and three daughters. I began keeping a journal in seventh grade and have enjoyed writing ever since. 'Dare to Dream' recalls the days when, as a young girl, I dreamed of being a ballerina." — BETH FIRESTONE

dream was being taken away from her.

Did they really expect her just to sweep it away like some broken vase? Did they really expect her to throw it all away like some outgrown dress? How had her life come to this?

At first it had all seemed so innocent. Her parents had wanted to light Shabbos candles on Friday nights and have a family dinner. A year later her mother had decided to keep a kosher kitchen. Maggie had helped her shop for new pots and pick out the pattern for the dishes. It had been kind of fun to do things a little differently. It had made her feel somehow more Jewish, and, to her surprise, she liked that.

Perhaps, thought Maggie, she should have seen the writing on the wall three years later, when she was eleven years old. She could remember the day well when her parents had announced that the family would be *shomer Shabbos.* Well, they didn't actually announce it. In all fairness, they'd called a family meeting to discuss what this implied. They had wanted Maggie and her little brother to understand that without Shabbos the Jewish people wouldn't survive. They had talked about how special and holy this day was. They described it as a day to stop and get off the "treadmill" of life, to be together with family and friends, to take time to think about God and pray. They talked about how sad they were that they had all missed out on so many years of Shabbaos. They talked about themselves as being *baalei teshuvah* — Jews who were returning to Orthodox Judaism.

At first it hadn't sounded so bad the way her parents described it. But when she and her brother learned that they couldn't watch T.V., listen to music, or go to ballet class or baseball practice on Shabbos...boy, her parents sure heard protests then.

But even that had worked itself out with time. They'd

arranged for her brother to play ball on Sundays with a group of Orthodox boys, and Maggie made up for her missed ballet class by taking two classes on Monday. Gradually she had gotten used to the Shabbos routine, and she had even learned to like it. Sometimes she'd invite a friend from school to spend the night, but eventually she started making new friends at the shul she and her parents started attending on Saturdays. She grew to really look forward to the long, quiet, lazy afternoons, no phones ringing, no music blaring, no homework, no household chores...just reading a good book or taking a long walk with her friends or even her family.

Their lives had changed so much, in fact, that when Maggie's parents asked her how she felt about changing from public school to a private Jewish day school, Maggie agreed. It felt like the right thing to do. She knew a lot of the girls already from shul, and, luckily, she wasn't shy and had made new friends easily. A Hebrew tutor had helped her the summer before the switch, and even though she was a little behind at first, by the end of her first year she had caught up. She liked her new school and new friends. Thank God, those changes had worked out all right.

There'd been other changes, too. At first she'd put up a fight, but eventually she'd gotten used to them. Like not being able to wear whatever she wanted to wear. She was prepared to wear a uniform to her new school. But when she learned that she could no longer wear shorts or pants...give up her blue jeans? No way! The day she found this out, she ran all the way home from school and burst into angry tears.

"Why didn't you tell me?" she cried, furious at her mother.

"I was getting to it, sweetheart. I just thought that you'd already made so many changes. I wanted you to take it slowly."

"You were scared to tell me," Maggie accused.

"Scared? Of what?" her mother, ever so patient, inquired.

"Scared I'd finally run away from home, like I should have a long time ago!" Maggie cried out, running to her room.

She didn't talk to her mother for two days after that. Finally, when she calmed down, she and her mother had one of their famous heart-to-heart talks. This one was about the Jewish idea of modesty.

"It's like all the other changes we've made — all the other mitzvos we've taken on," her mother explained. "The way a Jewish woman dresses is yet another area of her life in which she can better serve the Almighty."

"Kind of like keeping kosher and saying *brachos*?" Maggie said, feeling like she was beginning to understand. After all, if Jews even turned going to the bathroom into an opportunity to say a *brachah*, then it wasn't really that outrageous to turn the way a person dresses into an opportunity to serve Hashem, was it?

"Exactly," her mother said, pleased. "You see, you're more than just a pretty face and, in your case, a well-toned body. You're a daughter of Israel...a *bas Yisrael*. This is something you can be very proud of. Think of the Queen of England. She must always dress appropriately for the occasion because every eye is upon her. She must dress with dignity, as a queen should."

"But I'm not royalty."

"That's where you're wrong. Every *bas Yisrael* is a princess in the eyes of Hashem. When you dress modestly, you are making yourself something Hashem and the Jewish people can be proud of."

"I don't see why wearing skirts instead of pants makes someone any more modest," Maggie said, still wary about giving up her beloved wardrobe, especially her blue jeans.

"That's because we've become used to dressing immodestly. But I can assure you from experience that once you change the way you dress, you become much more sensitive to the lack of modesty all around you. After you've been dressing more modestly for a while, you'll see how self-conscious you feel when you try wearing what you used to wear. Believe me, I know."

Come to think of it, Maggie hadn't seen her mother in pants for some time now. It had never really registered that her mother had changed the way she dressed, probably because she'd done it gradually, like everything else in their ever-changing lives. As a matter of fact, gone were all her mother's short skirts, too.

"But I can't just change like that," Maggie said, snapping her fingers.

"You'll take it slowly," her mother reassured her. "The important thing is to keep your eye on the big picture. Remember why you're putting yourself through these changes. You see, when a woman dresses in a way that calls attention to her body, that's what people will notice about her. And even worse, that's what she'll value most about herself. But when she dresses modestly, it's as if she's giving others a message that she values what's inside herself the most, and so should they. And the truth is, when there are no flashy, revealing clothes to draw people's attention to her body, what do you think will happen?"

Maggie thought for a moment. "I guess they'll probably just be interested in her for who she is, not for how she looks."

"Precisely," her mother said with a big smile on her face. "Judaism teaches that what we should value most about a person is what's inside — the *neshamah*. Do you understand?"

And indeed, with time, Maggie had come to a better understanding of the role modesty played in a Jewish girl's life. Her mother had taken her out to buy new clothes, too, so that had made the transition easier. She really did start to feel differently about herself, and she liked the feeling, even if she did still wear her favorite old pair of blue jeans around the house sometimes.

But this was going too far. How could they expect her to quit doing the thing she loved best in all the world? Life without dance would be like...like life without flowers, and sunsets, and chocolate-chip ice cream, and good music, and...they might as well ask her never to smile or laugh again. They might as well just ask her to stop breathing.

Maggie wiped away her tears with the curtain, but they wouldn't stop. Eventually, the drape was so soggy that she just let the tears roll down her cheek and sink into the old cushion.

The next morning, Maggie was so tired from crying half the night that she slept through her alarm. Her mother peeked into her room.

"Mag, it's already 9:30. Come on, I'll take you to school."

"I'm not going."

"Are you sick?"

"I guess you could call it that."

Her mother came over and sat down on her bed. She reached over to stroke Maggie's hair, but the girl pulled the covers over her head.

"I know this was a real blow to you, honey," her mother said, "and I'm really sorry. I know how you feel."

"How can you know how I feel?" Maggie said from under her covers, starting to cry again.

"Why do you think your father and I waited this long to tell you? We put it off and put it off."

"Just go away."

"We put it off until we couldn't anymore. You're going to be fourteen in a few weeks. You're not a little girl anymore.

I guess we should have told you when you became bas mitzvah."

Maggie sat up angrily. Her eyes were puffy and swollen. She could see from the expression on her mother's face that it hurt her to see her daughter so upset. But feel her pain? No way. If her parents really knew how she felt, they'd let her keep dancing, no matter what Judaism said.

"Why did you and Dad have to go and change and drag us along with you?" Maggie demanded.

"Maggie, you're upset and angry. You're going to say things you don't mean," her mother said.

"I do mean them. I just want to dance. That's all I've ever wanted."

Her mother rose and walked to the door. "Stay home from school today. We'll talk later, after you've calmed down." With that, she closed the door and left Maggie alone.

Maggie stayed in her room all day. When her mother came by in the late afternoon with some food, she found Maggie still under the covers, head and all.

"Mag, please eat something. You must be starving."

"I'm not hungry."

"I thought at least you'd want to go to ballet. There's still time."

Her parents had given her two weeks to keep dancing. They said this would give her a chance to ease out and say goodbye to her instructor and friends. But Maggie thought this was a terrible idea. How could she go to class and give it her all, when she knew it was all for nothing?

"You just don't understand," she said, starting to cry all over again.

"Maybe I don't, Mag. Why don't you explain?"

Maggie knew when her mother was trying to get her to talk. Well, it wasn't going to work today.

"Okay, I'll go," Maggie said, getting out of bed. It was better than staying here, where she was beginning to suffocate from all the shoulds and can'ts and dos and don'ts. Maggie moved to her dresser and opened her top drawer. The one she had opened so many times before. The one filled to the brim with her many tights and leotards, knitted bun nets and hair ribbons, ballet slippers and toe shoes. She fought hard not to burst into tears again as she got herself dressed for class.

Over the next few days, Maggie felt more like a robot than a human being. She got up, got dressed, went to school, and came home just because that's what she always did and she had no choice. She'd lost her appetite completely, and she had no patience to sit and do her homework. Her parents kept their distance, "giving her space," as they called it. Thank God for that. The only thing she looked forward to was going to ballet each day after school.

On Thursday, Maggie stood at the barre in her ballet class, doing *developées*. Sweat was dripping from her face and neck and down her back. She was used to working hard. She looked in the mirror and was pleased with what she saw. How far she had come. How hard she had worked to perfect her form. With a scrutinizing eye she straightened her back a bit, tightened her knee just a little more, and pointed her foot a little harder.

"Beautiful, Maggie. Good work," her instructor, Mrs. Clark, called as she walked over to her. "Now, keep that form and take it to the side," she continued.

Maggie carried her leg carefully and diligently to the side as her instructor looked on approvingly. "A little higher," she encouraged. "You can do it."

Maggie used all her concentration and determination to lift her leg higher. She could feel beads of sweat pouring off her neck and falling to the floor. The music came to a stop, and the other dancers let their legs down to rest before the next exercise began. But Maggie still held her leg up, though the pain was becoming unbearable.

"Beautiful, Maggie, well done. You can let it down now," Mrs. Clark repeated.

But Maggie still held it high, though she was so tired her leg began to shake. The other students turned to watch. A few snickered. Maggie didn't notice. She was far, far away in a world of her own.

"Maggie?" Mrs. Clark shouted. When Maggie still didn't respond, Mrs. Clark gently took the girl's leg and wriggled it until it loosened.

At her touch, Maggie let her leg drop with a thump and began to blush when she realized everyone was watching. Finally, the stress of the past week was taking its toll. The sleepless, tear-filled nights, the days without eating, the dancing like there was no tomorrow...the room started to spin, and her legs began to buckle under her. The last thing she remembered was feeling like she was falling, falling, down, down, down, like she did sometimes in her dreams, having no idea where she would land.

When Maggie came to, she was lying on the couch in the studio office. Mrs. Clark was leaning over her.

"Did I faint?" Maggie asked.

"You most certainly did."

"Oh...wow...I always kinda wondered what that would feel like," Maggie said a little jokingly.

"Well, now you know."

Maggie could hear the music still playing in the studio. "Who's teaching?" she asked.

"Don't worry, I had one of the advanced students take

over. I've called your mother; she's on her way."

"She's the last person I want to see."

"Maggie, have you been starving yourself?" Mrs. Clark asked.

"Not purposely."

"Do you want to tell me about it?"

This was the moment Maggie had been dreading and putting off. To tell her teacher was to make it all real and final. If she didn't know, then Maggie could just go on pretending.

"Maggie, I know how dedicated you are. But you have to keep your strength up. You mustn't develop an eating disorder. You can stay thin without starving yourself."

"I'm not starving myself."

"So what is it?"

Maggie was about to explain, but they were interrupted by a knock at the door. Her mother peeked in. At the sight of her, Maggie felt all her anger rising inside again. She jumped up.

"Ask her to tell you!" Maggie stormed out of the office and into the dressing room, where she proceeded to burst into tears as all her ballet friends started piling into the room from class. When they saw her crying, they all gathered around. Maggie told them the news. A hush filled the tiny room. Finally, Maggie could stand it no longer.

"Will somebody please say something?"

One of her friends finally leaned over to hug her.

"Isn't there some way to change their minds?" her friend asked.

"It's not their minds I have to change, it's my religion. And that's impossible."

Then Maggie explained about the Jewish idea of modesty. Leaping around on stage in a leotard or tutu in front of a mixed audience, which after all was a big part of being a ballerina, went against the philosophy and laws of modesty in Judaism.

A few of the girls cried a little for Maggie.

"You were so good. You really would have made it," one of them said.

"Thanks," said Maggie.

Slowly the girls all started to change clothes and pack up their bags. The dressing room, normally buzzing with excitement and chatter, was eerily quiet. Maggie, too, dressed quietly, finding a small amount of comfort just knowing that finally somebody understood how she felt.

When Maggie came out of the dressing room, her mother was waiting for her.

"Come into Mrs. Clark's office. We want to talk to you."

Maggie followed her mother into the office. Mrs. Clark looked at her sympathetically. Maggie felt that she was going to start crying all over again, but she fought back the tears this time.

"Sit down, Maggie. Let's talk."

Maggie sat down, already knowing what her instructor was going to say. Maggie'd imagined this scene many times in the past week. Mrs. Clark would tell her that she wasn't that good anyway, that she'd never have made it. She'd tell her these things to make it easier for her to let go. She braced herself for the cutting words. Even if she believed in her own heart that they were false, it would hurt to hear.

"I know how hard this must be for you, Maggie," Mrs. Clark began. "You're one of my most dedicated students. I had high hopes for you."

Maggie was speechless. She wasn't supposed to be saying this. This was only making her feel worse. Tears welled up in her eyes.

"But you know, Maggie, you won't be the first talented dancer who has to give it up."

"Really?" Maggie asked, not at all comforted, but curious.

"I've known quite a few. And they were much further along in their careers than you. Imagine being a soloist in the American Ballet Theater and having to quit because of a terrible knee injury."

"But that hardly ever happens."

"It happens more than you think. Believe me, it isn't uncommon. And if it's not an injury, it's something else. Dancers are always fighting their weight. Some just can't keep it down."

"Yeah, but there's no telling if anything like that would have happened to me."

"No, there isn't. But that's not all you'd have to worry about. Even if you're talented, as you are, there are no guarantees. There's a lot of competition out there. Many, many dancers spend their lives training, only to find in the end that their best just isn't good enough. Better to be disappointed now than later."

Maggie was starting to feel antsy. She stood up, but there was no place to go in the small office. She just stood there, arms folded, nervously tapping her foot.

"I don't understand," she said. "I mean, if what you're saying is true, aren't a lot of your students just wasting their time?"

Mrs. Clark sighed. Maggie waited impatiently for her response.

"I don't know if I can answer that. Every girl out there loves to dance. They all have a dream. It's their choice. I'm just helping them along the way. I'm not responsible for how things turn out."

"Well, maybe you should tell them the truth instead of

letting them have dreams that will never come true!" Maggie blurted out, unable to control herself.

"Maggie!" her mother said sternly with a look to match.

"Sorry," Maggie mumbled, sinking into a chair.

"It's okay," Mrs. Clark said. "Look, Maggie, I don't mean to shatter your illusions, but this ballet studio is a business. If somebody wants to dance, all she has to do is pay for lessons, and we'll do our best to teach her. If somebody dreams of being a dancer, far be it from me to discourage her. I'm telling you the truth only in the hope that it may ease your pain a little."

Maggie rose to leave. Even though her parents had given her another week to keep taking classes, she knew this would be the last time she'd set foot in the studio. A thick sadness settled deep in her stomach.

"Maggie?" Mrs. Clark said softly.

Maggie looked over at her.

"You asked me if my students were wasting their time, and I couldn't answer you. But you know what? I don't think they are. And don't think you've wasted all these years either. Do you know why?"

Maggie shook her head.

Mrs. Clark continued, "Because you've learned how to truly dedicate yourself to something you love. You've learned to work hard for what you want. You've learned to discipline yourself." Mrs. Clark took Maggie's hands and squeezed them tight. "You're only what...almost fourteen? You have a lifetime ahead of you. Use those skills in other areas of your life, and you're sure to succeed in whatever you set out to do."

By the time Maggie and her mother left Mrs. Clark's office, it was dark outside. The other dancers had gone home, and the studio was empty and quiet.

"Can you wait a minute?" Maggie asked her mother as they passed the empty studio.

Her mother nodded and watched as Maggie walked to the center of the room. She stood there looking at herself in the mirror. As if to some music that only she heard, Maggie started to dance, at first slowly and self-consciously, then gradually faster and more fiercely, losing herself completely in her movements. Only when she was dripping with sweat and panting did she finally stop. Slowly, she looked over at her mother, who, to Maggie's surprise, stood crying in the doorway.

"What is it?" Maggie asked.

Her mother wiped her eyes and looked at Maggie, unable to speak for a few moments. "You dance so beautifully," she said at last. "This is hard for me, too, you know. I just hope that one day you'll understand all this, and you won't be so angry with me."

Maggie looked away. It hurt to see her mother crying...almost as much as she herself was hurting right now. The room was so silent, all she could hear was her heart beating. She knew she should say something to make her mother feel better, but she couldn't conjure up any words. They left the studio and drove home in silence.

The next few days seemed like a blur to Maggie. Without ballet to occupy her after school, she hardly knew what to do with herself. She thought of what Mrs. Clark had said about being disciplined and applying that to other areas of her life. But these days she couldn't even apply it to her homework. Finding it difficult to concentrate on anything, she spent most of her free time staring into space. She was lying on her bed doing just that when the doorbell rang. A few minutes later, there was a knock at her bedroom door.

"Maggie, there's somebody here I'd like you to meet."

The last thing Maggie felt like doing was having to smile and be polite to one of her mother's friends. Reluctantly she got up to open the door. Her mother was standing there with a young woman. She hardly looked old enough to be married, but she was wearing a *sheitel*. Maggie was struck by the woman's unique beauty. She was tall and thin, with delicate features and a warm smile. She reached out to shake Maggie's hand.

"Hi, I'm Batya. I've heard wonderful things about you."

Maggie looked at her mother quizzically. Who was this strange woman, and what had her mother told her about Maggie?

"You have?" Maggie said.

"Why don't we all go down to the kitchen? I'll make some coffee, and we can talk," her mother said.

"I'd love a cup of coffee," the woman said, following her mother down the stairs.

Watching from the top of the staircase, Maggie couldn't help noticing how graceful Batya was...almost like a dancer. Curiously she followed them into the kitchen.

"I heard you're a very talented dancer," Batya said as she sat down at the table.

Again Maggie looked over at her mother, wondering why in the world she would tell anybody that after all she'd been through these past weeks. Her mother just smiled at her. What was she smiling about? Maggie felt that familiar anger rising inside her.

"I was," Maggie said irritably. "But not anymore. I guess my mother didn't tell you I had to quit."

"Actually she did," Batya said kindly. "That's why I'm here."

Still with that strange smile on her face, Maggie's mother brought a tray of coffee and cake to the table and sat down with them.

"I had the good fortune of meeting Batya last night at that fundraiser I went to. If I'd known she was going to be performing, I'd have brought you, Maggie."

"Performing?" Maggie asked.

"Batya's a dancer."

Maggie's heart started to beat faster. Her hunches had been right. But how could it be?

Batya smiled at Maggie. "After my performance, your mother came running up to me in tears. She told me all about you and asked if I would come here today to talk with you."

Maggie's mind was racing with a thousand thoughts and questions.

"It was definitely *hashgachah pratis*," her mother said. "I never thought of the options."

"Options?" Maggie managed, still too surprised to say much more.

"There are ways to keep dancing if you really want to," Batya continued. "You'll have to adjust your dreams a little, but you'll still be dancing."

As they talked on into the late afternoon, Maggie found out all about Batya. She's already been dancing in a company when she discovered *Yiddishkeit* and started the slow process of becoming a *baalas teshuvah*. She'd finally come to terms with the fact that she had to quit the company. How difficult and heartbreaking that had been, even though she knew *Yiddishkeit* was much more important.

But she'd been determined to find a way to keep on dancing in spite of the limitations her religion placed on her. After all, Hashem wouldn't have endowed her with this special talent if there weren't some way she could use it to serve Him. Like music, dance could be used to bring people closer to the Almighty by heightening their appreciation of Hashem's beautiful creations. Watching a dancer was much like watching a beautiful sunset, smelling a rose, or tasting a delicious and rare fruit.

And so, convinced of her purpose, Batya had found a way to share her talent...and that's how Maggie's mother had chanced to meet her the previous night. In fact, she was now very much in demand by many organizations to perform at their fundraisers — for women only, of course. Maggie sat listening to Batya's story with fascination and admiration. But most compelling to her was what Batya confessed as her true dream: to form a women's dance company that would perform exclusively for women. She was currently teaching some *frum* girls who had promising futures and might one day become a part of that goal. This was all a distant dream, but one she didn't ever want to stop dreaming.

They talked about other options as well. There was something called "dance therapy" — combining special education and dance to help those with special needs and problems. And there was always the possibility of teaching dance to Orthodox girls who might otherwise never experience its joys. Maggie could even use her talents right now as a choreographer at her own school's yearly mother-daughter talent show.

Maggie felt she had truly met a kindred spirit in Batya. It was difficult to believe that only hours earlier she couldn't envision any future for herself. Now the future was filled with options. True, she'd have to adjust her dreams. But that was a whole lot better than giving them up altogether.

Evening was approaching, and Batya looked at her watch. "I better get going. I've really enjoyed talking to you, Maggie."

"Thank you so much for coming. You've been a tremendous help," Maggie's mother said.

"Wait..." Maggie said, clearing her throat. "There's just one more thing I want to ask before you go." The question had been simmering in her head for the past hour. She hesitated, then asked quietly, almost in a whisper, "Would you consider accepting me as one of your students?"

Batya smiled, "I was beginning to wonder if you'd ever ask."

That night, on her way upstairs to her room, Maggie stopped at the window seat. She thought of all the tears that had been shed there over the past few weeks. As she sat down in her familiar spot, she was surprised to find herself crying again. Only this was a new sensation — tears not of sorrow, but of joy.

Try Smiling

Author Unknown

When the weather suits you not,
  Try smiling.
When your coffee isn't hot,
  Try smiling.
When your neighbors don't do right,
Or your relatives all fight,
Sure 'tis hard, but then you might
  Try smiling.

Doesn't change the things, of course —
  Just smiling.
But it cannot make them worse —
  Just smiling.
And it seems to help your case,
Brightens up a gloomy place,
Then, it sort o' rests your face —
  Just smiling.

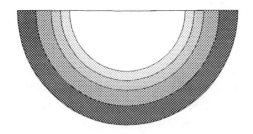

Twenty-Four Hours in the Life of a Klutz

Nachala T. Dworkin

Hi! My name is Nechama Klutz. At least, that's what my brothers call me. My teachers call me Nechama Katz, but my friends call me... Forget it; you get the point.

As you can tell from my exotic name, I am a klutz — a walking, talking bulldozer. Actually, forget the walking part — I never walk. I stumble.

Yesterday morning, I got up on the wrong side of the bed — literally. Any normal person can roll out of bed on one of two sides and land on the floor, right? Well, have you ever tried waking up with your nose stuck in the headboard? Don't — it hurts.

After I unstuck my nose, I hopped out of bed and stepped into my *negel vasser* bowl, of course. This is a morning ritual, and I was prepared.

NACHALA DWORKIN, the oldest of eight children, lives in Baltimore. A senior in Bais Yaakov of Baltimore, she is the news editor of her school newspaper. She has been writing since she was thirteen, with the encouragement of her parents, friends, teachers, and principals.

I crawled away from the wreckage (twenty-five bowls for the month of Adar so far) and pulled the towel off my desk. As I spread it over the lake on the wooden (oops) floor, my elbow struck my fifteen-subject looseleaf. Needless to say, it popped open, scattering papers to the four corners of the earth.

I raced around the room, scooping up papers as fast as I could. (I average 120 papers per minute.) After my entire looseleaf had been rearranged, I discovered that I would miss the bus in twenty minutes. For a normal person, twenty minutes is long enough to shower, eat, pack a lunch, and catch a bus, but not for a klutz...

Well, put it this way: I made the bus — only after I sprained my big toe and fractured my elbow. The bus ride was disastrous. Since I was the last one on the last bus, there were no seats left. Even the bus driver started davening when he saw I wasn't sitting. Each and every girl who travels on the last bus knows: Nechama Klutz + Late + No Seats = Disaster.

As I fell off the bus (ouch — there goes my other big toe), my looseleaf popped open *again*. This was pretty bad, even for a klutz. This time, I broke my record for looseleaf paper picking-up: 160 papers per minute.

Of course, I was late to class, and I had to get a note from the office. Mrs. Weiss was used to seeing me in her office, and we had a wonderful conversation concerning my unbroken record for lateness.

This, of course, did nothing to boost my morale, and on my way to class, I body-slammed two teachers and stepped on five people's toes. (What were they doing in the hall, anyway?)

During the break, I taped my looseleaf rings together. I was not going to test my looseleaf *mazel* anymore.

School passed by uneventfully — just the usual two overturned desks, five squashed fingers in my locker door, etc. As I was getting hopeful that maybe I wouldn't have such a rotten day, the inevitable happened.

It was the last period of the day, history. Mrs. Stein babbled for forty minutes on the pros and cons of Egyptian civilization. Then, as the minute hand on the clock drew nearer and nearer to 4:30, she stopped. The room was silent. (Maybe she should have played eerie music, just for effect.) And then...she asked for our homework.

No problem, right? Wrong! Remember when I taped together my looseleaf rings? Well, there I was, twenty-five seconds before the bell rang, with taped-together looseleaf rings and the only teacher in the whole school who abhors torn-out looseleaf paper. The Klutz strikes again.

Anyway, Mrs. Stein saw my predicament and told me just to rip the paper out and go home. I could just see her envisioning me sitting in the middle of yards of tape, the whole classroom in shambles. It's happened before.

This time, I got a seat on the bus. Everyone breathed a sigh of relief. On the way home, I walked into three lamp-posts. (There are only two between the bus stop and my house, but I bumped into the same one twice.)

If the bus ride was a disaster, last night was a catastrophe. Supper was fine: I spilled my juice only three times and my brother's only four times; my peas rolled off my plate twice; and once I squirted ketchup clear across the room!

Then my mother asked me to help her with the laundry. I very stupidly agreed, a decision I later regretted. I will mercifully spare you the gory details and will tell you only that I managed to pour bleach on my brothers' Shabbos suits as well as on my mother's new dress. Somehow, I also ended up losing five socks between the washing machine and the drawer. (I'll find them Pesach time — maybe.) While putting away a sweater, the drawer got stuck, and the whole dresser tipped over, causing my favorite *chatchkas* to plummet to their demise.

Homework was a calamity. What Mrs. Stein envisioned became reality. Aside from the fact that my looseleaf popped open, there was tape all over the place, and my room looked like a battleground. I ended up with a bloody nose, a sprained wrist, a shin splint, and approximately thirty bruises.

After my mother bandaged me up (she is an expert in first aid; she gives classes to pediatricians in the emergency room), it was too late to do any homework.

I crawled into bed, resolved that the whole world and I would be a lot safer if I stayed in bed the next morning. After davening that my *neshamah* shouldn't trip on the way to *shamayim* for the night, I drifted into nightmare land.

When I woke up this morning, I got tangled in my sheets. Maybe it would be safer for me to get out of bed after all, I thought. After four minutes and fifty-nine seconds of thrashing and kicking, I freed myself from possible suffocation and hopped out of bed. There went my *negel vasser* bowl — another Mediterranean Sea. The Klutz strikes again.

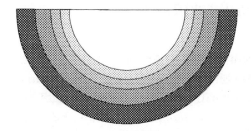

A New Reflection

Sheina Medwed

E sti looked in the mirror and sighed. She just never felt put together. No matter how much effort she put into her appearance, she always felt like a shlep. Especially next to her best friend, Sarah.

Sarah always looked just right. Tall and thin, she moved in a coordinated fashion. Her short, brown hair stayed in place no matter what the weather. Esti admired Sarah for her practicality and desire to help people. But she had to admit, she felt jealous of her appearance.

They were meeting today at two o'clock to go volunteer at the Sunflower Residential Center for Handicapped Children. Sarah had talked her into it. "Please come with me, Esti. They always need volunteers. A lot of these children have parents who can't come that often because they live far away. And anyway," she confided, "I'm afraid to go alone. I've never worked with handicapped children before, and I don't

SHEINA MEDWED wrote her first poem when she was in second grade. She now lives with her family in Jerusalem, where she writes part of the day. Mrs. Medwed has published her work in various publications. "A New Reflection" is dedicated, with deep love, to the memory of a special child whom her family took care of for over three years.

know how I'll react, if you know what I mean."

Esti saw Sarah at the bus stop and waved. On the bus they sat in silence, both wondering what it would be like. Esti was also wondering what it would feel like to be tall and thin and graceful. But as soon as the bus pulled up in front of the hospital, these thoughts were pushed aside.

"I didn't know it was such a big place," she said to Sarah.

"Neither did I," Sarah answered, opening her notebook to the directions she had jotted down. "Let's see, we enter through the parking lot to the door with the yellow frame. That's the children's ward."

Esti's heartbeat quickened as she saw the doorman sitting in a wheelchair.

"May I help you?" he asked with a smile.

"We're looking for Mrs. Astor, the social worker."

"She's in room 6, straight ahead through the double doors and then to the right."

The air had that unmistakable antiseptic smell of hospitals, but the walls were surprisingly bright and cheerful with pictures. They were full of pictures, and a large fabric rainbow spanned the length of one bright yellow wall.

"Sit down, girls." Mrs. Astor gestured to two wooden chairs. "I appreciate your coming. It's commendable to want to volunteer. That's the first step. Forgive me for being abrupt, but I want to get straight to the point. In my experience, not everyone is suited to work here directly with the children. Some can. Some can't. And some grow into it. This is a question only you can answer for yourselves. I will not expect any commitment from you until you've had a healthy trial period. And if you feel it's too much, well, we always have extra office work. I thought for a start that you could meet the babies."

Mrs. Astor led them to a very well-lit, airy room with

windows opening out to the forest. Crayon drawings, mobiles, and soft, stuffed animals were next to every crib. Two of the cribs were occupied.

"This is Leah. She is two years old. Her brain is perfectly normal, but we don't know if she will walk. Hello, *bubbaleh*," Mrs. Astor said, lifting a smiling, curly, black-haired Leah out of her crib. Her legs were in casts from recent surgery. "She loves reading books and will sit quite happily and watch you draw pictures. And if you like," suggested Mrs. Astor as she placed Leah on Sarah's knees, "you could take her outside to the swings.

"Now he," Mrs. Astor continued, moving to the next crib, "is our littlest birdie, Chananyah. We call him Nani. Poor kid. He has cerebral palsy as well as brain damage. He's three-and-a-half years old, but you wouldn't know it looking at him." Mrs. Astor sighed and gave Nani a kiss on his tiny forehead. "Nani understands one language — love. Chances are he'll never talk or walk," she said as she put him in Esti's arms. "But if you get to know him you'll discover that he definitely communicates. By the way, his hearing is excellent. He loves music and noisy toys. There's a tape recorder right on the shelf over here."

Esti sat down with Nani on her lap. She hadn't heard Bruch's violin concerto before, but apparently Nani had, because as soon as she put on the tape, he turned his head toward the music. As he nestled his little head under her chin, she looked down at him. His eyelashes were longer than any she had ever seen. His features were small and delicate. His skin was on the pale side but his cheeks were a healthy pink. His hands were curled in tight fists, but when she touched them they opened, and she got him to hold her fingers.

"Nani, Nani," she cooed to him, "do you know that a big

tzaddik, called the Chazon Ish, used to stand up for special children like you?"

Nani didn't smile, but he turned his head in the direction of her voice and opened his eyes wider. Sitting there with him, listening to the violin tape, Esti wondered about life and about children like...

"Esti, it's almost time to leave." Sarah's voice sounded a little impatient.

Esti looked up, startled. Had an hour passed already? She heard Leah crying in the background.

"Maybe you could help me. I took her outside, but she wasn't very happy, and now she won't stop crying."

"Okay, Sarah, just a minute."

Esti gathered up Nani and the tape recorder and walked across the room to Leah's crib. "Let's find a children's tape for her, Sarah. Here, *bubbaleh*, push the button and we'll hear more music." Esti put Nani back in his crib and kissed his forehead. *"Be'ezrat Hashem*, I'll see you next week." She felt sad leaving him, but she had to hurry because Sarah was already out the door.

As they waited for the bus, Esti said, "Thank you for asking me to come with you. Those kids — it really breaks my heart."

"I know how you feel," said Sarah.

They rode home in silence, each with images of the world they had just entered of their own will and left on their own two feet.

As Esti walked into the house, her mother was in the kitchen peeling vegetables. She turned around when she heard Esti's familiar "Hello, Ima."

"Why, Esti, what did you do today? Your face is shining."

"Really? I went with Sarah to the Sunflower Center for Handicapped Children to do volunteer work."

"Well, whatever you did, it also did something for you. I can see it in your face."

After dinner, Esti went to the dining room table to do her homework. She was just about to start an essay for her Jewish history class when the phone rang. It was Sarah.

"Sarah, is everything okay? You sound terrible. Are you crying?"

"Yes. I feel awful, and I just had to call to tell you I don't know if I can work with the children. And Esti, I'm jealous of you."

Esti couldn't say a word. Beautiful Sarah jealous of her?

"Esti, I just don't think I can handle it right now. The children, I mean. I get such a funny feeling. I don't know how to explain it. I get very, very nervous. I think I'll ask Mrs. Astor if I can work in the office for the next two months. Then maybe I'll be more used to the place, and I'll try it again. But you just took to that baby as if he were perfectly normal. You can't imagine how beautiful you looked holding him."

Esti could barely speak. "Sarah, I think you're terrific. I'm sure you'll get over it. I'm glad we're friends."

When Esti looked in the mirror that night, she still saw plain old Esti. But her mother was right. Plain old Esti was definitely glowing. Baby Nani had given her a gift. She knew something was different. And next week, when she went to hold him, she would have to remember to thank him.

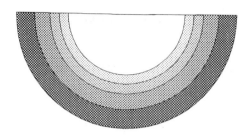

Four-Eyed, Freckle-Faced

Mindy Gross

Freckle-faced and four-eyed," they whispered. I would hear the giggles and, based on the description, know that they were directed at me. What could I do? I'd wonder to myself. This was how Hashem had created me.

Sometimes I felt Hashem had gotten stuck when He was sprinkling freckles, for it surely appeared as if I had gotten an overdose. When I'd pause before a mirror, my auburn hair was just perfect, but the effect was spoiled by the freckles and what seemed to be ten-inch-thick glasses... I'd walk away and sigh.

But I had some creative solutions to these two problems, which I will share with you now.

First, there was Mindy's fresh-squeezed-lemon-juice freckle remover. If lemon juice could lighten my hair and

MINDY GROSS has been writing since high school, where she served as the editor of the literary magazine and yearbook. Recently she has published a nonfiction work, *How Long the Night*, but after finally having three children, she is now considering a sequel, *How Short the Day*.

bring out my red highlights, I reasoned, then certainly it could help soften those little brown dots on my face. When my mom asked, "Mindy, did you see where all the lemons went that I bought yesterday?" my quick response was, "Sure, Mom — didn't we make a bunch of lemonade for the neighborhood kids?" My mother faintly smiled and moved on to other household mysteries. I knew I had told a fib (as we called it in my house, which means a little, bitsy lie), but what was a confirmed freckle-face to do? Could I confide to my mom the deepest fears of my adolescence? Who would want to marry a four-eyed freckle face?

The glasses proved to be more difficult. Of course I tried to buy the most fashionable frames in the hope that they would adorn my face like a piece of jewelry. Then, for awhile I wore clear frames, hoping they would appear invisible. And then, of course, there were some very pretty frames that I think would have added to my appearance, but the optometrist always explained that those were for young ladies with a weaker prescription. They certainly could not support the thickness of my glasses. If I took the glasses off out of pure frustration, it took no longer than a week for them to reappear on the bridge of my nose. The reason was simple: I couldn't see the blackboard without them, no matter how I squinted or leaned forward on my seat. Now vanity was one thing, but suffering in school was quite another. I may have had to be a four-eyes, but I didn't have to flunk out.

Interestingly enough, the freckle issue — if not the freckles themselves — faded as the years of my adolescence moved on. Freckles, society had determined, had character. They had personality. I guess by my high school years I had developed enough self-confidence in who I was to be unconcerned with those silly brown dots. I was a *"gingey,"* a redhead, and I was glad to be a member of the club. But my glasses were still perched on my nose as I went on to high school, and they had their share of breakages on the playing field during recess.

By the time my sixteenth birthday had arrived, so had the popularity of the contact lens. Every four-eyed female in my hometown was headed for the local shopping mall and optometrist's office to be fitted for contacts. Well, being a normal teenager, I asked my parents for contact lenses. Of course they would buy them — provided I would care for them: wash them properly, boil them, soak them, etc... So I went off happily to the doctor to be outfitted. Years of being a four-eyed soul were now about to be cast away.

I remember wearing those contacts with pride. I found caring for them a bit time-consuming, but it was worth the effort. Sometimes, despite my diligence, the lens burnt (in the little boiler that was provided as part of the kit). Occasionally I ripped or misplaced one (thank God for the insurance). But all in all, the contacts were great, especially when I started to go out on *shidduchim*. For what intelligent man would want a four-eyed young lady when contacts were available?

And so it came to pass that I started to date the man who is now my husband. And one evening, late into the date, my eyes started to burn. I turned quickly to Kalmen and excused myself for a moment. I yanked the contact from my eye, but now I could only see out of the other eye. So I made the fateful decision, my personal moment of truth: I took out the other contact and donned my horn-rimmed glasses. As I reentered the room, Kalmen quickly remarked with a smile, "Mindy, you look really great in your glasses — a real intellectual!" Those were the words I was waiting to hear. I knew the wedding band would soon be playing, for I was now loved as a four-eyed freckle-face after all.

Three side notes: The other freckle-faced, four-eyed girls in my class also got married. I have been wearing glasses since the week of my *sheva brachot* ended thirteen years ago. And I still use lemon juice every so often to lighten my hair.

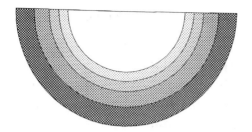

The Cable

Sheindel Weinbach

Approaching the postal clerk's table,
A man announced, "I have a cable
I wish to send across the ocean,
But how — I haven't the slightest notion.

"I wish to invite my only brother,
Because, alas, I have no other,
To attend the wedding of my first son,
And it's very important that he come.

"What shall I write? What shall I say?
To express myself in an effective way?

"I began my writing career in third grade with a notebook of poems. My first story was published in *Olomeinu* some twelve years later. I never thought I would be an author, but Hashem guides our paths, and when I came to Jerusalem, I put my love of language to good use. I have translated dozens of books and written a few of my own, including *Goldie's Toys Rebel*, *Shimmee and the Taste-Me Tree*, *The Friendly Persuader*, and *Cartons in the Air*." — SHEINDEL WEINBACH

"After writing the name, the city and street,
'Dear Brother,' I must surely greet.
'How are you and how's the weather?
It's really time we got together.
If you wonder why I send this cable,
It is to beg you — if you are able —
To attend the wedding of my son,

" 'Of all the guests, you're the dearest one.'
I'll include the date, the time, the place,
And 'I count the hours to see your face.'
I'll sign off with 'Your loving Chaim,
Waiting to drink with you a *lechayim.*'

"Now tell me, sir, what is the cost?
What? Two hundred dollars? Oh, go get lost!
You must be joking with such a figure,
Or else you're crazy, plain *meshuga.*"

"I'm sorry, sir, there's no mistake.
There's no way I can give you a break.
You must cut out a lot of stuff,
A word or two is not enough.
Your message must be very brief,
If you wish to find relief.

"Count every word, make sure to measure,
For words are a very costly treasure.
The less you use, the more they mean,
It's a lesson that's been tried and seen."

He read the letter, not knowing what
To leave intact — or what to cut.
But then he crossed out left and right,
Until the message felt very tight.
"Dear Brother" was quite unnecessary,
And the bit about the weather — very!
That part about drinking a *lechayim*
Could surely wait for another time.

Thinking about what he wished to say
Made a difference in every way.
When he showed the clerk the revised edition,
And heard the price — he gave permission
To send the cable overseas,
And said, "Why, writing it was a breeze!
Instead of sentences by the rows,
I was careful with every word I chose.
I took a little time to think,
And lo — that cable really did shrink!"

The lesson that we must derive
And remember well through our lives
Is to choose the words we wish to say,
Because for every word we will have to pay!

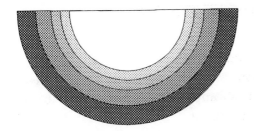

The Great Turnaround

Libby Lazewnik

Daddy? What's a turnaround?"

My father smiled down at Josh. "Where did you pick up that word, little fellow?"

"You used it just now on the phone. I heard you. What does it mean?"

I saw Daddy's face brighten as he lifted my kid brother onto his knee. A businessman he might be, but at heart, Daddy was a teacher. He spoke slowly and clearly. "I was talking business, Josh. A company suffers some reverses, see? It goes into the red and has no quarterly dividends to

LIBBY LAZEWNIK is the author of many books for young teens, including *Shira's Summer*, *Shira's New Start*, and *The Enchanted Circle*. Her newest book is *Anything Can Happen*, a selection of stories from her popular weekly page in *Yated Ne'eman*. The poem and stories she contributed to this book are also reprinted from that newspaper.

She recalls: "If I close my eyes, I can still see my first 'writer's notebook.' It was nothing much to look at on the outside — a scruffy spiral pad with a worn, blue cover — but inside! Inside were my poems about every topic imaginable. Poetry was my first love; books and short stories came later.

"When kids ask me how they, too, can become writers, here's what I tell them: All you need is a notebook, a pen, and a genuine love for words. And most of all, I tell them, '*Im lo achshav, eimasai* — if not now, when?' Do it now!"

pay its shareholders. A hard time, eh? But then, with good management and sometimes a minor miracle or two, there comes the *turnaround*. The company goes into the black, and everything's rosy again. Get it?"

"Nope."

Daddy tried again. "Well, say the forecast for a company's growth is gloomy. Sales are falling, inventory is piling up. And then, sales pick up. That's a turnaround. See?"

This time Josh didn't even deign to answer. He turned to me, a weary patience in his round, blue eyes. "Judy? What's a turnaround?"

"It's when everything sort of changes from bad to good."

Josh nodded and hopped off Daddy's knee.

What I know now, and didn't know then is that real life has its turnarounds, too. It wasn't until Cousin Ilana came to live with us that I learned that. I discovered how life *can* turn upside down in a flash — from good to bad — and then back to good again just like that. And it doesn't always take a miracle, either. Sometimes, all it takes is...well, just caring enough.

We'd always known we had a cousin Ilana, of course. Her father was Uncle Sol, Daddy's older brother. But they were far off in Israel. I'd been there as a baby, but my sister and brother had never been at all. Our folks left us with Grandma and Grandpa every few years and flew off to Israel to visit Uncle Sol and his family. I had a dim memory of Uncle Sol sitting at our kitchen table on one of his rare trips back "home": He was a tall, hearty man who drank lots of tea and told funny jokes. We'd never even met Cousin Ilana and her mother, Israeli-born Aunt Tamara.

And then, a few months after my eleventh birthday, the shocking news came: Aunt Tamara and Uncle Sol had been in a terrible car accident. They had both been killed instantly.

That left Cousin Ilana all alone, with no family in the world but us. Her mother, you see, had been an orphan, too. Ilana was only fifteen, too young to be on her own. So as soon as Daddy and Ilana's seven days of mourning had passed, Daddy cabled money and instructions to Israel. Cousin Ilana's home was to be with us!

I was only eleven, and I was the oldest. I couldn't wait to have an almost-big-sister of my own. At night I would lie awake imagining all the great times we'd have together. Each morning, I crossed another day off the calendar. The day of Ilana's expected arrival was circled in bright red.

The day finally came. My younger sister, Rachel, and I were busy blowing up balloons and hanging streamers until the last minute. Josh drew a large welcoming poster with his crayons, which we hung on the front door.

The house wore a dressed-up look, like a party about to begin. I guess we were pretty stupid. When you've just lost your mother and father, you don't really feel like partying. But we were so excited about Cousin Ilana's arrival that we didn't stop to think.

Well, you probably won't be surprised to hear that Ilana's face as she walked through the door was enough to deflate every balloon in the place. In contrast to the brightly colored streamers and posters, her eyes were sad, and her cheeks pale and drawn. She had springy, black hair, but that was the only lively thing about her.

"Shalom," she said quietly in response to our suddenly shy hellos. "So you're Judy, the oldest? And this is — Rachel? And you must be little Josh. I'm very pleased to meet you all finally."

Her English was careful, and her tone polite. She escaped to her room — our former guest room — as soon as she could.

We watched the door close behind her. There was a moment's silence as we looked around at the gaudily-decorated walls and then at each other.

"She looks," said Rachel rather forlornly, "like she might have a nice smile..."

"Give her time," my mother said. "She's just been through a terrible ordeal, poor dear — and it's not over yet. She needs time to adjust."

We were willing to give her time. We were willing to give her — oh, maybe even a whole week. But Ilana's manner remained unchanged for much longer than that. As the days passed into weeks and the weeks into long months, we grew used to Ilana's pinched, sad face and remote air. Used to it, but a little impatient also.

It wasn't that we kids didn't sympathize with her. We really did. It was just that we saw things from a different point of view. *She* was busy grieving. We were just waiting for her to finish.

Meanwhile, we went back to our pastimes. There was school and homework, and when the snows came early that year we had sledding parties up on the hill at the end of our street.

But my favorite, secret pastime was spying.

My two best friends, Debby and Esty, formed the rest of our spy ring. The "enemy" was the various delivery trucks that daily prowled our neighborhood streets.

There were J & B Fruits, Danny-Boy Florists, North-South Trucking, and a few others. Whoever spotted the enemy first would alert the others. Then we would follow the truck as best we could. Often, we'd lose sight of one only to recapture it — or a truck similar to it — on another block an hour later. We plotted the trucks' routes on maps we drew in the special spy notebooks we carried with us wherever we went.

Chanukah came, but the singing was subdued that year. How could we caper about in our lighthearted way with Cousin Ilana standing so silently, so obviously stricken, just behind us?

"When's she gonna lighten up already?" I groused later when the *latkes* had all been eaten, and Ilana had withdrawn as usual to her room with a load of schoolbooks. "She'd rather do homework — on Chanukah vacation — than hang around with us."

Mommy sighed. "She's hurting, Judy. Everything — especially every holiday — must remind her of her parents. How would you feel if Daddy and I went out in the car one day and never came back?"

I scowled. I didn't want to think about that. I wanted to have a a *real* cousin — almost an older sister — not a silent ghost who drifted around the house as if the rest of us did not exist.

Still, the next day I made an effort: "Mom says you lived in Haifa, Ilana. What's it like there?"

A tiny flicker of interest illuminated her face. She answered in her slow, careful English. "Oh, it's beautiful, Judy. Like a — a city in a fairy tale, overlooking the sea. I wish you could see it."

Encouraged, I groped for another question — anything to keep her talking.

"What do you miss most about Haifa?"

An instant later, I could've bitten my tongue. Her parents, of course — that's what she missed most! Now the shadow would fall back across her face like a curtain dropping, shutting her away from me...

But Ilana said in a thoughtful, faraway voice, "The flowers. It's the smell of the flowers that I miss. On summer nights, I loved to stand out on our balcony and breathe the air from the garden down below. It was dark, with so many tiny stars in the sky, and the flowers were invisible to me. But their smell filled the air, like the best perfume in the world. In the dark, I would imagine their colors: red and yellow and lavender and pink." She heaved a small sigh. "The flowers, that's just what I miss. There are no flowers here."

I was about to ruffle up indignantly — no flowers, indeed! What did she call the petunias and marigolds I myself had helped Mom plant along the side of the house?

But then, thinking over Ilana's words, I realized that she meant something else. There was something different in her voice. This had been the longest speech she'd made since her arrival. I decided to leave well enough alone.

"Flowers?" I echoed brightly. "Gee, that sounds nice, Ilana. Haifa sounds nice, too... Well, I gotta go now. See you later!"

And I was off at a run to meet Esty and Debby for another bout of spying on the enemy.

*   *   *

It wasn't until a raw, windy day in early March that we got caught.

We'd grown more daring in our spying. Instead of merely following the rumbling trucks in their slow journey through our quiet streets, we began to spy on them at their headquarters.

J & B Fruits had its main office in a warehouse somewhere at the edge of town, too far to walk. North-South Trucking had a cramped office beside the dry cleaners. Nothing very interesting ever seemed to happen there, though we lounged around outside for several days, watching hopefully.

But Danny-Boy Florists made up for that. You'd be amazed at the action in a florist's shop. We'd hide in the alley behind the store, watching the truck load up for its day's deliveries, and imagine the kidnapped princes and diplomats that could be hidden inside those enormous bouquets. It was hard to stifle our giggles as we let our imaginations run wild.

"See that rubber plant?" Esty whispered excitedly one afternoon after school, as we watched the sallow-faced truck driver, wearing denim overalls with "Danny-Boy" printed on the front, lug something huge and green and leafy out to the truck. "I'll bet Danny-Boy's hidden a microphone in one of those big leaves. I'll bet that plant's going to a foreign embassy, and he's planning to bug it — to learn all sorts of international secrets!"

"Yeah!" Debby's eyes sparkled as she took up the story. "And I'll bet he gets paid a fortune in gold from...from whoever wants to know those secrets."

"What *I* want to know," said a new voice suddenly, "is what you girls think you're doing here? Or do you spend all your free time snooping in alleys?"

It was a voice we knew. Towering over us, wearing the same dark-green overalls as the young truck driver, was the bushy-haired proprietor of the flower shop: Danny-Boy himself.

We spun around so fast we knocked over a trash can. It fell with an awful clatter, and as we hurried to right it, we heard the tinkle that said a customer had just walked in through the shop's front door.

Danny-Boy hesitated. Then he said gruffly, "Come into the store with me. I'll deal with this customer and then have a word with you."

Silently, we trooped after him through the back door.

An elderly woman stood near the houseplants, trying to make up her mind. While Danny-Boy attended to her, we whispered together nervously.

"If he phones my parents, I'll die. I'll — just — die!" moaned Debby under her breath.

"So will I," Esty agreed mournfully. "And couldn't you just die of embarrassment? I mean, him finding us in the alley like that!"

Maybe it was all that talk about dying that did it. I mean, for months I'd been learning that death is a pretty serious thing. Look at what it'd done to Ilana. And here were my friends, talking about *dying*, just because some small-time florist had found us out in a silly game we were playing.

That was when I stopped being so afraid and started thinking about other people — one in particular — and what I could do to help. It was then that I had the first glimmerings of my idea.

"Here he comes," whispered Debby, when the customer had finally paid for her plant and was turning to go. "We're dead ducks."

"No, we're not," I said calmly. "Don't worry so much. It'll be okay, you'll see."

My friends stared at me in astonishment, but there was no time to talk. Danny-Boy was back.

"Well, girls," he said, placing his large fists on his hips and watching us from under lowered, grizzled brows, "who's going to do the explaining?"

I took a small step forward. "My name's Judy Leiner, and we're sorry we were trespassing on your property. It was just a game we were playing. We didn't do any harm."

Danny-Boy (whose real name, it turned out later, was plain old Daniel Brown) considered for a moment before acknowledging, "I guess you didn't. But you had no business being here."

"You're right, we didn't," I agreed quickly. "But we do now."

All three of them — Esty, Debby, Danny-Boy — stared at me.

"Keep talking," Danny-Boy said curiously.

I told him all about my cousin Ilana. And then I outlined my plan.

We set a date one week away. That would give us time to prepare. I let my parents and sister and brother in on my idea, and they liked it as much as I did. If Ilana noticed the undercurrent of excitement in the house, she showed no sign. A mask of sadness still covered her face.

Sunday dawned clear and bright. Perfect! Mommy waited until we were all seated at the breakfast table and then said anxiously, "Oh dear. I was planning to do the shopping with Daddy today, but something else has come up. I don't think I can manage it."

"Can't Daddy go alone?" Rachel asked, on cue.

"I could," Daddy admitted, "but it goes much more quickly when there are two people to go up and down all those supermarket aisles." He turned suddenly to Ilana. "How would you like to come along with me? Between the two of us, we can go through the shopping list in no time at all."

Ilana looked startled, then resigned. "Uh, okay. I'd like to help. I'll be ready in a minute." She went upstairs to get her sweater.

We all stood in the driveway and watched as they drove off. Then we went into action.

A couple of hasty phone calls informed Debby and Esty that the coast was clear. Just as they rounded our corner, the familiar green-and-white truck came rumbling up our block. It stopped in front of our house. Danny-Boy himself was driving. When he saw me standing on our doorstep, he grinned and waved. I waved back excitedly.

He'd brought a worker with him — the young, sallow-faced one. Together they leaped down and headed for the back of the truck. Straining with effort, they began lifting out the flowers.

And what flowers they were! Danny-Boy had agreed to bring only the leftovers — the ones that remained when bouquets were made up and the weddings and bar mitzvahs were over. But it looked to me like he'd brought every flower he had in stock. There were masses and masses of them in every imaginable color: pink and mauve and purple and yellow and blue and white, and a million others. They came in all sizes and in every graceful shape.

And the smell...well, the sweet smell of them filled our street and our house and every room as the men carried them inside. But once they were placed in Ilana's room — where they took up every available space and even overflowed onto her windowsill — their fragrance could almost make you swoon with joy.

Danny-Boy and his assistant banked the flowers along all four walls, on the dresser, and under the window, and heaped them in profusion all over the rug. Then they started on the bed, the desk, and the chairs. When they were done, there wasn't an inch of room that was flowerless. We all took turns peeking in. The room was completely transformed.

You just had to smile when you looked at that riot of dazzling color and sniffed that heavenly scent. Yes, it smelled like a little piece of heaven.

"Good luck," Danny-Boy said as he returned to the empty truck at last. "I hope the little lady likes it."

"So do I," I told him. "Thanks a million."

"Yeah, thanks," chorused Esty and Debby, who stood beside me in the driveway.

"You girls are welcome to drop by the shop anytime," he

added, climbing into the truck beside his assistant. "Even to spy a little."

But all three of us shook our heads. We knew we'd put all that stuff behind us. It was no fun fighting imaginary enemies now that we knew there was so much we could do to make our real world a happier place...

The station wagon turned into the driveway a short time later. Daddy and Ilana carried some groceries into the kitchen. The rest of us ran out to help. Out of the corners of our eyes, we were all watching and waiting for the moment Ilana would feel she'd done her duty and return as usual to her lonely room.

We followed silently as my cousin, unsuspecting, walked up the steps. The fragrance was stronger upstairs. She seemed to hesitate at the top of the stairs, as if trying to puzzle out the source of the wonderful smell. Then she gave a tiny shrug and pushed open her bedroom door. We held our breaths.

We stood behind her as she surveyed the heaps and heaps of flowers. Her head moved slowly from side to side as she took it all in. And when at last she turned slowly to face us, I could tell that she thought it was a little like heaven, too...or was it Haifa she was thinking of?

Rachel had been right after all. Ilana did have the nicest smile.

My mother was standing beside me. I threw my arms happily around her waist, and some words of Daddy's came unexpectedly to mind: "The turnaround."

Daddy must have been thinking the same thing, for his smile was almost as broad as Ilana's as he said, "We're back in business, folks. So who's ready for some lunch? The scent of those flowers really whets my appetite!"

"Mine, too!" Josh agreed emphatically.

We all gave Ilana's room so many last admiring glances

that it was some time before we made it to the dining room table for the meal. Ilana took her seat last of all.

As she sat down, she looked around at each of us. Her eyes were brighter than I'd ever seen them. She didn't say anything — she didn't have to. Her thank you was clear. She was still wearing her newfound smile — and a daisy tucked into her hair.

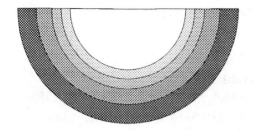

Tree of Life

Tamara Ruth Woolf

When I was young,
This was my home,
My "Climbing Tree."

It seemed so vast, exciting,
So full of long and twisting branches.
And I became adept at skimming up them
And jumping down.

Here were all my games:
Within these branches
Were Neptune's fork, an airplane,
A double-decker bus,
This was my fantasy and my reality.

TAMARA RUTH WOOLF is currently studying at Michlala — Jerusalem College for Women. She's been writing poetry since she was six years old and has won a number of Jewish poetry competitions.

She says: "I spent most of my childhood in just such a tree as I describe in 'Tree of Life' — climbing, daydreaming, picnicking, and enjoying my special bird's-eye view."

Now I am older,
I climb the tree slowly and carefully,
More appropriate to my age,
But still I feel a sense of overpowering lightness,
A surge of excitement and release.

And those branches which once I saw as being far too high
Are now within my reach,
And I nestle comfortably within them.
I look above and see yet more to be climbed,
To be conquered
Within the Tree of Life.

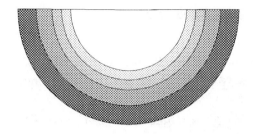

Growing Up, Slowing Down

Etti Abramcyk

Shushan Purim started out peacefully enough. It was midmorning when the sun's dazzling smile gently awakened the Hartstein clan from their post-Purim slumber.

One by one they wandered into the kitchen. Avi, the eldest, and Zvi, the next in line, came in together. They were playing catch and debating whose rebbe had been drunker on Purim. Sari, seven, her curly, blond hair hanging loose, was holding a brush and a few ponytail holders. Hennie, five, and Leah, three, were sitting on the floor in their pajamas, playing with their favorite dolls. Mommy was busy sorting out the nosh from *mishloach manos*, the baby in her arms.

Gitty was sprawled on her bed upstairs, gazing out of the window. I want this day to be really extra special, she thought, eyes sparkling. Then I'll have something to tell my friends at school, she smiled — *and* my diary.

ETTI ABRAMCYK is a *kollel* wife and mother who lives in Jerusalem. "Growing Up, Slowing Down" is based on an actual event and was the subject of an assigned speech she gave in sixth grade.

By the time Gitty appeared on the scene downstairs, negotiations were under way about plans for this precious day off from school.

Avi came up with the winning suggestion. "Let's go visit Totty's place!" he shouted, jumping over a chair and landing gracefully on Gitty's toe.

"Avi, be careful! Gitty, are you okay?" called their ever-alert mother from inside the pantry.

Gitty was fine. Being the eldest girl, with two big brothers and four younger sisters, she was used to just about anything. In fact, she often felt responsible for her mischievous older brothers.

Totty's place, she mused with a slight frown. That was what they called the basement where Totty stored his wholesale goods. It is a fun place, she thought. All kinds of interesting things — you never knew what you'd find. But I'm too old to run around like I used to. So what will I do there?

Her thoughts were interrupted by the impatient calls of her siblings.

"*Nu*, Gitty, we wanna go already!"

"Please help me put my shoes on." So Gitty spent the next half-hour getting herself and everybody else ready. By the time they were out the door, waving goodbye to Mommy, she was as excited as the others.

Off they raced into the crisp, sunny day, unbuttoned coats inviting the almost-spring winds in to warm their winter-chilled bones. Long braids flying every which way, the girls panted, trying to keep up with their brothers. Gitty felt too old to be running in the street, so she trailed behind with little Leah.

Fleet-footed Zvi was in the lead, smiling brightly, little dreaming that he was soon to be running home frantically, his smile long forgotten.

* * *

Totty was on the phone when they arrived. He smiled and waved them in, and, as if on cue, the action began. There were crates to jump on, broken clocks and radios to play with, and lots of secret nooks for hide-and-seek.

Everyone was having a great time. Everyone except Gitty, that is. She felt too grown-up for these games. I have to keep reminding everybody to stay clean and keep out of Totty's way. What a bore, she thought, and the kids don't even listen to me.

She sat in a corner by herself. What a way to spend a vacation day, she brooded. We never do anything. And nothing exciting ever happens to us. With a sigh, she reached for her diary and slowly began recording her frustrations, hopes, and dreams, oblivious to the noise and excitement all around her.

* * *

"I'm starving!"

"So am I!"

"Let's go buy pizza!"

"I want a *whole* slice for myself!"

"Ta, could we have money for ice cream, too?"

"Just one second," Totty called out. "I don't recall giving anyone permission to buy anything."

Avi spoke up. "Could we please go buy pizza for lunch?"

"I don't know," Totty said slowly. "I don't like the idea of you crossing all those streets by yourselves."

Gitty perked up. "The pizza shop is only four blocks away," she said, "and *I'm* already allowed to cross a two-way street by myself. Mommy let me this past Shabbos." She felt very grown-up.

"So Avi will hold my hand, Zvi will hold Hennie's, and Gitty will hold Leah's. It's perfect!" Sari announced with a satisfied nod.

"Please?" they all chimed in.

"All right," Totty conceded. "But be very careful..."

Before Totty even finished his sentence, Gitty was out the door, up the ramp, and halfway down the block. Had she listened to Totty a little more carefully, maybe things would have turned out differently. But she just *had* to be the first one across the avenue.

She took a quick look over her shoulder. The others were just coming out of the building. I'll cross the street myself and then cross back to help with the kids, she decided.

She stood at the edge of the curb. A big, brown station wagon blocked her view of oncoming traffic. She inched along the front of the parked car. Slowly, she stepped out into the street. But not slowly enough. A car was coming straight at her! A rush of fear, a flash of blue, a screech of brakes, and she was on the ground — unconscious.

"Call an ambulance! Whose little girl is that?"

Excited screams filled the air. "Zvi, run home and call Mommy. I'll call Totty," yelled Avi, running back down the road.

A quick-thinking woman whisked Gitty's three sobbing sisters away as Totty and the ambulance arrived on the scene simultaneously.

"Clear the way!"

"Don't move her!"

Gitty opened her eyes and saw white. A white-faced Totty and a crew of busy men all dressed in white. Movement. A siren sounded somewhere nearby. Movement stopped for a moment, and a red-eyed Mommy was there. "Mommy, I'm scared."

"Shh. Don't worry, I'm here with you."

Suddenly Gitty was being rolled faster and faster. More white appeared before her eyes. White walls, white nurses, a white sheet and blanket. Where are they taking me? she thought in a panic.

"Mommy!"

"I'm here, Gitty, walking right beside you."

Gitty relaxed. Mommy's here, Mommy's with me.

The tall, thin doctor finished the lengthy examination and turned to Mr. and Mrs. Hartstein. He relaxed his professional efficiency for a brief moment and shook his head in amazement. "She seems to be fine. No internal complications, no fractions, no lacerations. All I can say is, she is one very lucky little girl."

"*Baruch Hashem!*" Gitty's parents breathed at the same time.

"I guess Someone was watching over you closely today," Mommy said with a shaky laugh.

Nobody seemed ready to leave the room.

Gitty took a good look at her parents' haggard faces and felt a wave of love and guilt wash over her. How worried they must have been. "I...I'm sorry," she said quietly, head lowered.

Totty and Mommy glanced at each other and then at her.

"Gitty, what exactly happened?" asked Totty gently.

"I guess...I was in such a rush to show I could cross the street that I didn't look carefully enough," she said barely audibly. She didn't notice the long look her parents exchanged.

"Gitty," Mommy said softly, "from now on, please remember that there is no need to rush — not in crossing streets and not in growing up either. You're still a child, so enjoy your youth while it's here. Know what I mean?"

And quite suddenly, Gitty did. She hugged her parents hard and let them hug her back, feeling their love for her with overwhelming intensity.

She walked out of the room slowly between her father and mother. Tremendous relief filled her. What was it that the doctor had called her? A very lucky little girl? Oh yes, that was it exactly, she thought with a smile. I am one very lucky *little girl...*

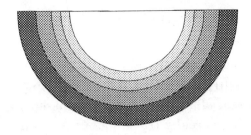

Some People Just Know How to Live

Malky Lowinger

Midwinter vacation starts tomorrow, and wouldn't you know it — I've got absolutely no plans. Five glorious days of vacation looming ahead of me, and the best thing my mother can think of for us to do is — get this — go out for pizza one night. I mean, come on. I was destined for bigger things, for better things, for excitement and adventure. No way would I take this sitting down.

"Mom," I began as assertively as I could, "this just won't do. All my friends are traveling all over the country this week, and I'm stuck here with my family and nothing to do. Why can't we go somewhere exciting for my vacation?"

Mom got that wrinkled-forehead look on her face, and I knew I was in for a lecture. "Now listen, Chaimele —" I know I'm in for it when she calls me that... " — you know that with a new baby in the house, we just can't pick ourselves up and

MALKY LOWINGER is a freelance writer whose work appears in the *Jewish Press, Kashrus Magazine,* and other periodicals. She began her writing career as a popular columnist in her high school newspaper. She and her family live in the Flatbush section of Brooklyn.

fly around the world. I'll try to make arrangements to visit a museum, maybe take a trip to the zoo. Or how about visiting your cousins on the other side of town? Besides, Chaim, let's be honest: Are *all* your friends really traveling out of town for vacation, or does it just *seem* that way?"

I tried to stay respectful, but I was really starting to lose my patience. "Yes, Mom, *all* my friends. At least my *best* friends. Dovi is leaving tonight to Miami. Chezky is going skiing in the mountains. And Ari got the best deal of all: He's going to spend a week in sunny California. Disneyland...Los Angeles...the works. What a lucky guy. Boy, some people really know how to live."

I could see that Mom was beginning to lose patience, too.

"Chaimele," she said crisply, "go to your room right now. I've heard enough. And while you're there, you can call your jet-set friends and wish them a happy and safe trip. At least that will keep you occupied for the next few minutes."

"That's just what I'll do!" I answered. "And while I'm at it, I think I'll ask them to take me along. I've had enough of this boring, stupid family!"

With that, I rose and stalked off to my room, slamming the door behind me. I could just see Mom's exasperated expression, her "What do I do with him?" look. It's not easy being ten years old and the oldest in the house. They expect me to be mature. They expect me to understand things and take responsibility. Meanwhile, I just want to be a kid like everyone else.

I grabbed the phone and called Dovi. If I hurried, I could still pack a bag and try to join his family as they drove down to Florida. I was sure it wouldn't be a problem. Dovi's parents always liked me, they called me "congenial" and "a great friend," so why not take a "congenial great friend" like me along to Miami?

"Hi, Dovi. It's me, Chaim. How's packing?"

"I'm so glad you called, Chaim. I wanted to say good-bye..."

"Well, that's why I'm calling. You see, I just had a brainstorm. How about if I go down to Florida with you? With just you and your brother, Tzvi, in the back seat, there's plenty of room. I'm sure your parents won't mind. What do you say?"

Dovi thought for a while. "You're right. My parents probably wouldn't mind at all. And we do have room. So I suppose I'll go ask them. There's just one thing, though, Chaim."

"What's that?"

"Well, I think you should know that this vacation isn't exactly all fun and games. You see, we're really going to Florida to visit my grandmother. She broke her hip last week, and she's in the hospital now. Tzvi and I will be spending a lot of time with her. If you come along, we won't have much time together."

I was speechless. Crushed. "Well, Dovi, I had no idea... I thought you were just going to have fun. I guess you're right. I would only be in the way. Listen, have a good trip and *refuah sheleimah* to your grandmother, okay?"

"Thanks, Chaim. See you in yeshivah next week. So long."

The situation looked pretty grim but definitely not hopeless. Without further ado, I dialed Ari. As the phone rang at his house, I sat back and pictured Mickey Mouse welcoming me to Disneyland with a huge bouquet of balloons...Yessirree Bob, this I could live with.

"Ari? It's Chaim."

"Oh, Chaim, I'm just so excited about this trip! I can hardly wait to see Disneyland!"

Neither could I. But I didn't say that to Ari. Instead, I said as diplomatically as I could, "Ari, do you know the one thing you really need to have along with you in California? Because I've been thinking, there's one thing you just might really want to have with you out there."

"What, Chaim? I can't imagine what I could have forgotten."

"*Me!!*"

"Excuse me?"

"Ari, just think of amazing, exciting Southern California, just think of all the adventure, and now think how much *more* fun it would be with a good friend like me there with you..."

I could tell I was being pretty persuasive, because I could practically hear Ari thinking it over in his mind. I was sure I was winning him over.

"Look, Chaim, I'd love to have you along, and you could probably still get a plane ticket. But how on earth do you expect to pay for it?"

Now it was *my* turn to think. That minor technicality had never even occurred to me.

"Well, how are *you* paying for your ticket?"

"I earned the money myself," Ari answered, his voice tinged with pride.

"Wow! How'd you do that?"

"Well, for the past few months, I've been helping out my uncle in his grocery story after school. I helped stock the shelves and make deliveries — I even manned the cash register for him when he had to go out. It wasn't easy, but I managed to save just enough for my ticket. That was the deal I made with my parents."

Now I was speechless. I suddenly remembered all those late-evening and Friday-afternoon basketball games. Come to think of it, Ari was never there. He must have been working in the store all that time. It dawned on me that Ari really deserved his California vacation. I really admired him, but I couldn't go along. I wished him well and hung up, but only after he promised to bring home a Mickey Mouse souvenir for me. Quite a guy, that Ari.

I stared at the phone. Two strikes, one more try. Chezky Abramson's family was going to spend vacation in a hotel in the mountains. They'd go skiing, skating, and sledding, he said. Though I prefer sunshine and tropical weather, I gave him a call to see if I could arrange anything.

"Hi, Chezk. What'cha doing? Polishing your skis? Sharpening the blades on your skates?" Maybe this was too direct, but I decided I had to get straight to the point.

"Chaim, hi! Am I glad to hear your voice! As a matter of fact, I'm not doing either of those things. I have to take my little brother to the park."

"The park? But Chezk, what about the mountains?"

"Oh that. Well, we cancelled."

"You *what*?" I shrieked

"Take it easy, Chaim. This is what happened. We were all set to go, but my mother found a few pimples on Surele this morning, and then Dr. Friedman said it was chicken pox. We can't travel if Surele is sick, and we can't leave her home alone, so we cancelled."

And that's just how he said it. As simple as that. He didn't scream, cry, or yell. So I did it for him.

"But Chezk, you were looking forward to this for weeks. You were so excited. Aren't you upset?"

"Look, Chaim, of course I'm not happy about it. But what else can we do? My father said we might go away in the summer instead. Right now I need to help my mother take care of Surele. That's why I'm taking little Tzvikie to the park, sort of to get him out of the way. Hey, Chaim, what are your vacation plans?"

By now, as you can well imagine, I was beginning to feel very foolish. If Hashem was trying to teach me a lesson in some not-so-subtle way, then I think He succeeded. I thought of my own family and how disappointed Mom was in me, and I told Chezky.

"Listen, Chezk, I'll meet you at the park in fifteen minutes, okay?"

"Chaim, that would be great! But I'll have Tzvikie with me, so we won't be able to play any basketball, you know."

"Oh, that's fine, Chezky. I think I'll take my baby brother out for a bit also. My mother's got her hands full lately. I should really help her out."

"That's just like you, Chaim. Always willing to help someone out. What a great *middah*!"

And who was I to argue with that?

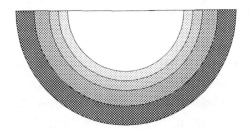

Her Greatest Role

Lena Spitzer

Simi clapped enthusiastically as she saw her friend Bracha walk slowly up the steps to receive her end-of-the-year prize.

"The Davis Memorial Prize for academic excellence goes to Bracha Rifka Weintraub." The citation was read out.

Simi cheered along with the rest of the class.

"I wonder what it feels like going up there," Ruthy asked, nudging Simi.

"Not much danger of my ever finding out!" quipped Simi with a grin.

Yes, Simi was used to watching other people get the prizes. Her own report cards bore remarks like "Fails to

---

"I am married to a *shochet*, and we live in Tottenham, a district of North London. We have, *k"h,* six children. For nine years I taught arts and crafts. Now I am training to be a special education teacher.

"I have written poems and songs for many years. I wrote this story primarily for reading to Shabbos groups for teenage girls. I have appreciated their feedback.

"My book *My Rock and My Redeemer* will be published soon by Targum Press." — LENA SPITZER

understand basic concepts" and, if her teachers were feeling kinder, "Simi tries her best." Simi was happy at school, though; her bubbly nature endeared her to her classmates, and they knew where to come when they needed a favor! But as governing boards don't give prizes for sunny smiles or friendly words, Simi was indeed very unlikely ever to experience the honor of stepping slowly up to the stage...

Summer came and went. Back in school, the autumn chill gave way to a winter freeze. The girls huddled around the classroom radiators at break time, discussing the Chanukah performance that was being planned.

"Nearly all the casting of the parts has been done now," declared Toby. "Bracha is the princess, I know that!"

Other girls chipped in with their information.

"Who's going to be the drunken messenger?" asked Esther.

No one had wanted that part. The girls fell silent.

"I'm doing it," Simi announced. She was trying to undo yet another knot in her trainers before the next P.E. lesson. Then, grasping Esther's flask of juice, she lunged forward in a comical, drunken stagger. Delighted, the girls clapped and cheered.

Simi smiled. Well, we can't all be princesses, she thought, but at least I can make them laugh!

Just that moment, a tremendous explosion ripped through the school! The walls shook in the echo of its aftermath, then the building came alive with noise.

The amazement on the girls' faces gave way to panic.

"What's happening?" yelled Esther.

They could smell smoke. The lights had gone out, and the fire alarms were screaming out their message. People were shouting and running, and doors were slamming. Someone downstairs was using a loudspeaker to tell pupils not to use the main staircase and to assemble in the back playground.

From their window, three stories up, the friends saw girls streaming out towards the playground from all the back exits.

Simi ran to the classroom door. She pressed her hand down on the handle, then withdrew it suddenly. "Ouch! It's hot!"

Esther and Bracha ran over to her, prepared to open the door.

"Don't open it!" yelled Simi with all her might. "It's hot! The fire must be very close. We don't know what's going on out there!"

Bracha was close to panic. "But we must get out fast!" she cried.

"Not that way, we won't," Simi said, trying to calm her own mounting fear.

"Quick, Bracha, get me some sweaters, jackets — anything! Come on, girls, Toby, Ruthy, help me," she called to the others, who were standing close to the window, seemingly in shock.

They watched as Simi hurriedly stuffed the clothing along the crack between the door and the floor. It was none too soon, either — smoke was already beginning to seep in under the door.

Some girls began to cry.

Esther whispered to Simi, "What are we going to do? We can't jump, it's too high..."

She was interrupted by Bracha, who was by now near hysteria:

"No one knows we're up here, girls! Do you realize? It's break time, and we're supposed to be downstairs in the hall. They won't know about us up here. They won't come... Oh,

Ribbono shel Olam, help us all!" she cried piteously.

Simi understood the significance of Bracha's words, but she chose to pretend otherwise.

"They have the registers, Bracha," she said quietly. "They will know who is not downstairs."

Simi looked at the door. The paint was blistering in the heat. She could hear crackling, but she said nothing. She ran to the window and made a quick decision.

"Esther," she called, "there's a ledge along the window. If we can just get a few feet along it, we can jump down from there onto the flat extension roof. It's not so high. We'll make it."

"No, Simi," said Esther. "Let's wait. We'll never get Bracha and the others safely along that edge; they're hysterical already. Listen! Can you hear the sirens? That's the fire brigade. They'll be here any minute now with ladders! Let's say *tehillim* and wait for help!"

Simi put her finger to her lips. With her other hand, she pointed towards the door. In a flash, Esther understood the danger they were in. It looked as if the fire could break through the door any moment. They had no time...

The room was beginning to fill with smoke.

"Listen, Esther and Toby," Simi said urgently, "when I open that window, we'll have to move fast. It will create a draft that will feed the fire. I will go first along the ledge with Bracha. Toby, you follow with Ruthy and the others, and Esther will go last."

Simi encouraged Bracha towards the window and explained how they were going to escape.

"Isn't there any easier way?" whimpered Bracha.

"It's the only way," Simi whispered. "Let's go."

Bracha was quiet now but pale with fear. Simi and Esther opened the window. While Simi perched on the outside ledge, Esther helped Bracha out.

"Come on, Bracha, we've got plenty of room, and it's not far..." Simi urged. "Go ahead — the others must get out, too!"

Bracha would not move.

Simi took a deep breath of fresh air and quietly began to sing one of the Chanukah choir songs to Bracha. It had a slow but steady rhythm.

"*Hinei lo yanum velo yishan, Shomer Yisrael.*"

At each beat of the tune, Simi edged her way a little further along the ledge and coaxed Bracha to do the same.

Slowly, slowly, *hinei lo yanum*...slowly, slowly, *velo yishan*. Bracha held Simi's hand and crept along the narrow parapet as the girl sang out.

"Halfway there now. Come on, Bracha, don't look down," prodded Simi.

Out of the corner of her eye, Simi could see Toby and Ruthy following slowly, inching their way along the narrow ledge. Suddenly, the extension roof was just a few feet below them.

"Jump, Bracha! Jump with me!" Simi shouted.

Bracha did not need persuading. Both girls landed safely on the roof below and waited till the others joined them.

"*Baruch Hashem*, we're all safe, Simi!" Esther cried as she jumped to join them.

But Simi had already seen what they had not. Smoke was pouring from the building below them, which was already on fire. They could not stay on this roof for very long.

Meanwhile, a cheer rose from the crowds below, who had spotted them.

"Stay there, girls. We'll get you down!" a fireman with a loudspeaker shouted up to them.

"Stay there, girls. We'll get you down."

The minutes ticked by. Softly, Simi began to recite any

tehillim she could remember. *"Mizmor leDavid, Hashem Ro'ee, lo echsar..."*

The girls heard her through the noise and smoke, and nothing could have sounded sweeter. Slowly, one by one, they joined in, calming the tearful ones as they waited...

Simi looked back fearfully towards the window through which they had just escaped. Flames were leaping through it.

" '*Gam ki eileich begei tzalmaves, lo ira ra, ki Atah imadi...*' Thank You, Hashem, for the courage You've given us all!" breathed Simi quietly.

But they were all still dangerously close to the fire. The girls were coughing from the smoke, and their eyes were streaming.

Then they heard the helicopter above them!

They saw firemen standing at the open door of the helicopter as it circled overhead. The noise of the whirling blades was deafening, but the helicopter could not come too close, nor could it land on a roof which was already in danger of collapsing.

Esther yelled over to Simi, "What's he going to do?"

As if in answer, a heavy canvas bag came flying through the smoky air and landed next to them.

"It's a chute!" Simi cried. "Quick, let's get it out and start sending everyone down!"

Esther and Simi unravelled all the ropes and metal hooks and anchored the top of the chute as best as they could. They then threw the other end down to be secured below.

Simi turned to her friends.

"Who's going to be Nachshon?" she asked with a grin.

"I will," Esther said bravely.

"I'll send Bracha down after you when she sees it's safe, and the others will follow," Simi said. "Keep your hands covered," she yelled to Esther, "so they don't cut on the sides, and tuck your head and arms in!"

Esther went flying down the chute and landed safely minutes later.

Bracha had to be helped onto the chute. She was crying fearfully, hardly knowing what was going on. Simi and Ruthy encouraged her to make the long slide to safety.

"We're up here holding the chute, and it's being held down there. You couldn't be safer," urged Simi.

Down Bracha slid to safety.

Trembling, Ruthy went next, then Rifki. Sounds of explosions could be heard from the building beneath their feet. The smoke was getting thicker.

"You go next, Toby," said Simi quietly. "I'm last."

There was no time to argue.

Toby went down, then Chana and Malka... They were all gone now.

Simi checked the anchorage of the chute. There was no one left to hold it securely for her now.

"*Hashem li velo ira*," she whispered.

Down below, the crowds cheered as the last schoolgirl reached the ground safely, minutes before the roof caved in.

Simi had never known such joy. She and her friends had been through a terrible ordeal, but, *baruch Hashem*, they had survived. That was all that mattered now. All around her, people were laughing and crying. They were all safe, and life had never seemed so precious or so wonderful!

*   *   *

Several weeks later, the Chanukah performance took place as scheduled in a nearby hall. Happy and excited, the girls put on the play they had worked so hard to produce, which their teachers had encouraged them to continue with even after the fire. As expected, Bracha and Toby carried off the main parts brilliantly.

At the end of the play, Mrs. Trager, the headmistress, appeared on stage, followed by all her members of staff and representatives of the parents' committee. Slowly the hall became hushed, and Mrs. Trager took the microphone to speak:

"We cannot end this evening without saying a special thank you and honoring a very special person. We wish to commend tonight the courage and quick thinking of a pupil who turned a day of disaster into a day of glory and thanksgiving. When fire broke out in the school, not only did she keep her head, but she encouraged her friends to such an extent that her common sense undoubtedly saved their lives. While we were davening for their safety down below, little did we know that Hashem had already prepared the *yeshuah* in the form of this wonderful girl, of whom the school is so proud. We are grateful to have her as a pupil.

"Would Sima Feld please come up now and receive a token of our appreciation?"

Amid thunderous applause and tumultuous cheers, for the first time in her life, Simi stepped slowly up to the stage...

ONCE UPON A TIME

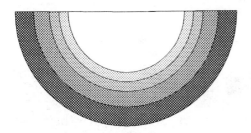

The Aristocrats of Sloof

Miriam Chaikin

People like to look at themselves. That's why there are mirrors. And cameras. For friends, people choose others who look like themselves. That's why there are clubs. And associations. And cities full of people with short noses. And towns full of fools.

Sloof was such a town.

Pilger the peddler went from town to town selling spoons: coffee spoons, teaspoons, soup spoons — you name it. One day he arrived in Sloof. He had never been there before. To him, it was the next stop, another town, a place to sell spoons.

He brought his horse and wagon to a stop in front of the inn. What a surprise he had when he got down from his seat and looked around.

On one side of the street, people were walking with their feet out. Like this:

MIRIAM CHAIKIN has written over twenty books of fiction, nonfiction, short stories, and humorous verse. In 1984, she won the Sydney Taylor Award for her "outstanding contribution to the field of Jewish literature for children." This story, copyright 1987 by the author, is reprinted with permission from MacIntosh & Otis.

On the other side, people were walking with their feet in. Like this:

Pilger didn't know what to make of it. He took his bundles and entered the inn. The thought of sleeping in a bed made him glad. The night before, there had been no room at the inn, and he'd had to sleep in his wagon.

The innkeeper, a heavy woman, was standing behind the counter.

Pilger went up to her. "Tell me," he said, "why do the people here walk so funny?"

"What do you mean — *funny*?" she asked.

Pilger told her about the feet.

The woman came out from behind the counter. She stood with her right foot pointing to 3 o'clock and her left foot pointing to 9 o'clock.

"Those fools!" she said. "They stick their feet in and think they're aristocrats!"

Pilger looked down at her feet. "I notice your feet stick out," he said.

The innkeeper gave a short bark of a laugh.

"This is how a true aristocrat walks," she said.

Pilger saw what was what and kept his mouth shut. He had come to Sloof to sell spoons, not to make enemies.

"You have a room for me?" he asked.

She pointed upstairs and gave him a key. Pilger picked up his bundles and went up the stairs. He remembered that it was the end of the month. Time for his wife to pay the rent.

He had to send her some money at once.

Pilger leaned over the banister. "Can you send me somebody to write a letter for me?" he called down.

"I'll get Velvel the orphan," the innkeeper answered.

Soon Pilger heard a knock on his door.

"Come in," he called.

Velvel entered with a small writing case. Pilger watched the boy walk across the floor and sit down at the table. Velvel's feet were straight!

"How come you walk straight?" Pilger asked.

Velvel smiled. "I guess I'm not an aristocrat," he said.

"What is it here with the feet and the aristocrats?" Pilger said.

"There are two main families here," Velvel said. "One thinks aristocrats walk with their feet in, the other says they walk with their feet out."

"Two families?" Pilger asked.

"Large families," Velvel said. "Cousins marry cousins..."

"I see..." Pilger said. He looked at Velvel. "How can you stand it here?" he asked.

"I don't mind. I write poems," he said. "They don't come near me. If they pass me on the street, they dip their bodies the other way."

"Don't you get lonely?" Pilger asked.

"No," Velvel said. "The writing keeps me busy. And the poems keep me company."

Pilger stuck out his feet and slapped himself on the belly. "*Oy!*" he said.

Velvel laughed. The sound had taken him by surprise. He had never heard himself laugh before.

"*Nu,*" Pilger said, looking at the ceiling. "Thank You, God, for leading me to Sloof. If the people here want to be aristocrats, I know just what they need. And thanks for sending me Velvel. With his help, I'll be able to pay the rent and maybe even buy my wife a new winter coat."

"How can I help?" Velvel asked.

"I'll tell you later," Pilger said. "First, let's write a letter to my wife."

Velvel took out a pen and some ink.

"Dear wife," Pilger began.

Velvel wrote down everything Pilger said. Pilger told his wife where he was. He sent her money and told her to give half of it to the landlord. With the other half, he told her to buy a number of things, naming each one.

Velvel finished writing and gave Pilger the letter to sign.

"You said something about my help before?" Velvel said.

Pilger took him by the arm. "I have an idea," he said. "How would you like to be my partner, my friend?"

Velvel shivered with delight. No one had ever called him a friend before. His eyes shone as he sat listening to Pilger spell out the details of the plan.

In the morning, Pilger took a box of spoons and went to sell them to the pharmacist. The pharmacist bought two spoons. Pilger told him they were lump pressers. You'll soon see why.

Pilger and Velvel waited for the things the peddler had ordered to arrive. As they waited, Velvel taught Pilger the alphabet and how to sound out easy words.

In a few days, lots of cartons and boxes arrived. Pilger, Velvel, and the wagon driver dragged them all up to the peddler's room and stacked them up neatly against the wall.

"The play begins," Pilger said to Velvel. Running out into the hall, Pilger leaned over the banister to speak to the innkeeper, who was standing and speaking with some of her feet-out cronies.

"I'm expecting A VERY IMPORTANT PERSON," he called down. "He's coming with his SERVANT."

The innkeeper nodded and went on talking.

Pilger closed the door behind himself and opened a box. He took out a gray tunic, gray stockings, a gray hat, and a frilly, yellow shirt.

"Here, put these on," he said, tossing them to Velvel.

Pilger opened another box and took out a long, white fur cape, a pair of shiny, black boots, and a yellow hat shaped like a crown. He put them on.

The two partners looked at each other and laughed.

"Let's go," Pilger said, taking hold of a long walking stick.

"Wait!" Velvel cried. "The people here know me. They'll recognize me."

"No, they won't," Pilger said. "Fools don't look in a person's face. They look at what he wears."

"But the innkeeper knows us," Velvel said.

"Don't worry," Pilger said. "She'll think we're Pilger's guests and that she didn't notice us come in."

Pilger pushed open the door and stepped out into the hall.

"Goodbye, Pilger!" Pilger shouted into the empty room. Then he bent over at the waist, like a broken toothpick. Velvel lifted up the back of Pilger's cape and followed him down the stairs.

The innkeeper and her feet-out cronies stared and bowed.

Outside, everyone stopped to look at Pilger and Velvel. They were quite a sight, Pilger bent in two and Velvel walking behind him and holding the hem of the cape. They walked to the town square, to the edge of the woods, then back to the town square again. Then Pilger went into the pharmacist's shop.

As planned, Velvel remained outside. He knew the Sloofi-ans would soon appear with their questions. And as he waited, he studied the sky. It was blue as could be. A small, white cloud looked down at him. Velvel made a note to write a poem about it later.

A moment later, the Sloofians began to arrive, one by one. Each conversation Velvel had was the same:

"Who is the gentleman in the pharmacist's shop?" he would ask.

"A great nobleman," a passerby would reply.

"Why does he walk that way?"

"He is an aristocrat. All aristocrats walk that way."

"What is he buying in there?"

"A lump presser."

"A lump presser? What is that?"

"If you were an aristocrat, you'd know what it was."

At last Pilger came out.

Velvel went behind Pilger to lift the hem of the cape. "You were right," he whispered. "They all wanted to know who you were and what you were buying."

"Good," Pilger. "Now let's get back to the inn and wait."

Pilger hobbled along. "*Oy!* My feet are killing me," he said. "My wife didn't have enough money for boots, so she sent me hers. They're way too small..."

"Look!" Velvel said.

Pilger and Velvel could hardly keep from laughing. Already half the town was walking bent over at the waist. A man bent like a broken toothpick came rushing up to Velvel.

"What did the aristocrat buy in the pharmacist's shop?" he whispered in Velvel's ear.

"A lump presser," Velvel whispered back.

"What is that?" the fellow asked.

"It's for aristocrats," Velvel said. "Walking the way they

do, they sometimes bang their heads and get lumps. They press down their lumps with a lump presser."

"Hmm, lump presser," the fellow said, rushing off.

"Let's hurry," Pilger said. "My back is killing me, too."

Next to the inn was a dark alley. Pilger and Velvel ducked inside, took off their outer clothes, and rolled them into a bundle. Pilger took off his wife's boots and straightened up.

"My feet and my back are sending me kisses," he whispered to Velvel as they entered the inn.

Five minutes after Pilger and Velvel entered their room, there was a knock at the door. Pilger ran to open it.

The pharmacist, a feet-in aristocrat, entered. He was out of breath from running.

Pilger shoved a chair under him. "What's up?" he asked, as if he didn't know.

"Remember the lump presser you sold me the other day?" the pharmacist said.

"What about it?" Pilger asked, putting a little anger into his voice.

"I need more," the pharmacist said. "Lots more." He fanned himself with his hand.

Pilger winked at Velvel.

The pharmacist rose. "I can't believe it," he said. "Until I met you, I never heard of a lump presser. Now, suddenly, everyone wants one."

"Aha!" Pilger said. "Didn't I tell you it was a popular item?"

The pharmacist shook his head. "It's a regular epidemic," he said. "Every forehead has a lump. Everyone wants a lump presser."

Pilger glanced at the cartons against the wall. "How many do you want?" he said, trying not to sound excited.

The pharmacist bought every carton. Not a spoon was left.

Pilger sat staring at the table in his room. Velvel sat opposite him. The table was covered with money.

"Isn't that nice?" Pilger said. "Everybody's better off. I sold all my spoons. The pharmacist did a good business. And the people of Sloof have something new to think about."

Velvel smiled. "There's a new group of aristocrats here now," he said.

Pilger divided the money into two piles and slid one pile over to Velvel.

"Here, partner, this is yours," he said.

Velvel slid it back. "I don't want it," he said.

Pilger stood up and looked at him. "But you earned it. It's yours," he said.

Velvel took two coins from the pile. "This is all I want," he said. "I'll buy some good writing paper."

Pilger scratched his head. "All right," he said, starting to unpack. "You'll come home with me. I'll open a store, and you'll be my partner."

Velvel got up. "Thanks, Pilger. But I'm staying here," he said.

"With all these fools?" Pilger said.

"I have a good life here. Nobody bothers me." Velvel held up his pad and pencil. "This is all I want or need," he said.

Pilger stared at Velvel. Then he took him in his arms and gave him a hug.

"I never knew what a poet was," Pilger said. "It's a wonderful thing, too."

"I never knew what it was to laugh," Velvel said. "It's a wonderful thing, too." He tore a sheet from his pad and gave it to Pilger. "Can you read that?" he said.

Pilger squinted at the paper. He studied the words, then read aloud slowly:

A slice needs a loaf,
A moo needs a calf,
A heart needs Pilger
To teach it to laugh.

Pilger brushed away a tear. He had never been able to read before.

"My house will always be open to you, if you change your mind," he said.

Then he tied the ropes around his valise, and he and Velvel went downstairs.

The innkeeper was bent over at the waist. She held a lump presser. Pilger looked at it.

"I know something about lump pressers," he said. "The one you have there is a dandy."

The innkeeper smiled. "I like only the best," she said. She looked at Velvel and shook her head.

"Look at this boy," she said. "He can read and write. But what good does it do him? He doesn't understand the first thing about aristocrats."

Pilger looked at Velvel. "Shame on you," he said.

Velvel smiled.

Pilger paid his bill. His horse and cart were outside. He put his bundles in back and got up on the seat.

"Goodbye and good luck, Velvel," he said.

"Goodbye, and thanks, Pilger," Velvel said.

Pilger clucked the horse onward.

"Goodbye, Feet-In and Feet-Out," he called as the horse rode away. "My wife thanks you for the new winter coat."

He waved to Velvel and rode on.

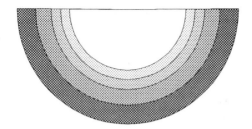

Koppel

Chana Ungar

Many years ago, in a distant village in Russia, there lived a wealthy innkeeper named Koppel. Koppel's inn was known by travelers and wayfarers for miles around for its tasty food. Koppel's wife, Freydl, was a fine cook, and she stood in the kitchen morning, noon, and night, preparing the finest delicacies. People came from far away just to taste her delicious cooking, and the inn was always filled with travelers.

Those who couldn't come to taste came to smell.

On Friday, when Freydl prepared her Sabbath delicacies, Avremel the tattered orphan liked to stand outside the kitchen window just to catch a whiff of the challos and *bobkas* as they emerged from the oven crispy and brown.

But, alas, Avremel could only enjoy the scents. He was never invited in to taste the food. Freydl feared that the dirty orphan would frighten the inn's fancy guests. Avremel didn't

CHANA UNGAR adapted this story from a traditional Jewish folktale that she first encountered in the book *Jewish Times* by Bob Simon. There it was related by Julius Lucius Echeles and ascribed to his mother, Della Leibowitz Echeles, *z"l*.

mind. Even though he had only stale crusts of bread to eat and water to drink, he was glad just to imagine himself dining at the inn and partaking of Freydl's fine cooking. The smells seemed to nourish him, for despite his meager diet, Avremel was a strong, strapping lad. His ragged trousers were bursting at the seams, and he was constantly rummaging through rag bags to find a new pair that would fit his growing body.

Koppel and Freydl had only one child, a son named Sasha. Sasha was the apple of their eyes. Freydl stayed up late at night preparing tasty treats for him — strudel, honey *tayglach*, and sugar cookies — which he lapped up heartily. You'd think that with Freydl around, Sasha would have been big and strong and even a bit on the fat side, but Sasha was as skinny as a rail. It wasn't that he didn't like to eat. He wolfed down huge helpings of Freydl's fine food. But it just wouldn't stick to his bones. The more he ate, it seemed, the thinner he got. His trousers got looser and looser, until he needed to wear two pairs of suspenders to hold them up.

Koppel and Freydl were very worried. They took Sasha to all kinds of doctors. Every doctor had something else to say.

Koppel and Freydl tried all their suggestions. They forced Sasha to swallow foul-tasting medicines and gulp down thick, oily liquids. But, alas, nothing helped. Sasha just got skinnier and skinnier.

Then one day, a traveler from the great city of Warsaw came to their inn. After a good meal, he started to chat with Koppel. Koppel's heart was heavy with worry about his son, and he spilled his troubles to the stranger.

"In my city there is a famous doctor," the stranger said. "Every day, hundreds of people come from miles around to see him. His time is very scarce. He can only give you one sentence of advice, but his words are more precious than gold."

Koppel ran into the kitchen to call Freydl. "This traveler says there is someone in the great city of Warsaw who can help Sasha. We must see him."

It was a month's journey by coach to Warsaw. (Airplanes hadn't been invented yet.) Yet that very night, Koppel and Sasha packed their bags and set out, while Freydl stayed behind to run the inn.

After traveling long and hard, they reached the doctor's office. They took a number and waited in line. Finally, their turn came. A very stern-looking assistant ushered the father and son into the specialist's inner chamber.

The specialist took one look at Sasha and said one sentence:

"The boy is not getting the essence of the food."

All through the long trek back, they tried to figure out what the doctor had meant, but neither father nor son could make heads or tails of the advice.

After a difficult, seemingly endless journey, they returned home on Sabbath eve. Just as he was about to open the door, Koppel spied Avremel the orphan standing outside Freydl's kitchen window, sniffing the odor of her cooking.

"This is the smell of paradise," Avremel sang. "If only I could try it with my mouth instead of just smelling it with my nose," he thought.

Suddenly a light went on in Koppel's head. "The essence of the food," he thought. "This must have been what the doctor meant."

Koppel snuck up on Avremel from behind. "Thief!" he shouted at the top of his lungs.

Avremel didn't know what to think.

"Excuse me, Reb Koppel, I was not stealing," he said. "I

was merely enjoying the smell."

"But that is the essence of the food. You are stealing the essence of the food from my poor, starving Sasha. Look at you. You are big and husky, while Sasha — his pants hardly stay up even with two pairs of suspenders."

Before he knew it, Avremel was sitting in Koppel's coach, being driven off to the police station.

Koppel barged into the police station with Avremel in tow.

"Arrest this boy!" he demanded of the police chief.

The chief brought out his handcuffs.

"What did he take?" he asked.

"He stole the essence of my son's food."

"What does that mean?" asked the chief.

Koppel explained how he'd caught Avremel red-handed outside Freydl's kitchen window, sniffing her Sabbath food.

"I'm sorry, Reb Koppel," said the chief of police. "I'm afraid I can't jail Avremel for that. Why don't you take this matter to your rabbi. He is a wise man, and I'm sure that he will advise you well."

So Koppel and Avremel left the police station and went to the rebbe's court.

Because it was Friday, the court was quite busy and filled with people, but Koppel the wealthy innkeeper was an important man in town, so the rebbe agreed to see him right away. The entire court gathered round to listen as the rebbe spoke to Koppel.

"So," said the rebbe, pulling at his long beard, "what is the problem, Reb Koppel?"

Koppel recounted how he'd caught Avremel red-handed outside Freydl's kitchen window, sniffing her Sabbath cooking.

"Aha," said the rebbe. "This is a very serious matter

indeed."

"Yes," Koppel agreed. "Can't you see how big and husky Avremel is? That is all because he sniffs the essence of Freydl's food. And our Sasha, he grows thinner by the day, eating food with no essence left in it," said Koppel woefully.

The rebbe then turned to Avremel.

"Is it true what he says?"

"Yes, I'm afraid it is," said Avremel.

"This is a very serious matter," repeated the rebbe. "We will have to punish you. Pay up one hundred silver rubles."

"But I'm an orphan with hardly a kopeck to my name!" cried Avremel, by now close to tears.

"Don't worry," said the rebbe. He called out to his beadle to pass around a collection plate. Everyone in the court threw something in, and within no time at all one hundred rubles had been raised. The rebbe emptied the coins into a large sack.

"Come here, Reb Koppel," the rebbe called.

Koppel was very satisfied that Avremel would soon get his just desserts.

Then the rebbe did something very strange. He took the sack and jingled it next to Koppel's ear.

"Do you hear the coins jangling?" the rebbe asked Koppel.

"Yes," said Koppel.

"You've been paid. Avremel smelled the essence of the food. You heard the essence of the money. Justice has been done," said the rebbe.

All the hangers-on in the court cheered loudly, and the rebbe let Avremel keep the money.

Suddenly Koppel felt very foolish.

To make amends, he invited Avremel to join him at his Sabbath table.

Avremel accepted. "It has been my dream to taste your wife's food. I'm so grateful that I will at last be able to," said Avremel.

He and Sasha became very good friends, and Avremel was invited back to Koppel's home again and again.

Within a short time, Sasha started gaining weight. His trousers began to stay up with only one pair of suspenders and then no suspenders at all, until he was bursting out of them.

Koppel and Freydl were so grateful that they adopted Avremel as a son. And every Sabbath eve, they invited all the hungry, homeless people in their town to enjoy Freydl's delicious cooking.

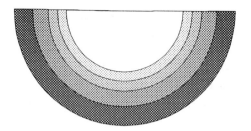

The Repentant Burglar

Naomi Cohen

I am Bert the former burglar. So why, you may ask, did I stop being a burglar? Let me tell you my story:

It was a cold English evening in early March. There was very nearly a full moon, and there was a feeling of merriment in the air. And I could hardly believe my luck — the decorator at 14 Adar Street had left his ladder against the back bedroom window!

That very evening, I climbed up the ladder and stole into the house. I cut my hand while smashing the window, but it didn't seem to matter much — all that sparkling jewelry would surely fetch a good price at the Hanging Gallows pub. So I stuffed the necklaces into my pockets and crept down the stairs, as I was a little scared to go back down the ladder with my injured hand. I had just reached the bottom step, when the Jewish house-owner approached me. He didn't run away, nor did he hit me — he didn't even seem frightened.

"Ever since I was a child I have enjoyed writing, and I have tried to weave stories out of many curious situations. Many of these have been published in various Jewish periodicals. Now I am a busy housewife, married to a lawyer in Manchester, England, and my own children relish their prolific stock of old stories." — NAOMI COHEN

"Come in," he greeted me in a chummy voice.

I stood still. Was it a trick?

"Show us your act," he beamed, "and you can warm yourself with some whisky."

I was startled and about to flee, but I'm never a man to refuse a good, strong drink. So I followed him into his living room, where he was entertaining a few friends.

"*Nu*, let's see your act, then," beckoned the owner. "The better you perform, the more money we'll pay you. Don't be shy!"

Me, Bert the Burglar, shy? But I was beginning to feel a little shy, a little awkward. This kind Jew didn't realize I had just burgled his house.

"Come on, a song perhaps?" he encouraged.

I opened my mouth and delivered my best rendition of "The Laughing Policeman," a ditty burglars sometimes like to sing.

"*Yasher koach!*" shouted the audience (I think that must be a Jewish way to say "Bravo" or "Thank you.")

"And for which charity are you collecting?" asked the host.

"Oh...for the old people," I mumbled. (I'm quite old myself, you see — all of thirty-seven.)

One man handed me a shiny coin, another gave a cheque, and the host presented me with a charity voucher. (What do you do with those?) He told me to help myself to his whisky, and of course I did so. For who else has ever invited me to drink my fill? Are these Jews always so generous?

Then somebody noticed my bleeding hand, and the wife brought some antiseptic and a bandage. How odd! I could not believe that this was all happening to me, Bert the Burglar.

"Thank you, thank you," I added, using my little-practiced manners. It seemed the right thing to say, since these

Jews were all so polite.

I was about to slip away when the doorbell rang, and three policemen entered, laughing and carrying drums. They started dancing and banging and tried to draw me into their circle of strange song and dance.

This was just too much for me.

"Aaaaaah!" I screamed. Freeing myself from their embrace, I fled into the street, howling and emptying my pockets of all the jewelry and money. I ran all the way home.

On second thought, as I mused later, these may not have been genuine policemen — they were not very tall, and I certainly did not recognize them as policemen who had ever arrested me. Were they in disguise, and for what reason?

This whole weird experience shook me to the core. Those Jews were so warm and welcoming and — I repeat myself — they even cheered me with free liquor. Why steal from them? I would not like others to steal from me, would I? I felt rather ashamed of myself and my way of life.

Since that strange March night, life has taken a new direction. I've abandoned my thieving evening forays, and I have never since been tempted to burgle a house.

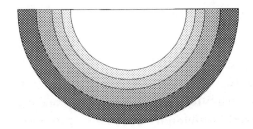

Carrot-Top

Esther Van Handel

As soon as learning was over for the day, Reuven ran to see the newborn lamb in his neighbor's flock. A group of children were already gathered round the pen. When they saw Reuven coming, they called out, "Carrot-Top! Here comes Carrot-Top!"

Reuven ran home crying.

"What's the matter?" everyone in his family asked.

"The children made fun of my red hair again," said Reuven.

"What do you care what anyone says about you?" said his big brother Nachum.

"I think you look very nice," said his sister Channah.

"It's not the person's hair color that counts, Reuven," said his mother. "It's his *middos* and good deeds."

Reuven wiped his eyes and tried to forget the incident.

The next week, Reuven went to market with his mother. The spice vendor smiled when he saw Reuven and asked,

ESTHER VAN HANDEL and her children enjoy writing books for, about, and by children. They include: *Secret of the Leaves, Benjy's Room, Farmer Greenfield's Big City Adventure*, and *Children's Treasury of Holiday Tales*.

"Where did you get that bright red hair?"

Reuven burst into tears.

"He's just trying to be friendly," said his mother.

Reuven didn't see anything friendly about it.

A few hours later, a new little girl appeared in their house. Strangely enough, she was already married, for her hair was covered. Who could it be? Reuven's mother studied the face carefully.

"Reuven!" she exclaimed. "Why are you masquerading?"

"I just wanted to cover my red hair," said Reuven.

"Boys are not allowed to wear girls' clothes," said his mother. "Off with them immediately!"

Reuven's father was a *sofer*. One day he sat down to write a mezuzah, but the inkwell in which he dipped his quill was missing. He searched all the rooms of the stone house and even the courtyard. He didn't find the inkwell, but he did find Reuven.

"Reuven!" cried his father in amazement. "What happened to your hair?"

Reuven's hair was black as a raven, black as the night, black as...ink.

"Please don't be upset, Abba," said Reuven. "I know I shouldn't have taken your ink without permission, but I just had to do something about my red hair."

Reuven's hair stayed black until Friday, when he took a good bath in honor of Shabbos.

After Shabbos, Reuven's father told him, "Pack some clothes. Tomorrow night, we're going on a trip."

"Where?" asked Reuven.

"To the king," replied his father. "The king is wondrously wise and kind. Perhaps he will be able to solve your problem."

Very early the next morning, Reuven and his father davened and ate breakfast. Then they loaded a few loaves of bread, a skin of water, and their best clothes on the backs of two donkeys. They said goodbye to the family, mounted the donkeys, and set off to see the king.

For a full day they rode. They passed rocky, terraced hills, gnarled, old olive trees, fields of golden wheat, flocks of goats and sheep, and fragrant, broad-leafed fig trees. They met people riding camels and donkeys and walking on foot. Toward evening, they came to the capital, where they made their way to the house of Uncle Menachem.

The next morning, they put on their best clothes, and Uncle Menachem took them to the palace.

They walked through a splendid garden and came to a palace built of stones as tall as a man. They passed through a huge hall lined with uniformed guards. After walking and walking, they came to a large room filled with people waiting to see the king.

At last, Reuven and his father's turn came. They were shown into a magnificent reception hall, where the king received the many people who came to him for advice or help. Reuven and his father bowed down and said, "Peace be unto Your Gracious Majesty."

"Peace be unto you," said the king in a gentle voice. "Rise, my faithful subjects."

Reuven and his father rose. But Reuven, overcome with shyness, kept his head down. He admired the king's golden step stool and the edge of the purple garment that cascaded down to it.

Suddenly, the same gentle voice asked, "How are you, my son?"

Slowly, Reuven raised his head. He was awed by the royal robes draped over the golden throne. Lifting his head a bit more, he saw the golden scepter in the king's hand. Mustering all his courage, Reuven looked up toward the king's face. Beneath a dazzling, gem-studded crown was a face full of love and concern, with penetrating, twinkling eyes...and a long, red beard. The king was a redhead!

"Is there some problem you would like to discuss?" asked the king kindly.

"N-no thank you, Your Majesty," said Reuven. "I think my problem has just been solved."

THE SOURCE OF EVERYTHING

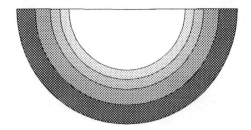

Heaven-Scent

Gila Gershenfeld

Why so glum?" Zaidi asked Miri as she plopped down on the couch across from him.

"Dovid, Dovid, Dovid. That's all I ever hear about," Miri blurted out.

Zaidi put down his *sefer* and swiveled around in his chair. He was surprised to find his usually bubbly, smiley, fresh-as-a-daisy granddaughter looking very unlike herself. Miri's normally shiny blue eyes were red-streaked, her brown ponytail didn't have its usual bounce, and her freckles lacked their fresh glow.

"How about some chocolate chip cookies? Bubby just made them this morning," Zaidi offered. He had a feeling he was dealing with serious business here.

Zaidi brought a pouting Miri a plateful of cookies and sat back down. He stroked his white beard and leaned back in his chair.

"Now tell me, what's all this about Dovid?"

GILA GERSHENFELD lives in Jerusalem with her family. She says: "Fantasy is a great thing. It gives a voice to all your best and highest hopes and dreams, and it gives you the impetus to make those dreams reality."

Miri fidgeted in her chair, not quite sure how to continue.

"In a few weeks is Dovid's bar mitzvah, and there's lots to do."

"Yes, I know," Zaidi said. "What has that got to do with you?"

"Well, the problem is, I'm the one who always has to do everything: 'Miri, can you please watch the little ones while we go out to buy Dovid his new hat?' 'Miri, please try to keep the children quiet while Dovid has his bar mitzvah lessons. You know he can't concentrate when the kids make a lot of noise.' 'Miri, we have to make a quick run to look at the invitations. Please set up for supper. You're a doll. We don't know what we'd do without you.'" Miri's imitation of her parents' demands ended with a "you see what it's like" humph.

"I see what you mean," Zaidi said understandingly. "You have a lot of responsibility in the house, and your parents count on you. It's a busy time for everyone. Do you think you can hold out for just a few more weeks?"

"It's not just the bar mitzvah, Zaidi," continued Miri, her words gushing forth from a heart bursting to release its painful load.

"It's not?"

"No. Then there are school problems."

"This is getting complicated," Zaidi remarked.

"Every day different girls are sick or absent," Miri explained. "And even though some girls say they are going to visit them and bring over the material we learned in school, they don't. So I end up calling and visiting these girls every day, because I know how bad I feel when no one visits me to bring me the stuff we learned that day."

"That's really special of you, Miri," Zaidi said, a touch of pride in his voice.

"And then there's Mrs. Perkof, our neighbor. When she was diagnosed last week with her serious illness, Ima thought it would be a good idea if I organized a *tehillim* group among the girls at school. So now I'm forever busy reminding the girls to say their *pirkei tehillim,* and when some girls tell me they can't do it, I end up saying their *perakim.* Sometimes, I'm saying *tehillim* for over an hour!

"I don't mind doing it," Miri quickly added. "It's just that when friends call me up to play, I always end up saying I don't have time. It seems I'm always doing things for others and have no time for myself." Miri's chest heaved, and her voice started to break.

"Sometimes I feel like I just want to stop being Miss Nice and do what I want to do. I don't think anything would happen if I let a few mitzvos go undone. What do you think, Zaidi?" Miri's watery eyes were fixed on Zaidi's face.

Zaidi's deep brown eyes were sympathetic. He tried to remember what his own daughter had been like at that age. When Miri's mother had been eleven years old, he recalled some difficult moments when life seemed to get a little out of control for her.

Zaidi leaned forward in his chair and spoke with a soft voice. "Sometimes special, caring people take on more than they can handle. In such cases, it's a good idea to do a little less in order not to feel overwhelmed."

"Doing less sounds fine to me," Miri agreed.

"But one should not look forward to doing less," Zaidi added. "Rather, one should view it as a temporary rest in order to be able to continue to do more mitzvos. Miri, you must know one thing. You asked what would happen if you let a few mitzvos go undone. Lots would happen." He paused, lost in thought. "I've got a story I think you'll want to hear."

Miri settled back on the couch and nibbled away at the chocolate chip cookies. She loved hearing Zaidi's stories.

Zaidi swiveled back in his chair and, with his hands folded over his stomach, began his story.

*   *   *

Rivki's class was going on a Lag Ba'Omer picnic to a national park. The park had many picnic sites and play areas, and a huge forest. Her class was typical, made up of twenty-eight lively, happy Bais Yaakov students. Actually, everyone was typical except Rivki. There was something very unusual about her. Every time she did a mitzvah, a very special, sweet smell would emanate from her, sort of like a mixture of roses, lily of the valleys, and lilacs. Most people thought she put on perfume every day. Of course, Rivki never told anyone about her strange condition. But somehow her friends found out about it and accepted it.

Twenty-eight excited girls arrived at the national park laden with heavy canteens, bulging lunch bags, balls, jump ropes, and an assortment of books and games.

The girls scampered about, each one finding her own spot to put down her things. After everyone had scouted out the site, a few girls suggested playing ball.

"Great idea," said Dina, always one to join the action.

"I love playing ball," chimed in Rivki.

"So do I," called out Tzivia as she finished drinking some juice from her canteen.

A group of ten girls found a large, empty grassy area and started to play. The girls tried to throw high, long pitches.

"Rivki, quick, try to get this one," Dina called out. "It's coming in your direction!"

Rivki saw the ball flying way above her head. She knew that to catch it she would have to run toward the forest. She dashed for it, running as fast as she could. She wasn't even paying attention to where she was going. Her eyes were following the small, blue ball in the sky. And then all of a sudden, she couldn't see it anymore. She had entered the forest, and all she saw were thick branches around her. Tripping over some rocks, she felt her tights rip on a thorny bush.

"I wonder what happened to the ball," Rivki said to herself. "I guess I'll get out of this forest and ask the girls where they saw it fall."

Rivki tried to make her way out of the forest, but instead she seemed to be getting deeper and deeper into it.

"Oh my, could it be that I'm lost in this huge forest?" Rivki asked herself, afraid to answer. "How could that be? It seems like just one minute ago I was with my friends in the open field — and now all I see is trees, bushes, and rocks. I'll keep walking, and I'm sure I'll find my way out," she reassured herself with attempted confidence.

Rivki kept on walking. "After the next tree, I'm sure I'll see the grassy area where we played ball," she told herself. But the next tree, and the ones after it, just led to more forest. After a few more minutes, her worst fears were confirmed. She was lost.

Rivki sat down on a huge rock. "Well, I can either cry or try to think of what to do," she thought, surprised at her own maturity.

Suddenly, a brilliant idea crossed her mind. "I know," she said. "I always thought it was strange that I have a sweet smell whenever I do mitzvos. But maybe Hashem made me this way just for this purpose. If I can find lots of mitzvos to do, then the smell will get stronger and stronger, and hopefully the girls will follow the smell and find me." Her spirits lifted with her new plan.

"Now, how does one find mitzvos in a forest?" Rivki's plan momentarily seemed like it might not work as well as she had originally thought.

"Oh, I almost forgot!" she exclaimed. "I've got some cookies in my pocket." She reached into her skirt and pulled out her mother's homemade jelly cookies. She said a *brachah* and took a bite. They tasted great, and she realized how hungry she was. A slight, sweet smell started to permeate the air.

As she was munching on the cookies, she strolled around looking for more mitzvos.

From a distance she heard gurgling. She followed the sound, and sure enough, in a small clearing just up ahead she saw a small stream flowing through the rocks. "Great," she said with glee. "Not only am I thirsty, but I can say another *brachah*."

She bent over the stream, cupped her hands, scooped up some fresh, clear water, and made a *brachah*. The sweet smell became even more noticeable.

"Oh, look over there," she told herself. "There is a fig tree and some wild berry bushes growing alongside the stream."

She dashed over to the spot and found a plump, juicy fig. "I can say another two *brachos* — *shehecheyanu* (I haven't had a fig in over a year) and *Borei pri ha'etz*. I know the berries are not poisonous, because our teacher gave us a lesson before we went on the picnic so we would know which ones to pick. I can even say another *brachah* — *Borei pri ha'admah*."

Rivki said three more *brachos*, and the sweet smell grew stronger. Rivki was enjoying her lunch immensely when she realized she could now say two after-*brachos*: *al hamichyah* and *Borei nefashos*. By now, Rivki was smelling like a full-fledged flower garden.

"I hope the girls are looking for me," Rivki thought to herself. "It's soon going to be dark, and I'm going to be very afraid being here by myself." A chill ran up her spine at the thought of spending a cold night alone in the huge, lonely forest.

"Let's see if I can find more mitzvos to do," Rivki encouraged herself. A plan of action was definitely better than worrying.

Butterflies flew past her, and she heard the chirping of birds. Lizards darted near her feet, and parades of ants made their way along the dirt floor. Suddenly, she heard a rustling of leaves behind her. She jumped. Who knew what wild animals lurked in the forest? She looked in the direction of the noise and saw movement on the floor. Slowly, she moved closer. A white, fluffy rabbit was caught in a thorny bush. Blood was oozing from his leg.

"Poor little rabbit." Rivki's heart went out to him. "Let's see if I can get him out of that thorny trap."

Carefully, she pulled aside the thorns and released the rabbit from its snare. In a flash it hobbled away.

"I guess it wasn't hurt too badly if it could hop away so fast," she thought. The sweet smell became stronger, and she realized she had just done another mitzvah — relieving *tzaar baalei chaim*.

A patch of beautiful flowers was just up ahead, and Rivki made a beeline for them. She said yet another *brachah*, *Borei isvei besamim*, and took a whiff. "Mmm, delicious." She breathed in their fresh, delicate fragrance.

Rivki started to feel tired. She sat down on a nearby rock and leaned against a tree trunk. She watched the sun shine through the high branches and play games on the forest floor. She hoped her friends were looking for her.

In the meantime, Dina and the girls had immediately informed their teacher that Rivki had disappeared while playing ball. They called the forest ranger, and together they set out on a search. The ranger equipped the girls with walkie-talkies and instructions on how to proceed. Everyone was divided up into small groups, which were given their own areas to cover.

"How will we ever find Rivki in this huge forest?" asked Leah, fear noticeable in her voice.

"Don't worry, I'm sure everything will be all right. Have bitachon in Hashem, and keep your eyes open," practical Sara replied, a walkie-talkie dangling from her skirt belt.

The girls walked together in groups, each one looking behind every rock and tree. Perhaps Rivki was sleeping or was hurt and could not call out. All sorts of scary pictures played on the minds of the girls. They kept moving even when they felt tired and achy.

"Rivki! Rivki!" they called out. "It's us."

But no reply.

They had been walking for about two hours when all of a sudden Dina called out, "Girls, do you smell something unusual — or rather, usual?"

The girls took a big whiff of the air.

"Yeah, it smells like Rivki's perfume!" exclaimed Tzivia.

"That must mean she's nearby!" Dina cried out. "Let's go, girls. Follow your noses."

"I'll radio the others on the walkie-talkie," offered Sara.

The girls continued to follow the sweet smell, all the while noticing it getting stronger and stronger.

"I'm sure we're getting closer," said Miriam. "It's much stronger than before."

"Come on, girls. This way," directed Dina. "It's really getting stronger!"

The girls kept moving.

It was starting to get dark, and Rivki decided to say minchah (as much as she remembered by heart; she knew Hashem would understand if she didn't know every word) and some tehillim. Her smell was growing stronger and stronger. She finished davening and was trying to think of another mitzvah when she heard voices. She listened carefully. They sounded like girls' voices.

"Rivki! Rivki!" she heard them cry out.

"*Baruch Hashem.*" She breathed a sigh of relief.

"I'm here. Hello. I'm here!" she screamed at the top of her lungs.

She heard the girls' voices getting closer and closer. She yelled as loud as she could, "Hello! I'm here!"

And then she saw Dina's pigtails bounce as she jumped over a rock and nearly bumped into her.

"We've found her!" Dina called out to the group, as she gave Rivki a big hug.

"Oh, Rivki, we've been so worried about you. Are you all right?"

"*Baruch Hashem*, I'm fine, and thanks to the power of mitzvos, you found me before it got dark," Miri reassured them.

"I'll radio the ranger and the rest to tell them the good news," Sara said, pulling out her walkie-talkie.

Soon the ranger arrived and escorted everyone out of the forest. The girls piled onto their bus and, after a very eventful afternoon, were happy to head back home.

*   *   *

"That was a great story, Zaidi," said Miri. The plate of cookies was empty. "But I don't see the connection between

Rivki and me. When I do a mitzvah, there is no sweet smell in the air."

"Ah, that's what you think," replied Zaidi, a twinkle in his eye. "Every time a Jew does a mitzvah, the world is a much sweeter place to be. The Shechinah is brought into the world with each mitzvah we perform, and what could be sweeter than having Hashem's presence closer to us? The more mitzvos we do, the happier Hashem is with us, until one day we will be *zocheh* to the coming of Mashiach."

Miri was lost in thought. "That really sounds beautiful, Zaidi."

"It is beautiful, Miri. Once you realize that every time you do a mitzvah, you are making the world a better place and quickening the coming of Mashiach, then each mitzvah is a powerful privilege to perform.

"Wow, I never thought of it that way."

"So now, back to your problems," Zaidi continued. "You might want to tell your teacher the difficulties you're having with your sick classmates, and maybe she can pick a few other girls to go visit them. And perhaps you can choose an assistant *tehillim*-sayer when too many girls forget to say their *perakim*, so you don't end up feeling overburdened with everything. As for Dovid — well, the bar mitzvah is almost here. Try to pitch in for just a few more weeks. If you'd like, I'll let your parents know you're feeling a little overloaded right now."

Miri smiled. "You know, Zaidi, somehow my problems don't seem like problems anymore. Actually, I'm kind of happy to be able to do all these things."

She glanced at her watch. "Oh, I'm late! Ima asked me to be home to watch the kids while she did some errands."

Miri said an *al hamichyah* and got up to leave.

"Two mitzvos, just like that," smiled Zaidi. "The world smells better already."

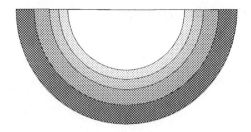

Rosh Chodesh Av

Aidel Stein

I want to tell you about something that happened Rosh Chodesh Av. It wasn't a big adventure, but it made us think.

On Rosh Chodesh I came home early. My mother was in the kitchen, dishing out lunch. The baby, Benny, was hanging onto her leg and moaning. My mother was talking to him.

"Okay, Benny, one minute. See, I'm just serving lunch. Some for Chaim, some for Shoshie, some for Shlomo, and

---

"I never imagined myself as a writer," says AIDEL STEIN. With two sisters, an aunt, a grandfather, and a husband who have published as well as a father in publishing, Aidel was the one who never put pen to paper. "First of all, no one could read my handwriting!"

She started writing in her early thirties while working on a now-defunct magazine with a friend, "proving," she says, "that you can start writing anytime. I wrote my first story because we needed to fill in some space."

"The best foundation for good writing is reading," Aidel tells aspiring writers. "I learned to read when I was four and haven't had my nose out of a book since."

Aidel lives in Jerusalem with her family. The characters in this story are based on her children. In addition to this story, she has authored: *Stars in Their Eyes*, *And the Winner Is…*, and *Ima Come Home* in the *Baker's Dozen* series and some stories and poems in *Eager Readers* magazine. Aidel Stein is a pen name.

some for yoooooooou!" She looked up. "Hi, Chaim! Come sit and eat, fast. We're going out."

"Where to?"

"The Kotel."

I thought that was a good idea, good for Rosh Chodesh Av. I told my mother so.

"I'm glad you approve." She picked up the baby and put him in his high chair.

I went into my room to hang up my schoolbag. My little brother Shlomo (you have to call him Shlomo, never Shlomie) was playing with his cars. If there was ever a kid who loved cars, it's my kid brother. I squatted down next to him.

"Do you want me to show you something?" I asked.

"No." He didn't even look up.

"Come, let's park all of the cars."

He shrugged one shoulder and pouted.

"Chaim! Shlomo! Come eat! Now!" my mother shouted from the kitchen.

Shlomo kind of slumped on the floor and got his stubborn look on his face. You could tell he didn't want to come.

"Come on," I said. "Let's bring some cars to the table."

"Don't want," he said.

"Come," I said as I got up. "Let's go and feed the jeep." He didn't answer.

"The jeep and the tow truck." I added, "The tow truck is so-o-o hungry."

He looked up at me, "Also the shovel truck," he said.

"Okay." We picked up the trucks and went to the table. "Here's Shlomo!" I said. I felt very pleased with myself.

"Good," said my mother. "Now eat. I want to get out of here already."

I started eating fast. Whenever we go somewhere, I get the feeling that my mother has been trying to leave for hours.

That's why I ate fast. Shlomo gave one bite to each of his trucks and then took one himself.

"Where's Shoshanah?" I asked.

"She should be home any minute." My mother was trying to get the baby to eat. He was busy smearing the food all over the place. He has good ideas for peas. He puts them on the table one at a time and mushes them with his finger. Then he gives them a few good bashes and pushes them off the table.

The door swung open with a bang. Shoshanah was here.

"What's for lunch?" she said.

"Hi, Shosh! Welcome home," said my mother.

"Peas? I hate peas!"

"How are you?"

"And fried fish? Again? We always have fried fish, always! I hate to eat this stupid fried fish."

My mother stood up. She had that look on her face. She took Shoshanah by the shoulders and steered her out the door. "Try again," she said, and she closed the door.

The door flew open again. Shoshanah came in and stood next to my mother. "Hi, Shosh!" said my mother. "How are you? It's good to see you."

"Hello, Mommy."

"Come and eat; we're going to the Kotel."

"We are? Oh goody!" She ran to put away her schoolbag, then sat down and began to eat.

I don't think I'll ever understand my sister.

"Don't you think the shovel truck has had enough to eat?" My mother was trying to get Shlomo to hurry.

He thought for a minute. "No," he said.

"I'm done," I said.

"Good! Say a *Borei nefashos*, then go and fill up the water bottles, please."

"Right."

"My tummy is full," said Shoshanah.

"You hardly ate."

Shoshanah slid down in her chair and closed her eyes.

"Three more bites," said my mother.

Shoshanah opened one eye.

"How can I buy ice cream for you if you don't eat lunch?"

"Oh, okay."

My mother took the baby out of his chair and cleared off the table. "We'll clear up the kitchen later," she said.

"Can I take my trucks?"

"I think they'd get lost," said my mother. "Go park them."

Shlomo put his trucks in their box. He's very neat.

In the meantime, my mother put on her *sheitel* and was going through her handbag and talking to herself. "Where is that...oh, there it is! I can't ever find anything in here. Shosh, run and get me a diaper!"

Shoshanah ran to the diaper bag.

"Shlomo, pull up your pants! Chaim, where are those water bottles? Who's seen the baby's hat?" My mother put a hat on each of our heads. I don't really like my hat, but it didn't look like a good time to argue.

"Shoshie, wash Shlomo's face!"

"No! I do it!" Shlomo ran to the sink.

"Chaim, did you fill...oh, here they are. Right, everyone out! *Oy*, Shlomo, you're wet! Never mind, it will dry. Out!"

We all ran out the door except my mother and Benny. We stood on the steps and waited. And waited. I was about to go back in when my mother and Benny burst through the door.

"Sorry," she said. "Last-minute diaper change." She locked the door. "Better late than never." She grinned at all of us. "Onward!" We ran down the stairs with the stroller bump,

bump, bumping behind us.

My mother can walk fast. Shlomo had to run to keep up.

"I hope we didn't miss the bus."

"So do I!" said Shoshanah. "What if we did?"

"We'll take the next one."

"Oh."

"We're going on a bus?" That was Shlomo.

"Yup!"

"I wanna go in a taxi."

"So do I," said my mother. "But we don't have the money. Maybe we'll take a taxi home."

When we got to the bus stop, my mother took Benny out of his stroller and folded it. A lot of mothers bring the whole thing on the bus, baby and all, without folding, but my mother says it takes up too much room. She says she doesn't mind saving the extra fare either. She put Benny on the bench.

"I'll take the baby. Everyone, take a water bottle. Shoshie, you hold Shlomo's hand. Chaim, you take the stroller, and here's the children's bus pass. Three fares, got it?"

I nodded and picked up the stroller.

"You don't have to pick it up yet. Wait until we see a bus."

I put down the stroller.

"Look, here's the bus!" shouted Shoshanah.

I picked up the stroller.

"It's a 16," said my mother.

I put down the stroller.

"Here's another one!" shouted Shoshanah.

"It's a 35! Let's go!"

I picked up the stroller and got on the bus. We went to the seats that face each other. We like them best because we can all sit together. My mother got there just as the bus started and fell into the seat with Benny on top of her.

Shoshanah and Shlomo took the window seats. This bothered me, as I am always last on the bus (except for my mother), so I hardly ever get a window seat. I didn't say anything, but I wasn't happy.

"Here, Chaim, you take the window seat."

I was really surprised. "Thank you, Shosh!"

"You're welcome!" She turned to my mother. "Right, that was a mitzvah?"

"Yep! Well done!"

"That's because we're going to the Kotel. Right, you have to do extra mitzvos in the nine days, especially *bein adam lechavero*? The Beis HaMikdash was ruined because of *sinas chinam*."

She looked very pleased with herself. This type of behavior annoys me, but I try not to complain. I have a friend whose sister lets you know all the time what kind of *tzaddekes* she is. Shoshanah only does it once in a while. And she *did* give me the seat.

Shlomo spoke up. "The goyim broke the Beis HaMikdash, and we have to ask for a new one."

"That's right, Shlomo," said my mother, and she pinched his cheek. "When we get to the Kotel, you daven to Hashem for a new one, okay?"

"Okay," said Shlomo, looking at my mother with big eyes.

"Oish, Mommy, when will Mashiach come already? I can't wait!" Shoshanah bounced in her seat.

"Neither can I," said my mother.

We changed buses. This next bus was very crowded, so I stood.

It's really good to get off a crowded bus. We're not always the last ones off the bus, but we're always the last to leave the bus stop. By the time my mother gets Benny in the stroller and we have drinks and put on our hats, everyone else is gone.

While my mother was fixing up us kids, I watched the bus driver. He was inspecting the empty bus for suspicious-looking objects. It made me feel funny. When he finished, he drove to the pick-up spot, where the people stand who want to leave. The bus looked so empty, but you could feel it getting ready for its next "big meal." By the time the bus swallowed all those people, it looked pretty stuffed. I'm glad I'm not a bus; I wouldn't mind trying to drive one, though.

"Chaim!"

I had to run to catch up.

We all get very quiet at the Kotel, sort of an excited quiet if you know what I mean. It's also a quiet that's a little sad, a davening quiet, a thinking quiet. If you've ever been to the Kotel, then you can understand.

Down the stairs and through the gates. Our bags were checked. No bombs.

"I should say not," said my mother.

At first you don't see the Wall, just the big area in front of it. Then suddenly, it's there; it's huge, and you feel so small. I wanted to stop for a minute, but my mother went straight to the tap where you wash your hands.

"Chaim, are you coming with us or going to the men's section?"

Oh boy, what'll I do? I thought. "I think I'll go to the men's section."

"Okay." My mother gave me such a look. I think she was pleased. "We'll meet right here when we're through. See ya later!"

They went down to the women's section. I went to the left. It really wasn't an easy decision. On the one hand, I didn't like being alone. On the other hand, I didn't want to daven with the women; I'm really a bit big for that.

I walked down the men's ramp. It wasn't so crowded in the men's section, but I'll bet there were about a hundred people there. I felt like stopping where I was and going back, but when you're at the Kotel it makes you act bigger than you feel, so I kept going.

I like to daven in the front corner by the gate that goes inside. I hope you don't mind if I don't tell you about my davening; it's personal. I guess it's that way for everyone.

When I got back to the fountain, no one was there yet, so I found a place to sit. I looked for my mother. I know she davens a lot for us. I hope Hashem hears her. I'm sure Hashem hears my mother...

When they finished, I went to meet them.

"Did you have a good daven?" my mother asked me.

"Yep," I said.

We stood and took one last look at the Wall.

"Right, that's the Kotel?" asked Shlomo.

"Right," said my mother. "Let's go."

"Are we going home now?"

"I thought we'd explore a bit." My mother led the way through Sha'ar Ha'Ashpos. "We'll take the bus from the second stop."

On the way down, she showed us the remains of an arch that once supported a bridge. Then we stopped by the entrance to the diggings to look at the pictures there. My mother showed us what the bridge looked like way back when. Shoshanah wanted to buy a picture like that, but my mother said she didn't have enough money with her.

We came to the second bus stop and sat down to wait. Benny started kvetching, so my mother took him out and began to fold up the stroller. Shoshanah walked around the bus stop. She stopped by my mother.

"What's that?" she said, pointing up towards the Old City walls.

"What's what?"

"All those rocks and things."

"More diggings."

"What are diggings?"

"Hundreds or even thousands of years ago, people lived here. What you see up there is all that's left of their houses. People called archaeologists dug them up to learn what life was like then."

"Can we go up there?"

"I'm a little tired, *buba*..."

"Pleeease?"

Going up there seemed like a good idea to me, so I tried to help. "Please, Ima?"

"The bus is coming..."

We could tell she was beginning to give in.

"Please!" Then I had a great idea. "Come on, Ima, it will be educational."

My mother began to laugh. I don't understand why. She's always pleased when something's educational, but why did she laugh?

"Yes, Ima," Shoshanah nodded. "Very educational."

"Okay, guys, you win." She opened up the stroller and strapped Benny in. "Come on."

"Goody," said Shlomo.

As we were climbing up, Shoshanah turned to me and asked, "Chaim, what does 'educational' mean?"

"Shh!" I said. "I'll tell you later."

But my mother heard her. "It means we'll learn something from it." She began to laugh. "You people are really something else." I wish I understood what was so funny.

Shoshanah found a sign. She's good at that, finding things. "Ima, what does it say here?"

My mother leaned over the sign. "It says that these were houses at the time of the second Beis HaMikdash.

"Really? Wow!"

We climbed around for a while. My mother showed us different things, like what might have been a kitchen, a *mikvah*, and stuff like that.

"The rooms are so small."

"People were smaller then, or so they say."

"But Moshe Rabbeinu and Yirmeyahu were supposed to be huge," I said.

"I have to admit I don't know that much about it." She sat down on a rock. "Whew! Look, I'm going to sit here with Benny, and you can look around some more."

This didn't bother us much as we can go much faster without my mother and Benny.

"Look," said Shoshanah. She'd stopped at a house that wasn't in such bad shape. "Let's play here. I'll be the ima, you can be the *abba*, and Shlomo the big boy. You'll be a *kohen* and work in the Beis HaMikdash."

We found rocks for plates and dead weeds for food. (My mother says flowers are not ours to pick.)

"Good morning, darling," said Shoshanah. "Come and eat."

"No time. I've got to get to the *avodah*."

"Oh. Can you take little Yirmi (let's say that Shlomo's name is Yirmi), can you take little Yirmi to cheder?"

"Sure," I said. "Come on, Yirmi."

I took Shlomo/Yirmi to another room. "Pretend that this is your cheder," I told him. "A special cheder for boys of *kohanim*. Soon go back to Ima, and tell her I'll be late."

"Okay." Shlomo is good at playing; he takes things seriously.

Then I went further and *shechted* a few *korbanos*. There was a *shailah* on a *moom*. I was thinking I should be the *kohen gadol* rather than a *kohen hedyot* when Shlomo called me.

"Shoshanah's crying," he said.

I ran down the rocks. It's probably nothing, I thought. She cries about everything! When I got to our "house," there she was in the kitchen, crying her eyes out.

"What happened? Are you okay?"

She just cried louder. "Did you hurt yourself?"

She shook her head and kept on crying.

My mother showed up. "What happened? Shoshanah, why are you crying?" she asked.

Shoshanah flung herself into my mother's arms and kept on crying. My mother held her.

"What? What? Shh, honey, tell me what happened. Did something scare you?"

After a while Shoshanah began to calm down.

"*Nu?*" I said.

"Hush, Chaim!" said my mother. "Shoshanah, do you want to tell us what happened?"

Shoshanah sniffed a couple of times. "I was playing that I was the *ima*, and I was cooking — there's the stove — and I thought about what the sign said and how people used to live here when there really was a Beis HaMikdash. And then I thought that maybe really a mommy sat here and an *abba* went to work at the Beis HaMikdash with his little boy, and I thought how their house is all ruined and how sad they must have been and...and..." She started to cry again.

At first, my mother just stared at Shoshanah. Then she held her tight, rocking slowly, eyes closed. Shlomo and I just stood there. I felt like I couldn't move. I saw one tear slip from my mother's eye.

I looked up and around at all of those ruins. People, real people, Jews...like us...like me...I could almost see them. I thought of Yirmeyahu on the road to Yerushalayim, seeing the smoke and thinking it was from the *ketores*...but it wasn't.

My mother began to sing softly: "*Nachamu, nachamu, ami, yomar Elokeichem. Dabru al lev Yerushalayim, vekir'u eilehah...* Be comforted, My people, be comforted..."

She gave Shoshanah a kiss. "Come," she said. "Let's go."

We climbed down to the stroller, strapped Benny in, and went down to the bus stop. We were all very quiet.

By the time we got to the bus stop, Shoshanah had cheered up a bit; she never stays sad for long. My mother folded up the stroller, and I took it. She still looked very thoughtful. She sat down with Benny. Shlomo sat with her.

"Ima?" he said.

"Yes?"

"Ima, right, the goyim broke the Beis HaMikdash?"

"Right."

"Right, we're very sad?"

"Right, doll."

Shlomo sat for a while, swinging his legs. Then he turned again to my mother.

"Right, Mashiach is gonna come?" he said.

Ima smiled. I felt like a big load rolled off me. She smiled at Shlomo and ruffled up his hair.

"Right, my boy, right indeed!"

"Here's the bus!"

We got on the bus and went home.

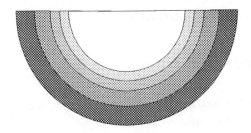

Thunder and Lightning

Joanne Jackson Yelenik

Summer,
Washington in July,
when you can taste the heat on your parched lips.
    We are seated in our car,
your father and I in the front seat,
you and a school friend in the back.
We are laughing and talking, having
played miniature golf,
a summer's night's entertainment,
relaxed and easy.
Suddenly, the sky is alive with lightning,
a summer storm,
vital and strong.
    I turn and ask,
"What is the blessing for a storm?"

JOANNE JACKSON YELENIK is a teacher who writes and a writer who teaches. This all began when she was very young and someone told her the most important thing in her education was to read, and another person said, "Writing well is the key to being educated." So she became a reader and a writer. She lives with her family in Washington, D.C., where there is plenty to read and write about.

Without pausing, you and your friend reply together,
"*Oseh maaseh bereishit.*"
Just as suddenly as the storm's start,
we are transported to another age,
a different time and place.
You are two old, white-haired men with beards
riding in a horse-drawn carriage; we are in Poland;
you are robed and garbed in the dress of Spain's Golden Age.
You are with me at Sinai
or in Egypt's clay pits.
It is summer in Washington,
but the blessing changes the scene,
adding to it holiness
and God.
We speak an ancient tongue;
we are a tribe,
a people young yet ageless.
Lightning illuminates the bright threads on your *kippah*.
I say the blessing, remembering where we are,
And wait still for the Messiah.

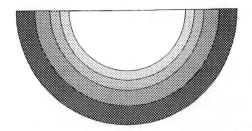

A Gift to You

Esther Cohn

I sent a gift-wrapped package to Hashem. Enclosed was a variety of worries and woes. Feeling insecure, acknowledging the reality of being overweight and overworked and thinking almost constantly of others' problems, left me so helpless and tense one night.

Sleep eluding me, I decided to send it all to Hashem. I sent Hashem my worries and anxieties — direct flight. I gathered them all together: my insecurity, my friends' problems, the (seeming) injustice in the world, the sadness etched in people's expressions, the tensions, all of it...wrapped in a huge, square box with black, shiny wrapping paper adorned with a large, red ribbon...to Hashem.

Hashem can cure, Hashem can bring an end to suffering. I cannot. I can't change the world. So I left it in the box, the

ESTHER COHN lives in Jerusalem with her family. "A Gift to You" embodies a tool Mrs. Cohn learned in a workshop given by EMETT lecturer Miriam Adahan. Mrs. Cohn, who has been writing since she was a teenager, advises young writers: "When you feel strongly about something, just pick up a pen and write, as if to yourself. If your writing is not part of you, it will not interest the reader. You must be honest in your writing. You can always rewrite and polish your original thought or idea."

box of belief, of really feeling Hashem's presence, trusting Him to send my gift Above.

I left it to the Source...of everything.

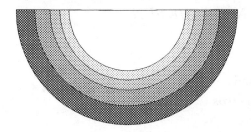

Better Than Magic

Bracha Druss Goetz

What's better than magic
And within your reach every day?
You can make things *disappear*!
They'll vanish right away.

What's better than magic?
Here comes another clue.
Every moment there's a chance
to start off clean and new.

When you have done something wrong,
this tool can fix your mess
(no matter which bad thing you've done.)
What is it? Can you guess?

It's far better than magic,
'Cause no one gets a trick deal.
It's far better than magic,
'Cause it's amazing *and* for real!

BRACHA DRUSS GOETZ has written several children's books. She published
her first poem when she was thirteen years old.

In just one *tiny* second,
Big mistakes can be erased.
Watch it wipe out your *aveiros*
Without leaving *any* trace!

And that isn't all —
For when its full powers are found,
Aveiros change to mitzvos,
Turning *completely* around!

It's TESHUVAH that does more
Than pulling rabbits out of hats.
Teshuvah can make *you* over,
And no magic can beat that!

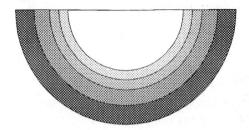

Possibilities

Rhona Silver

We left the Belzer Clinic in Mekor Baruch, Jerusalem, and jaunted down Malchei Yisrael, the main artery of Geulah.

My youngest skipped ahead, ponytail bouncing above her oversized, black-and-white-checked jacket, hands drawn into the sleeves for warmth, gas mask slung over one shoulder, hanging down to her knees and banging merrily against them with each step.

The hood of our eldest's red, wool coat, tightly tied, hugged her head. She held the long, black, plastic straps of her gas mask wrapped around one hand so she could dance over the cracks of the sidewalk, gawky and graceful at the same time.

The edges of their noses were red-tinged, and their breath puffed into the winter air.

RHONA SILVER was an assistant professor of English at Temple University in Philadelphia. She is now a freelance writer and artist living in Jerusalem with her husband and children. Her story "Command Performance" appears in *More of Our Lives*. She has loved to write since she was in second grade, and even admits that, as a child, she used to read the dictionary for fun!

My husband strode with firm steps, his brown, leather jacket open, carrying both our gas masks on one shoulder as if the large, cardboard rectangles weren't even awkward.

I limped quickly, only slightly behind my husband, my hands stuffed comfortably into the pockets of my purple down jacket, rejoicing in the rhythm of my feet hitting the pavement and the expanse of my lungs filled with cold, moist Jerusalem air.

Normally, the streets would be filled beyond capacity with traffic and shoppers. But it was the second week of the war, and although sirens had sounded only at night, the streets were clear because the possibility of a daytime attack felt very real. An isolated figure or two would pass us on the sidewalk or duck into one of the few open stores. For the most part, the heart of Jerusalem, already our girls' familiar backyard, belonged to us.

We had been in Israel for six months — long enough to have a favorite falafel shop, housewares store, *tichel* stand, and tape vendor. I was still awed that my daughters now possessed the same mental map of Jerusalem that I had carried for over twenty years in America, which had always made my eyes moist when one of its street corners would bump into my consciousness.

We were hungry. My husband surprisingly ushered us into a small, unfamiliar grocery and proceeded to order a child's fantasy: one hundred grams of anything tempting on the wide, worn, wooden table near the register. He passed over *garinim* and peanuts in favor of pistachios, cashews, smoked almonds, and three types of chocolate squares whose contents we could only guess. Each selection was packed in its own miniature, brown, paper bag. What daring! I admired my husband's flair.

We rushed to the closest #1 bus stop and then settled in

for the wait. I molded myself into an orange seat, my husband stood watch to my left, and the girls played games with curbs and storefronts. We waited for close to an hour, worrying that perhaps the bus service had been suspended. But the bus finally pulled up, almost nonchalantly, and we soon found ourselves seats facing the girls. I had to remind them repeatedly to shift their mask boxes higher on their laps so the cardboard edges wouldn't dig into my knees.

We looked around us. Although the buses travelling this route were usually jammed, today there were only a handful of passengers. Each was elderly; each had that going-to-the-Kotel look of determination and serenity; most had masks. We always enjoyed the slight danger of riding through East Jerusalem on the way to the Old City — the low-key thrill of passing through "enemy territory" and emerging unscathed, with Hashem's help.

Today the shops were all bolted, and no one wandered the streets because of the curfew the war had dictated. We rounded the massive Old City walls and hunched closer to the windows. My youngest never wants to miss Sha'ar HaRachamim; my eldest always tries to catch a glimpse of Yad Avshalom and Kever Zecharyah. Today we all stared to our right until Sha'ar HaRachamim had flown past. These weren't ordinary times.

The approach to the Kotel was empty. The Kotel itself was practically deserted as my husband walked around to the men's side of the *mechitzah*. Was it considered unsafe to be here, foolhardy to expose children to the open? I took a worn, blue, plastic-and-chrome chair and pulled it close to the Wall, followed by the girls, and we slid our mask boxes to our feet.

It was much colder here than it had been downtown. I was curious what my reaction would be, standing at the Gate of Heaven in the throes of war. I knew I wasn't at all afraid. This suddenly seemed the safest place to be. I knew the girls felt the same when my youngest leaned her cheek on the freezing stones and quietly said that they keep her warm.

When the girls were settled in comfortably with their Tehillim, I was left alone with my thoughts. First, as usual, I stole a furtive glance high at the upper left of the Wall, remembering stories of the Shechinah appearing as a woman dressed in black, mourning the destruction of the Holy Temple. And as usual, I was embarrassed at myself for even presuming to look. Not yet. Just a soft, gray sky.

It was about then that I noticed how happy I was. I had come here to daven in a crisis, and here I was smiling — no, grinning — from ear to ear. I tried to ignore the phenomenon, pulled my Tehillim from my black, canvas bag, said our "sealed room" *kapittels*, and turned to "*Shir HaMaalos*." It didn't help; I was still wonderfully happy. I couldn't stop grinning. If the girls had looked up at me, they would have found it quite odd: my eldest resigns herself to being uncomfortable when I habitually cry several tissues to shreds each time I daven here; my youngest looks forward to her self-appointed job of helping me erase the embarrassing mascara trails from my cheeks when I am finished, like a mother cat fussing over her kitten.

Yet here I was grinning while peering all around, trying to memorize every detail of the *ezras nashim* — the wave of the *mechitzah*, the pattern of the paving stones, the heft of the lintel stone to the far right, the muted tones of the doves — as if it were the cherished face of a dear old friend soon to metamorphose into a princess under the *chuppah*. I had the gut feeling I would never see the Kotel like this again — a kind of nostalgic euphoria.

Oh, I had pictured Mashiach coming before: an awesome, hazy blur of trembling and dancing amid the faceless surge of my people. But this was totally different. Replacing my vague cluster of tzaddikim suffused in a soft, white light was a friendly jumble of bus drivers, second-grade rebbes, accountants, kindergarten teachers, dental technicians, the lady in the maroon *tichel* three houses down, my second cousin (waving to me), and my husband's dry cleaner, all moving noisily to the right of the Kotel, climbing the steps (one-two-landing, one-two-landing) by the southern wall, a few short of breath. It wasn't out of time at all, this vision, more like 3:35 P.M. next Tuesday afternoon. Today felt more surrealistic than this dream.

What caused the change? The answer had already formulated itself. It was the precious gift of this war-that-was-not-a-war that had managed to bring home to me how tangible possibilities really are. Possibilities had become ingrained in my everyday reality.

I knew for certain that it was entirely possible for a deadly gas bomb to drop straight on our heads. I also knew for certain that it was entirely possible for Hashem to send us an open miracle tonight to intercept that bomb. I knew that it was entirely possible for Hashem to send Mashiach — not in the year 6000 or some Tishah B'Av in the fog of the not-so-distant future, but today, or Wednesday morning, or three weeks from this *motza'ei Shabbos*. It is entirely possible that I will be sitting in the kitchen at the *milchig* counter, wearing my black-and-white sweater dress and my ponytail *sheitel*, stuffing tuna pitas for our girls' lunch into little sandwich bags, when I will hear the call of the shofar above the blast of our *"Deveikus"* tape.

And then I will hurriedly leave a message for my husband, put my ArtScroll Tehillim in my black, canvas bag, grab my purple jacket, make sure the girls have their hats/hoods on tightly, and run with them across the street to catch the first women's #2 bus with standing room and become part of the crush of the privileged crowd on the way to the *ezras nashim* in the *azarah*.

It is possible that, in His infinite kindness, Hashem deems it time for us to be redeemed, even though we are just who we are, in all our glaringly mundane detail.

I was still beaming as the girls interrupted me for the customary rummage in my bag to find *kvittel* paper and pens. They did not like to show me their private messages to HaKadosh Baruch Hu, but I did get hints.

"Ima, how do you spell Mashiach?"

"Ima, how do you say 'peace' in...oh, yeah, never mind."

Going home, we huddled in the last seat of the bus, passing the little, brown, paper bags back and forth between us, munching as our toes slowly thawed, our rectangular cardboard reminders of possibilities stacked near the mud-flecked, foggy window. The vault of the sky had already fallen, splashing happily and haphazardly on the ground, as we headed down the straight stretch of Rechov Kanfei Nesharim.

FRIENDS &
STRANGERS

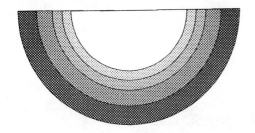

Miriam the Motivator

Leah Subar

I was sitting on the recliner in the family room — big cushions, fluffy headrest, orange juice in one hand, bag of chips in the other — the third day in a row.

Not that I'm lazy. It's just that my friends were all junior counselors at Camp Rina or up in the mountains for the summer. My sister, Shani, had plans to go to seminary in Jerusalem in the fall, so naturally, she had three million things to do.

And there I was, deciding whether or not to get up for yet another orange juice. I just didn't have the motivation. Then I started thinking...

Surely I'm not the only one in this predicament, I thought. Probably dozens or even hundreds of girls are sitting home just as bored. They just need a little push, a gentle nudge. They need...

I dashed to my room and pulled out all the colored markers.

MIRIAM THE MOTIVATOR, the first sign read. Boring.

MOTIVATION'S MY MIDDLE NAME. Tacky.

LEAH SUBAR was born in Denver and lives in Jerusalem with her family.

DO YOU NEED MOTIVATION? I was getting closer. Finally...

motivation*motivation*motivation
MOTIVATION UNLIMITED
You have the potential...
but you need a friend
Call Miriam Blobstein
655-8899
she'll motivate you!

I made five signs and posted them up around town: two in the mall, one in Mr. Stein's pizza shop, one in Kosher Kitchen, and one by the pool.

That night the phone rang.

"Hi! Is this Miriam Blobstein?"

"Yes."

"Er — I saw your sign today in the pizza shop — the one about...motivation?"

"Oh, yes, would you like me to motivate you?"

"Er — yes, I guess so. I feel sort of silly calling. Do you go to Bais Sarah?"

"No. Bais Devorah."

"Oh. Well, I go to Bais Sarah. You motivate Bais Sarah girls, too, right?"

"Of course," I said. "I motivate anyone. What's your name?"

"Rivki."

"Okay, Rivki, how can I motivate you? Are you sitting home bored? Is that the problem?"

"No, I'm afraid my problem's more complicated than that."

"Really?"

"You see," she said slowly, "for the past four years...I've... well...I guess you could say I've been a little overweight. The truth is, I'm downright chunky. Oh, you see? I can't even admit it to a stranger! I'm a blimp, that's what I am — a blubbery, flubbery blimp!"

"So go on a diet!" I blurted. Rivki was silent. "Hello? Rivki," I said, "have I helped you yet?"

"No, you haven't. See, I've gone on about a dozen diets. I know what I'm supposed to eat and what I'm not supposed to eat. I've read six books in the last two months on nutrition. I could probably write my own book!"

"Really?"

"That's right. There are approximately 20 calories in one medium-sized apple, 30 calories in an orange, and nearly 60 in just ten grapes..."

"So many?"

"...walking for one hour burns 50 calories, jumping rope burns 100, swimming burns 600, and...am I boring you?"

"Not at all."

"Good. Sugar is an empty calorie, whole grains are vital, and fruit is most easily digested when eaten before the meal. That's in the Rambam."

"You really know a lot."

"Sure. But I'm not motivated enough to follow it. I never exercise, and I'm addicted to chocolate. I'm hopeless."

"But you know so much — you could teach others."

"I can see it now. 'Hello. Let me, the fattest girl in the world, teach you how to be thin and healthy.' Fat chance."

"Wait a minute," I said. "You said before that you could write a book with all you know."

"I sure could."

"And the Torah says we must watch our health, right?"

"So?"

"So...you could put together a pamphlet with lots of information about health. And you could write it in a way that Bais Devorah girls *and* Bais Sarah girls would enjoy."

"Hmm, that sounds like a pretty good idea. And maybe my principal could write the introduction, explaining how important it is that we, as Jewish girls, take care of ourselves."

"That's a great idea, Rivki."

"This is so exciting! I can't believe...wait a minute!"

"What's wrong?" I asked.

"I'll tell you what's wrong. What's wrong is that it doesn't matter if I write an entire book about health. And it doesn't matter if every girl I know reads it. Don't you see? I'll still be fat! FAT! FAT! FAT!"

"Oh, Rivki," I said, "you don't understand. Every time you feel like eating, write a few lines for the pamphlet instead. By the end of the summer, you'll have written so much, you'll have the whole thing done! And by then you'll be thin!"

"That's interesting. I think...I think that just might work. Every time I get a craving for a box of chocolates, I'll write instead. I can write about how many calories are in a box of chocolates. Or I can write about how long you have to jump rope to burn off a box of chocolates. Or...or..."

"Wonderful, Rivki! You're going to help all of us girls stay healthy."

"Right."

"So that we'll study harder!"

"And do more mitzvos!"

"Go to it, Rivki! And send me a copy when you're finished."

"Thanks, Miriam. Thanks a lot."

Over the next several weeks, the calls just kept coming in. After the first dozen, my mother suggested I make appointments to see the girls personally so the phone wouldn't be tied up all day. I put a small table and two chairs out in the backyard under the big oak tree.

I was organizing a filing system for my clients when someone knocked on the door. Her name was Nechama, and she was twenty minutes early.

"Am I in the right place?" Nechama asked, taking off her sunglasses.

"Are you looking for motivation?"

"Y-yes, I am."

"Then you're in the right place." I led her to the backyard, but when we got to the door, she stopped.

"Would you mind if we spoke inside?" she asked. "It's very important that no one sees me here."

"No problem," I said. We made ourselves comfortable in the family room.

"I'm not here for myself," she began.

I'd heard that one before.

"It's my sister, Tzipora. I mean, nothing's really wrong with her. She's just, well, she's a little different, that's all. And since I'll be going to Gateshead in the fall, she'll be all alone."

"What do you mean? My sister is also going away this fall."

"Listen," she said. "My sister has no friends. She comes home from school and talks to me. When she's having a fit of depression, she cries on my shoulder. When she has good news, though it doesn't happen often, it's me she runs to tell — and in less than two months I'm leaving."

"That's very sad," I said, "but how can I help?"

"Well, your sign said you motivate people."

"Yes..."

"So," Nechama said, "motivate my sister to make friends — starting with you."

"Me?" I'd never been anyone's first friend before.

"Tzipora walks to Gateway Park every day at four. She likes to watch birds. That's where you can find her."

"Watching the birds?"

Nechama glanced at her watch. "If she finds out I was here, she'll be furious! Do you have any questions before I leave?"

"Leave? But you just arrived."

"I know. But Tzipora will wonder why I took so long. And by the way," Nechama said, "I have a very nice reward awaiting you if you succeed."

I didn't know what to say. I wasn't interested in receiving a reward. Being a motivator was just a nice way to spend the summer.

"Reward?" I asked blankly.

"If you succeed."

The next morning, I took a bus to the library. I took a huge stack of books from the shelves and plopped down at a table. I figured that, to succeed with Tzipora, I'd better have something in common with her. I'd spend all morning gathering information and then dazzle her at the park that afternoon. The topic: Birds.

I memorized all the parts of a bird, but I kept getting the scapulars mixed up with the wing coverts. Then I studied a few birds in depth so she would know that my knowledge wasn't just superficial. After three hours of hard work, I was prepared to meet my client — or so I thought.

Kids were playing frisbee in the park that afternoon, and some little boys were riding bikes. No sign of Tzipora. I checked the picnic benches, the sandbox, the swings. It was nearly ten after — I was getting worried. I tried watching birds, but somehow a robin redbreast was easier to identify in the book.

"Excuse me," a voice called out. "You — with the green blouse — hello!

"Yes, I'm speaking to you," the voice continued. "Up here! Don't you see me?"

I looked up, half-expecting to see a blue jay speaking to me. But she wasn't blue. And she wasn't a bird, though her name *was* Tzipora, and she *was* sitting in a tree.

"Oh, good," she said. "I thought you'd never look up."

"Sorry, I don't usually talk to people in trees."

"Is there something wrong with us?"

"No. I mean, I don't usually see people in trees."

"Oh. Well, that's because you don't look up. Listen, can you do me a favor?"

"Okay."

"Do you see a pair of binoculars down there?"

I knew I'd forgotten something! What kind of bird-watcher goes to the park without her binoculars? I was ruined.

"These?" I asked.

"Those." She stretched out her hand.

"Would you mind coming down?" I asked. "I can't reach you."

"Can't you climb up? It took me a long time to find this place."

"I'm sure it will be there when you return."

"You don't understand," she said. "I'm perfectly comfortable."

I could see this wasn't going to be easy. But I was on a mission to make her my friend.

"Look," I said, "I wouldn't mind climbing up, but I'm not wearing the right shoes. I'll slip."

Tzipora eyed my shoes. "Okay," she said, "I'll come down."

Next time I went to the library, I'd have to look up tree-climbing.

"Thanks," she said. She grabbed the binoculars and headed up the tree.

"Wait a minute," I said. "What are you looking for?" She was already halfway up.

"Who says I'm looking for anything?"

"Well, you have binoculars. What do you expect to see?"

She looked at me for a moment. "Birds," she said.

Now was my big chance. I could ask her if she'd seen any of those sharp-billed, white-breasted nuthatches flying around. Or maybe a ptarmigan, whose plumage would surely be brown this time of year instead of whitish, as it was in the winter. Or...

"Excuse me," Tzipora said, "why are you still standing there?"

"I think I hear a meadowlark! Have you seen one?"

"How should I know?"

"Oh. Well, you must have seen a lot of those North American juncos flying around."

"I don't know what you're talking about."

"Didn't you say you're looking for birds?"

"So?"

"So don't you know anything about birds?"

"No, not a thing."

"Where are you going?" I asked as she climbed down the tree and began walking away.

"I'm going to a different tree."

"What's wrong with this one?"

"Nothing. But I can't concentrate while you're here."

"Wait a minute," I called out. "What's your name?"

"Why do you want to know?"

"Well," I said, "it's nice to know the names of the people I meet."

"But you didn't meet me."

"So what's your name?"

"Why do you want to know?"

"So...so I can meet you."

"My name's Tzipora," she said. Then she ran as fast as she could until she was out of sight.

I was going to run after her, but I changed my mind. After all, I didn't want to overwhelm her. She told me her name — that was enough for today. Tomorrow I would tell her mine.

"Oh, it's you again," said Tzipora the following afternoon.

"That's really a warm way to greet a friend," I said.

"Who says you're a friend?"

"Who says I'm not?"

"Guilty until proven innocent."

"Guilty of what?"

She didn't answer that one, and I wasn't sure what the question was. But that's how Tzipora and I spoke.

"Why did you run away from me yesterday?" I asked. "Is there something wrong with me?"

"I was busy, that's all."

"Oh. And are you busy now?"

"Extremely."

"Then I'll just tell you my name. It's Miriam. Miriam Blobstein."

"But I didn't ask. It's very annoying to receive unwanted information."

"Oh, sorry. I take it back."

"Too late," she said. "You can't take it back. Now I'll always know your name. I'm very busy, so if you don't mind..."

"I just want to ask you one thing..."

"What?" Tzipora asked with a sigh.

"If you're such a serious birdwatcher, how come you don't know anything about birds?"

"Who says I don't know anything about birds?"

"You did! Yesterday. You said..."

"Oh, that. I only said that to keep the conversation short. I happen to know a lot more about birds than you do."

"Oh?" I said.

"How many times do birds blink per minute?" Tzipora asked.

"What? You must be joking."

"Oh, no, I'm not! Thirty-three. I've counted many times. And how many worms does a hungry bird eat in one hour?"

"How should I know? That's not important."

"It's important to the birds!" Tzipora protested. "They eat four-and-a-half or else three plus breadcrumbs. You see? I know much more than you."

"But I know all the names and all the parts and..."

"Sure — the names, the parts, this and that. Do you think the birds care what you call them? I watch the birds every day. I really know all about them."

I swallowed hard. I had spent an entire morning at the library studying birds. I never studied so hard for finals! Nevertheless, I was here to teach Tzipora the virtues of friendship. Giving in, just a little, would probably be a good first lesson.

"Tzipora," I said with as much sincerity as I could pinch together, "would you like to teach me what you know?"

She looked at me, baffled. "Teach you? It's not something

that can be taught. You have to sit and watch, like I do. But in a different tree! Now, no more questions."

"All right, I'm leaving." I turned and began walking away.

"But you can come back tomorrow," said Tzipora softly, "if you want."

I did return the following day. And every day after that. I found out that Tzipora had a coin collection, her favorite color was blue, she enjoyed baking, and she didn't mind washing dishes. And she told me interesting facts about birds: the kind you don't find in books.

Tzipora told me she liked my freckles. She said she once rubbed lemon juice all over her face for a week because she read that lemons give a person freckles. It didn't work, and girls called her "Sour Face" for a month afterward. I got the feeling they called her other names, too.

One day, we were sitting in my kitchen. The time had come to start encouraging Tzipora to be more outgoing.

"Let's make cookies for my neighbors," I said. "They're making a bris this week."

"*Mazel tov*! I love baking cookies!"

"You do? Maybe you should join a cooking club. Does your school have one?"

"I don't know."

"Our school does. And an art club and a creative writing club. That's the one I joined. Do you belong to a club? It's a great way to make friends."

"Well, I already have enough friends."

"Sure — me and the meadowlarks."

"That's not very nice, Miriam."

"I'm sorry, Tzipora. I just get the feeling you avoid people. They don't bite, you know."

"They don't?"

"People can be very nice. I am, for instance."

"Yeah, my sister also assumes it's my fault."

"Me? Assume?"

"Maybe in your school, the girls don't talk behind each other's backs, and maybe they care about each other's feelings. Well, my school is not your school..."

The doorbell rang.

"End of round one," I said. "Keep going with the cookies."

I opened the door expecting to see the mailman or a neighbor. It wasn't the mailman, though it was a familiar face. After a second, I realized whose it was.

"Hi!" she said. "Remember me?"

I leaped out the door, shutting it behind me.

"What's wrong?" she asked. "You look like you've seen a ghost. Anyway, I've come to congratulate you. I didn't think it was possible."

"Shh..."

"Well, anything's possible. What I mean is..."

"Wait a min —"

"I just came to give you your reward. Remember? I told you if you succeed, you'll receive a very nice reward. Well, you did it. You've befriended Tzipora. She comes home every day and goes on and on about you..."

"She's here!"

"You're a huge success! You actually befriended my sister. Now stop being so modest and...what did you...?"

Nechama looked past me. Suddenly her mouth dropped open. There in the window beside the front door stared two almond-shaped eyes.

"Surprise, Nechama," Tzipora said, opening the door.

"What are you doing here?" Nechama asked.

"I thought I was visiting a friend."

"Just a minute," I said. "You have to let me explain."

"I don't have to do anything, Miriam. Except congratulate you. You've succeeded in making a fool out of me."

"It's not the way it seems."

"Don't tell me that! I heard every word. Now what are you waiting for, Nechama? Give Miriam her reward! Go ahead!"

"Listen, Tzipora," Nechama said, "if you'll just let me explain — it's really very simple..."

"I'll tell you what's simple: I can't trust *anyone — ever.*"

"It's not true!" I pleaded.

"Don't say another word to me, Miriam Blobstein. You're worse than all the girls in my class. They don't play games. They tell me they don't like me, and that's that. But you — what you've done is the cruelest trick ever!"

Tzipora's eyes filled with tears as she ran out the door.

Mr. Stein's pizza shop smelled delicious, but I hadn't come to eat.

There was my sign — Miriam the Motivator. I didn't want to do any further damage, and with school starting soon, there wouldn't be time for a side occupation. It was pretty tattered, anyway. I took it down.

I didn't do much of anything for the next two weeks. The whole family went to the airport together to see Shani off. Another day I spent a few hours looking through a pamphlet I received in the mail: "Guard Your Health," by Rivki Rosner — a sixteen-page article about health, complete with calorie charts and food diagrams. I guess the "motivation" business wasn't a complete failure.

One day my mother asked me to go shopping at King's Grocery. On my way home, I passed a group of girls.

"I don't understand," one of the girls said. "Why does she

have to be so strange?"

"She was born that way," another girl said.

"She'll always be that way," the girls giggled.

"You know what I think?" one girl said. "I think Tzipora Kleinman should be sent to Siberia!"

My heart pounded. They continued cackling until I could no longer hold back.

"*Stop!*" I shouted.

"Are you speaking to us?" the tall one asked.

I gulped hard. My toes curled under. "Y-yes. Ahem. I'm speaking to you," I said. "I heard what you said about Tzipora Kleinman and..."

"And what?"

"It's not true."

"You know Tzipora Kleinman?" one of the girls asked.

"Yes," I responded. "She happens to be my friend."

"Friend? I didn't know she had a friend." They giggled.

"Well, she does. Tzipora's one of the most special girls I know. She's smart and funny and a loyal friend. If you'd just speak with her, you'd see that I'm right."

"Speak with her?" one girl said. "She doesn't let anyone near her!"

"That's only because of the way you treat her. If you'd be nice, you'd see that she would be nice, too."

"Who are you?" the tall girl asked.

"My name's Miriam Blobstein."

They all looked at each other and giggled.

"What's wrong?" I asked.

"Are you the one who put all those silly signs around town?"

My heart beat faster. "I didn't think they were silly..."

"You *are* the one! What a big joke!"

"Now just a minute..."

"No wonder you're friends with Tzipora," the tall girl said. *"You're as strange as she is! Ha! Ha! Ha!* C'mon, girls, let's get out of here. We're being invaded by strange people!"

The girls rushed past me, knocking me over. I brushed myself off and realized that, once again, I'd made things worse. Not only do the girls in Tzipora's class think she's strange, but they think her friends are even stranger! I knelt to pick up my purse and the grocery sack. I hoped the eggs weren't broken.

"Don't look so sad," said a voice. "You tried your best."

I stood up slowly and found a smiling face.

"Aren't you going to say hello?" she asked.

"Tzipora!"

"I should have warned you about those girls. You really made a fool out of yourself, you know?"

"Thanks."

"And you did it all for me."

"I'm afraid I did more harm than good."

"It was amazing the way you told them how wonderful I am."

"Yes, Tzipora. Believe it or not, I really like you. And I've missed you like crazy!"

"I can't wait to call Nechama and tell her. She's in Gateshead. She left last night. Oh — that reminds me," Tzipora reached into her pocket. She took out a small box and placed it in my hand. "Open it," she said.

"What's this?" I asked.

"Nechama promised you a reward if you befriended me, right? Well, you certainly did the job."

"Tzipora..."

"Nechama gave it to me when she left. It used to be wrapped."

"But..."

"No arguing, silly. Open it."

"Tzipora!" I exclaimed. "It's beautiful."

"You can try it on at home. It's a pendant."

"I know."

"It's for Shabbos. Or whatever. Now put it away, and tell me where you were headed before you got ambushed."

"I...I guess I was going home," I said. "I need to drop off this grocery bag. Why — you want to go to Gateway?"

"I was sort of in the mood to make cookies for your neighbors. We didn't really finish, did we?"

"But the bris was two weeks ago."

"Oh. Too bad," Tzipora said. "We'll just have to eat them ourselves."

"Hmm..."

"And if they come out good," Tzipora said, "we could go into business."

"You know what, Tzipora? I've had enough of business for a while. Let's just go watch the birds, okay?"

"Well, only if you really want to. Say, it's funny that of all the people my sister could have hired to be my friend, she chose someone who likes birds as much as I do. Isn't that a strange coincidence?"

"Eh..." I paused. I figured there'd be lots of time to tell her all my secrets. "Yes, Tzipora," I said, "that's a very strange coincidence."

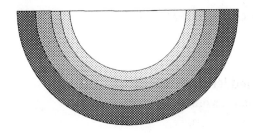

A Boy Named Sam

Libby Lazewnik

Sammy lives at the end of our street
He has two eyes, two hands, two feet.
In some ways he's not like me,
But in others — different as can be.

Sam can't think like you and me
His mind is very young, you see
And when he speaks, it's plain to tell,
It's hard for him to do it well.

His face is round, his eyes are small,
He can't play catch — he drops the ball.
He can't crack jokes, although he's tried;
But Sammy's smile is big and wide.

The other kids, they stay away
They never call to Sam to play
And when they see him, they just run,
Or else they'll stay to poke some fun:

If you want to read about LIBBY LAZEWNIK, turn to page 49.

"Oh, Sammy, what do you learn in school?"
"Do you know two plus two, you fool?"
And then they warn him nervously,
"You stay right there — away from me!"

Some mornings when I pass his house
He's out there, quiet as a mouse,
Whispering and playing games
With make-believe friends who have no names.

Other times he swings his gate
As we rush by (we never wait),
And calls out, "Hi, there!" if he dares.
But no one listens. No one cares.

One day, a group of children played
Near the house where Sammy stayed.
And he ran out to stare and stare
(I passed by then and saw him there).

Sammy went out into the sun
To watch the children have their fun;
And as he stood there in his place
A friendly smile came to his face.

"Hello!" he shouted, loud and clear.
But no one looked, no one came near.
Sammy waited, puzzled; then
"Hello!" he shouted once again.

The kids threw him a sideways peek,
Then went on playing hide-'n-seek,

And then went on to Cop and Bandit.
Sammy couldn't understand it.

"Hello, hello!" poor Sammy cried.
The kids got scared and ran to hide.
His face grew red as he watched them go —
"Hello, hello, hello, HELLO!"

Suddenly to my surprise,
I saw hot tears gush from his eyes.
And then Sam started to crawl around,
Looking for something on the ground.

He found it then: a little stone
And in a flash poor Sam had thrown
That rock as far as it would go
At those kids who wouldn't say hello.

He threw it at those fleeing backs
(It wasn't much of an attack)
The stone fell harmless to the street,
Far from the kids with the running feet.

And then I heard a new voice say,
"Come, Sam"; and Sammy turned away.
He shook his head and sobbed some more
As he went to his mother by the door.

"What happened, Sam?" she gently asked.
He pointed to those fleeing backs.
"Did those children cause you pain?"
He nodded but could not explain.

Then she saw me standing there
And beckoned me to come up near.
"Did you see what occurred, young man?
Tell me about it, if you can."

I thought about what I'd just seen,
And all at once I felt so mean,
Because I realized, don't you see?
That any of those kids might have been — me.

I hung my head and spoke real low.
"All Sammy did was say hello.
All he wanted was to be heard!
But those kids wouldn't say a word."

She nodded, "And do you know why
My Sammy then began to cry?"
"Yes," I whispered, "it's clear in the end:
Sam just wanted to make a friend."

"I see," she said, "you understand.
Sam will never be a man.
Sam will always be a child,
But a good-hearted one, friendly and mild.

"The world is very strange to him
Because his mind is weak and dim
But though he cannot think like you,
My Sammy's heart is good and true."

I took a real look at Sammy then
And knew I'd never be scared again;
I need friends, I like to play,
And Sammy feels the exact same way.

I tried to show him I understand;
I went and shook him by the hand;
I wanted him to know I'd heard;
And so I spoke a single word.

"Hello," I said — and Sammy smiled.
His face grew calm, his eyes were mild.
"Hello!" he answered, beaming so,
"Hello, hello, hello, hello!"

These days, whenever I chance to meet
The boy who lives at the end of our street,
"Hello!" I call, approaching near,
And Sammy smiles from ear to ear.

We cannot play, we can't discuss;
Sam, you see, is not like us;
His face is odd, his thoughts are slow;
So many things he'll never know;

But in a way that's deep and real
I know the way that Sammy feels;
He wants to build friendship, not a wall.

We're not so different after all.

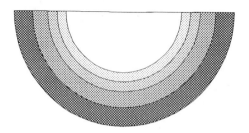

Buttonholed

Sheindel Weinbach

Brochele's big, blue eyes looked up trustingly at the man on the ladder. "My mother said I should ask you. You have good taste."

Mr. Gutfarb pushed his glasses farther up on his bushy, gray hair. One of these days he would have to get bifocals. It was a nuisance taking his glasses off each time he had to read a label or price. He climbed down to the little customer, rubbing his forehead in wonder.

Good taste? How did the woman know he had good taste? Had he ever advised anyone in the store on dressmaking or design? All he did here was fetch button boxes and put them back, unroll ribbon, measure it, cut it, and put the roll back in place. He hardly even used the cash register. Besides, most customers knew exactly what they wanted and chose by themselves. They were fairly good seamstresses and not too particular about frills. With so many kids, he thought to himself, they probably did not have the time or money.

Climbing down the ladder, he felt somewhat lighter

If you want to read about SHEINDEL WEINBACH, turn to page 46.

than when he had climbed up. Was going down that much easier? he wondered. He looked at the swatch of material in the little girl's hand and said, "Now, what was it you needed?"

"My mother is making a dress for me for my brother's bar mitzvah. She wants beautiful buttons. She said that you had good taste and would choose better than I would."

There it was again. Good taste. He was intrigued. When in the past two years had he exercised his famous artistic skill? His designer craft was long buried, together with Gadi.

Alex Gutfarb lived in Tel Aviv. He had come there as a young Holocaust victim and married a woman who had also been through the concentration camps. He and Rosa had considered themselves lucky when Gadi had been born; the doctors had given them no hope of having children.

Gadi had been their wonder child. They drowned their sorrows in love for him. They doted upon him, pampered him, treated him as if he were the Jewish people's only hope. And no wonder, for of both their shtetls in Poland, they alone had survived.

Gadi grew up as a typical Israeli boy. He joined the Tzofim, the Israeli version of Boy Scouts, went on many outdoor hikes, trekked the length and breadth of the country, and loved its beautiful scenery. At the age of eighteen, he enlisted in the army, where he trained as a pilot. *"Hatovim latayas* — the elite for the Air Force" was a motto that appealed to him, for he had always excelled in school, leadership, and every other area of his life. He was a model student, a model son, a model pilot.

And then came the black day when Gadi's plane was shot down. Gadi had died a hero's death, steering his limping plane towards an enemy aircraft to retaliate with a well-aimed bomb which had downed it, Samsonlike, along with his. The I.D.F. had awarded him a posthumous medal. Mr.

Gutfarb treasured it. But it could never bring Gadi back to life.

All hope, all thoughts of any worthwhile pursuit in life withered before Mr. Gutfarb's eyes. The abyss he had glimpsed during the Holocaust came back to haunt him. A successful fashion designer up to Gadi's death, he quit his job, and for many months he sank into deep depression, refusing to speak to anyone, even Rosa. He took to drinking because it helped him forget.

Though she was no less stricken by her son's death, Rosa still held onto her sanity and found some consolation in volunteer work. This did not bring in money, however, and she could not think of taking a steady job at her age and state of health. But they had to live on something.

When Alex's unemployment insurance proved too little even for their meager expenses, she pushed her husband into finding a job. She realized that he could not go back to being a fashion designer. His creativity and ambition were gone. And he drank too much.

Mr. Gutfarb found a job advertised for a pensioner. It fit the bill. He would work only morning hours, and his duties required no skills. The half-hour trips to and from the sewing store in B'nei Brak would also help pass the hours that hung so heavily on his hands. In his heart of hearts, he really did not want to drink. But he did not want to think, either, and when he was not occupied with anything, drinking was his only way of banishing those aching memories of his beloved Gadi.

He did his work mechanically. What pride could one have in button boxes aligned neatly in rows, arranged by color and size? There was no challenge in his work, but he was grateful for that. He would work all morning, and then, at about two o'clock, the store owner, Mr. Gelb, would go home for lunch. Mr. Gutfarb would finish picking up the loose threads, literally and figuratively, and then lock up and go to the nearest pub. That was in Tel Aviv, of course. He would spend all the loose change in his pocket, get drunk, and return home to sleep it off.

And then things changed.

It began with the blue-eyed little girl asking him to match some buttons for her.

Mr. Gutfarb could not remember having been addressed personally for months. It was always "put this away" or "bring me that box from the shelf up there," as if he were a robot.

But now this customer was asking him to use his judgment. His good taste. Something snapped to attention inside him. There was a challenge. He took the swatch of material in his hand and let his eyes rove up and down the rows of button boxes, rejecting one after the other. Finally his gaze settled upon a box in the corner with novelty buttons of unusual shapes.

"Why don't you try these out? If your mother doesn't like them, you can exchange them."

Would Little Miss Blue Eyes' mother be ready to set a trend? The way he envisioned the new dress, it would be the envy of all the girl's friends.

"Here, tell your mother to add a touch of this ribbon by the collar and sleeves to match your blue eyes, and the dress will be nice enough for a wedding. I'll give you a few centimeters so she can see what it will look like."

"I'll tell her you said so." The little girl looked up at him gratefully.

Mr. Gutfarb went back to his simple tasks and soon forgot about the buttons and bows. He swept, emptied the waste basket, and closed up shop at two as usual.

The next morning, the little girl was back. "Hello, Mr. er..."

"Gutfarb." It was nice to have a name again, thought the

man behind the counter. The name Alex Gutfarb had once meant something to Tel Aviv fashion houses.

"And who are you, little girl with the blue eyes? Since you are such a steady customer, you might as well introduce yourself, too."

She smiled up at him. "I'm Brochele. You know, my mother was very pleased with your suggestions. She said she wanted one-and-a-half meters of that ribbon you sent along. She said I should ask you if the dress would look better with pockets or without. You would know. You have good taste."

Mr. Gutfarb glowed with the compliment. "Wait a minute, Brochele." He found a piece of scrap paper and sketched a dress. It had the buttons she had bought yesterday, ribbon around the collar and wrists, and interesting pockets that seemed to match the shape of the buttons. "Tell her to try this. And here are some extra buttons to put on the pocket." He fished out some coins from his own pocket and put them in the cash register. "A small gift from me."

It would mean a drink less, but so what?

Brochele came back the next day. "Mr. Gutfarb, my mother wants to thank you for your excellent tips. The dress came out beautifully, and a neighbor asked her to make one just like it. We could use the extra money. Moishe will be bar mitzvah soon. Anyway, my mother bought this material for the dress and wants to know what would go well with it."

Mr. Gutfarb's eyes narrowed as he studied the fabric. Brochele would not want her friend to be dressed exactly like her, would she? Besides, this material called for a different style altogether. He quickly sketched another design and filled in the details with different trimmings.

"Tell your mother to try this ribbon and make the pleats going this way instead of that, with a twist of material here, like this."

While Mr. Gutfarb was advising Brochele, another customer was peering over her shoulder. "That is very clever of you. I like that. Could you suggest anything suitable for a dress I bought? I feel it's missing something. A bow or a flower or something..."

Mr. Gutfarb went about his work that day with a spring in his step. He felt better than he had in months. As he was straightening out the show window, he added a few touches here and there that gave it a fresh appeal. He noticed with satisfaction that some women outside stopped to look, and some even entered.

He was very busy that morning, serving customers, advising, bringing out dusty boxes with sewing notions that had lain forgotten, matching and mixing. When the store was finally empty and Mr. Gelb had gone home after a busy morning, Mr. Gutfarb saw boxes piled high on the counter and general disarray. He set to work rearranging items that were in greater demand so they would be in easy reach. Then he strung up some ready-made appliqués from a decorative hanger above the counter, like a mobile, and stood back to study the effect. He was pleased.

Mr. Gutfarb puttered about the store putting things to right. He was still busy when the owner returned at ten to four for the afternoon hours. Mr. Gelb was pleasantly surprised to see him still there.

"Since you haven't gone home yet, Alex, perhaps you would like to go out for a sandwich and come back for the afternoon shift. There is plenty of work to do, I see."

Mr. Gutfarb nodded. That was an idea. Who said he had to drink away his sorrows when he had work to do? It helped him forget just as well.

He went out, found a luncheonette and ordered something. Seeing everyone wash, he went over to the sink and did the same. He had nothing against religion, really. It just had never fit into his life, so he had drifted away from practicing the mitzvos. After the Holocaust, that is. But he was not a "*lehachis-nik*," one who spitefully rejects the mitzvos. One could not very well work in B'nei Brak and dislike the people there; they were so decent and good.

At Mr. Gelb's suggestion, they alternated watching the shop that afternoon and going out to *minchah*. Mr. Gutfarb had not davened for years; it was nostalgic. Memories did not always have to be painful, he realized. He felt at home in the *shtiblach*, where people jostled one another for room but found the time to answer questions, give directions, lend advice or money, and execute myriad transactions before, after, and around the half-dozen minyanim forming with kaleidoscopic rapidity and variety.

Mr. Gutfarb returned home sober and told his wife of the day's experiences. She was thrilled to see him take an interest in things and hoped it would extend to the following day as well.

The next day Brochele came in again, this time with her mother.

"Hello, there. My daughter says you are the one with all those creative ideas. But you are not the owner, Mr. Gelb, at all!"

She turned to Brochele. "See, he wears glasses, and Mr. Gelb doesn't. I thought at first that she had made a mistake. She did, actually. But I am not in the least sorry. Your taste, Mr. Gutfarb, is really the best."

Mr. Gutfarb pulled himself out of his depression and found new expression for his creativity. He never did go back to fashion designing; he was already too old for that. But he did return to something else. His roots. And he found that helping others, in his unique way, was really the best way to help himself. In a sense, he had found the right button for his empty buttonhole...

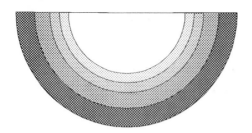

The Whisper

Lena Spitzer

I only told to it to a friend
I'm ever so discreet
It was something that I knew
She wasn't likely to repeat.
Then like seeds a-blowing in the wind,
It flew on and it grew...
Because it was so interesting,
And she said that it was true!

Here a whisper,
There a chat
Some said this...
And some said that...
People I have
Never known
Heard the tidbits
On the phone.
Words flew on
And without doubt
Reached the ears
Of the "talked about"

If you want to read about LENA SPITZER, turn to page 75.

And when they came to check it out,
And landed at my door...
The finger pointed straight at me,
I could have fallen through the floor!
They feel so sore — and say I'm to blame
And honestly, I'd say the same!
An aggrieved heart — who can repay it?
Once a word is said — you can't un-say it!

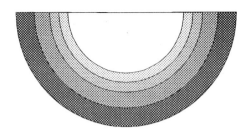

Leave a Message after the Tone...Please!

Bracha Druss Goetz

Left on call waiting, and no one came back.
It took so long that I sent out a fax.
The most sophisticated communication ever seen.
But all I get to talk to is an answering machine.
Advanced communication. There's one problem only.
How come more people than ever are lonely?

If you want to read about BRACHA DRUSS GOETZ, see page 135.

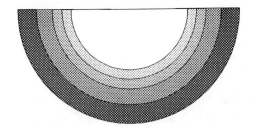

A Special Friend

Sheryl Prenzlau

S hifra awoke feeling very excited. She blinked once. She blinked twice. And then she suddenly remembered! Today she would be going to sleep-away camp for the very first time! She looked over at the corner of her room as if to confirm the thought and make sure she wasn't still dreaming. There, neatly bundled and labeled, stood the suitcase and duffel bag that she and her mother had finally completed packing late last night.

She said *"Modeh Ani,"* hopped out of bed, and quickly washed her hands. Then she dressed in the clothes she had carefully prepared before collapsing into bed around midnight. After combing her hair, she remembered to pack away her comb, brush, toothpaste, and toothbrush for her three-week stay at Camp Rayus.

"As a kid, I used to write all kinds of funny poems. I never tried writing stories until I got my computer last year. It made erasing all my mistakes so much easier. Since then, I've been working hard organizing this book. It certainly looks easier than it was. I am also busy writing some of the *B.Y. Times Kid Sisters* books. My advice to anyone who wants to try writing is: Go ahead — you might be as surprised as I was to find out that someone likes the way you write!

"P.S. My family and I moved to Israel from Denver ten years ago and we love it here!" — SHERYL PRENZLAU

She would really have to hurry up if she wanted to be at the bus by ten o'clock.

Shifra went out on the porch with her siddur. She always felt that just looking at the beautiful hills of Yerushalayim helped her have more *kavanah* in her davening. Sometimes she would close her eyes and picture Avraham Avinu walking with Yitzchak to the *akeidah*. Maybe over these same hills. Or David HaMelech marching with his army — right over there, or...

"Enough daydreaming, Shifra," she reminded herself. "You're always imagining things and wasting time. It's eight-thirty already, and Devory and her mother will be picking you up in less than an hour." Shifra often spoke to herself like that when no one was listening.

She finished davening, kissed her siddur, and packed it into the corner of her bag, so she would know just where to find it. She would need it soon to say *"Tefillas HaDerech."*

Beep. Beep. Beep.

"Ima, I think it's Devory!" Shifra called, running over to the window to look out. "Oh, I'm so excited! Goodbye, Esti, Avromi, Rifky, Yanky, and especially *you*, baby Chaimel!" Shifra gushed, hugging the squirming baby. "Be good, and don't forget to help Ima double while I'm away."

Shifra and her mother pushed the heavy bags into the hallway and waited impatiently for the elevator. Somehow they managed to squeeze themselves and their bulky bags into the small elevator.

"Hi, Shifra. Are you as excited as I am?" cried Devory as she jumped out of the car and rushed to greet her friend.

"Are you kidding? Today is the happiest day of my life!" Shifra exclaimed. "Well, almost the happiest," she amended, remembering her bas mitzvah just three months before. "Let's hurry up so we can get good seats on the bus. My neighbor Chevy is babysitting, so my mom can wait with us till the bus comes."

So Shifra and her mother, Devory and hers, and all the suitcases and bags and extra little packages squished into the Tennenbaums' car and headed jauntily for Binyanei HaUmah, the Yerushalayim pickup point for Camp Rayus.

The parking lot was crowded. It seemed that Camp Rayus was not the only camp that had designated the famous Yerushalayim convention hall as its meeting place. Several groups were standing around the lot. But Shifra and Devory had no trouble finding theirs. Even in the heat of the summer, the girls of Camp Rayus were dressed modestly, befitting true *b'nos Yisrael*.

Mrs. Tennenbaum parked the car between two other half-loaded station wagons, and together they all began struggling with their clumsy bags.

"Need a hand?" four of the girls asked, coming over with big smiles.

Devory and Shifra smiled awkwardly at each other, signaling with their eyes how uncomfortable they felt, since they didn't even know these girls. Shifra and Devry had been best friends since kindergarten and could almost read each other's thoughts by now.

"Are you new to Camp Rayus? Is this your first time?" one of the girls asked as she heaved Devory's bag aboard the bus.

"Yes. I'm Devory Tennenbaum, and this is my best friend, Shifra Schulman," introduced Devory.

"And I'm Leah, and this is Malky, Freidy, Chani, Chedva, and Tzippy," chirped a bubbly redhead, who seemed to be at the center of the group. "We all went to Camp Rayus last year, and you're going to love it — right, gang?"

"Right!" chorused the other five.

Mrs. Tennenbaum and Mrs. Schulman grinned at each other and knew they were right in choosing Camp Rayus for their girls. They had heard that this camp attracted girls with good *middos,* and what the women had just seen confirmed it.

Both girls hugged their mothers and kissed them goodbye.

"We'll see you in only a week-and-a-half on visiting day, remember?" Mrs. Schulman told Shifra. "And I'll try to call you before Shabbos so you won't be homesick."

"And don't forget to write a few postcards," added Mrs. Tennenbaum to Devory. "That is, if you find time between all your activities."

Climbing onto the bus, Shifra and Devory found seats together near the back. They opened the window and leaned out. "Bye! Shalom!" they called to their mothers.

"So long! *Lehitraot!*" Mrs. Schulman and Mrs. Tennenbaum answered, waving.

The bus pulled slowly out of the lot and into the busy street.

Shifra leaned back in her seat. "You know, Devory," she said with a sigh, "I'm a little nervous about meeting all these girls. Since kindergarten, we've always had the same kids in our class. I've never met so many people at once. Do you think it will be hard to remember all their names?" Then she asked the question that really seemed to be bothering her. "Do you think we can really become their friends?"

Devory looked straight at her best friend. "Shifra, you know we'll always be best friends. But I think it's kind of exciting to meet new people, and I'm really looking forward to it. Maybe you're just tired."

Shifra smiled at her friend. "You're probably right, Devory. I barely slept last night with all the excitement of the trip on my mind. I'm probably just 'making a mountain out of a molehill,' as my father always says. I guess he means that I always picture things as much worse than they really are." And with that, Shifra sat back again and closed her eyes to rest.

Devory was glad the bus was air-conditioned. The heat of the Jordan Valley would have been unbearable otherwise on such a hot day.

As the bus began driving down the hills toward Maaleh Adumim, Michal, the camp director, spoke into the microphone: "Girls, it's time to say *'Tefillas HaDerech.'* " "I'll say the *brachah*, and you can all just answer, 'Amen.' "

Shifra sleepily listened to her words and said, "Amen," along with the other girls on the bus. Soon, despite all the singing and noise, she drifted off to sleep.

Leaning forward in her seat, Devory was able to hear Chani and Chedva playing a word game. "*Alef* is for Ahuvah, *beis* is for Batya..."

"May I play, too?" Devory asked.

"Sure," Chani answered. "Your letter is *gimmel*. Can you think of a girl's name that starts with it?"

Devory thought for a second and came up with the name Gitta. "Is that the way to play?"

"You've got it," Chedva smiled.

The game continued through three more rounds, until no one could suggest names that hadn't already been mentioned.

"I'm really glad we'll be in the same bunk," Devory said happily. "It's a little scary to go to a camp with strangers, but I almost feel like I've known you both for years."

Chedva's eyes twinkled with delight. "That's the nice thing about Camp Rayus," she said. "Everyone is so-o-o friendly."

Chani joined the conversation. "Tell me, is it true that you and Shifra have been friends for ten years?" she asked.

"And that you've hardly ever been apart?" added Chedva curiously.

Devory hesitated, thinking about the time in second grade when she and Shifra had had an argument and hadn't spoken to each other for a month. Then she answered, "Yes," deciding not to bring up bad memories. "We've been together since kindergarten — we're almost like sisters." But to herself, she silently added, "Sometimes, though, we're too close. If only Shiffy wouldn't be so jealous when I make other friends." She glanced guiltily over at her sleeping friend, afraid for a second that maybe they *could* read each other's minds.

"*Od Avinu chai! Od Avinu chai!*" The singing grew louder and louder, as row by row of girls joined in. The bus itself seemed to be singing along! Soon Chedva could hardly hear what Devory was saying anymore and decided they might as well sing, too.

Sliding out of her seat carefully, so as not to disturb the sleeping Shifra, Devory stood in the aisle, where she began harmonizing to a slow, flowing tune about Yerushalayim. Soon she was caught up in the lilting and graceful music. They sang and sang for another half an hour, with Devory enjoying every minute. And then, exhausted, she plopped down into the empty seat next to Malky, near the front of the bus.

"I'm enjoying myself so much, Malky — and camp hasn't even begun yet!" Devory exclaimed, catching her breath.

Malky grinned. "I know what you mean. Ever since last summer, I've been looking forward to camp again. Camp Rayus is just great — you'll see!"

At the mention of *rayus* — friendship — Devory looked

back. Shifra was awake, sitting upright and staring out the window.

Shifra had actually been up for five minutes already. The singing and clapping had jolted her awake. Immediately, she had begun a frantic search for Devory, finally locating her sitting at the front of the bus next to Malky. Shifra gulped noiselessly, feeling queasy and uncomfortable. Her stomach filled with butterflies. She felt like crying.

Just then, Leah leaned over and asked: "Do you mind if I sit here?"

Looking at her, Shifra thought for a second and said: "Okay, but Devory might come back."

"That's all right," answered Leah with her friendly smile. "I can move when she comes. Would you like a drink? My mother gave me three cans of juice — let's share one."

Sitting back in her seat, Shifra gratefully accepted the juice and sipped it quietly. The cool liquid began to soothe the lump in her throat.

The bus drove lower and lower into the desert valley, the fields and buildings of neighboring Jordan actually visible across the border fence. Occasionally, soldiers in jeeps passed by as they patrolled the no-man's-land between the two countries.

Soon Leah and Shifra were chattering away, deeply involved in discussing their doll collections. The longer they talked, the more they found they had in common — like their love for quiz games, dancing, and writing poetry.

The three-hour trip flew by. Before anyone realized how late it was, the bus passed through the small city of Beit Shean. Suddenly, the girls came alive with exclamations of delight as they caught their first glimpse of the glistening waters of the Kinneret. What a wonderful three weeks this would be!

Camp Rayus echoed with happy voices again. Its twelve cabins, dining hall, sports fields, and gym once again bustled with dozens of girls struggling to transport their luggage to their rooms and acquaint themselves with the lovely campgrounds. Bunk 5 was soon filled with ten girls all talking at once. Climbing over the piles of suitcases stretching from one end of the room to the other, they began filling the shelves near their beds with all the things they had carefully packed the previous week.

"Boy, will I be glad when this is all finished," said Mindy, the junior counselor, balancing on top of two duffel bags.

"Don't worry," answered Shani, the counselor, as she tripped on some shoes. "During supper, they'll collect the luggage and store it in the barn until we leave in three weeks."

Scanning the crowd for her best friend, Shifra quickly looked away when she saw Devory and Malky saving beds together by the window.

"Here, Shifra, this one's for you," Devory called. She felt guilty when she saw the look on Shifra's face.

At the other end of the bunk, Leah was waving, "Shifra, come! Let's sleep near each other over here!"

For a moment, Shifra stood still. She looked over at Devory and Malky and then back at Leah.

"Okay, Leah, that sounds great," Shifra replied half-heartedly. She dragged her bag (which suddenly seemed much heavier) across the room, seemingly indifferent to Devory's shocked stare.

"Oh, no. Now I've asked for it again," Devory thought to herself. "How can we be so close and yet sometimes so far apart? I wish Shifra weren't so sensitive and could realize that it's possible to have more than one good friend." But outwardly she just smiled as Racheli took the bed she had saved for Shifra.

"Here are my shirts, and I'll put my socks and pajamas here," thought Shifra. But louder than these thoughts were the confused ones racing through her mind: "How could Devory do that to me after all these years?" She swallowed hard and held back tears.

Leah slipped in beside her. "Come, I'll help you," she said. "I've got a great system for doing this real fast."

"In fact, Leah has a system for just about everything," Chani added brightly.

"Come on, Chani, you promised — no teasing," answered Leah. "Shifra hardly even knows me, and already you're giving her ideas."

Chani gave Leah a quick hug and laughed. "Everyone knows I'm just teasing you, Leah — we're all crazy about our favorite redhead."

In ten minutes, Leah had accomplished what she'd set out to do — help Shifra unpack and distract her from her homesickness and confusion about Devory.

"Let's all go play *machanayim*," called Malky.

"Wow, what a great idea!" Tzippy exclaimed. She rushed out the door, the rest of the girls quickly following behind.

Two other bunks heard the screams and sounds of the game, and within just a few minutes the whole courtyard was filled with laughing girls and flying balls.

Shani and Feigy, the counselor of neighboring bunk 6, sat together watching the game.

"I think this summer will work out just fine," Feigy said, stretching out on the warm grass.

"I hope so, Feigy," answered Shani. "But I'm afraid there's a small storm brewing in my bunk." Suddenly she wasn't so comfortable on the grass; she could feel the bumpy little pebbles beneath her. "We'll just have to wait and see how things develop," she finished with a sigh.

The afternoon continued uneventfully, and soon the girls were told to wash up for *minchah* and supper. All the bunks began filing into the noisy dining hall to sit around their assigned tables.

By now, Leah seemed almost glued to Shifra, who certainly wasn't complaining. But when she saw Devory surrounded by three chattering girls at the washing area, Shifra was suddenly quite homesick and also a bit lonely for her best friend. She quickly sat down between Leah and Tzippy, not wanting Devory to see her waiting and feel that she *had* to sit near her.

Devory and the other girls washed and found their way to their table. Surprised to see Shifra already sitting, Devory managed to squeeze her way in and sit down directly across from her. After swallowing a few bites of bread, Devory smiled uncertainly at Shifra.

"Everything okay, Shiffy?" she asked quietly, looking straight into Shifra's eyes.

"Sure, Devory. Why do you ask?" Shifra replied, convinced that the whole camp could hear her heartbeat pounding in her ears.

"Come on," Devory insisted. "I know you better than that."

Shifra gulped, avoiding Devory's stare. "Well I *thought* you did, too."

Devory shifted uneasily in her chair. "Okay, we'll talk later," she whispered.

Both girls finished their first meal in camp smiling on the outside, but with heavy hearts.

Late that night, after all the girls in her bunk seemed sound asleep, Shifra crept out of the cabin and sat down on the steps. She shivered a little in the chilly night air and hunched her shoulders together. The minutes passed. Shifra's mind was cluttered with thoughts of the previous day. She was sad and confused but, surprisingly, also a little happy when she thought of Leah and Tzippy and all the new friends she had made that day. She was so caught up in her thoughts that she didn't even hear the door open. She jumped slightly when she felt someone sit down next to her.

Devory looked over at Shifra. "Is it okay if I sit with you awhile?"

Nodding, Shifra continued staring straight ahead.

"Shiffy, I wish you'd tell me what's wrong," Devory said quietly. "I've tried so hard today to see what's bothering you, but you keep shutting me out."

"*I'm* shutting *you* out?" Shifra asked in disbelief. "All day long, you haven't even come near me!"

"What? I can't believe it!" Devory croaked in surprise. "I saved you a bed next to mine, but you went with Leah instead. I came into the dining hall to find you, but you were already sitting with Tzippy and Leah. I asked what was bothering you, but you wouldn't even talk to me. We've always been so close, but sometimes I don't understand you at all." Devory's eyes filled with tears.

The door creaked. Both girls turned around quickly. Shani stood behind them in the doorway.

"Would you girls mind if I joined you?" Shani looked at their teary faces and added, "Maybe I can help with whatever is bothering you."

Both girls looked down and then nodded.

Shani sat down between them and put an arm around each of the shivering girls' shoulders. "Maybe we can work out this problem soon, so we can all get back into our warm beds and get some sleep."

The two girls took turns describing what they thought had happened that day. Shani listened carefully to each girl's story, remaining silent until they'd both finished, and their tears had almost dried.

"You know, girls," she began softly, "I think we have a true misunderstanding here. Each of you feels hurt by something she thinks the other has done to her. Each of you is confused, and I think it's important to clear this up before it goes any further.

"I think Shifra feels Devory doesn't want to be with her anymore and prefers the girls she met today. Is that right?"

She looked at Shifra, who nodded silently.

"And if I understand correctly, Devory feels that even though she *did* make friends today, each time she tried to be with Shifra, she was already busy and seemed happy with *her* new friends. Am I right, Devory?"

Devory nodded.

The camp echoed with evening sounds of cricket choirs and owls. But the two girls, absorbed in their counselor's words, barely noticed.

"I think both of you need to realize two things," Shani continued seriously. "One is that we can all be good friends, and the other is that no one wants to split you two apart. You have been so close for almost your whole lives and probably will remain close for many years to come. You have a very special friendship...but there's always room for new friends for each of you.

"Shifra, you told me how much you and Leah seem to have in common. And Devory, you told me how you enjoyed discussing your favorite books with Malky. But that doesn't make you like each other any less." She smiled. "I think you both need to see how much you can gain by meeting all types of girls this summer. And remember, you'll always still have each other.

"Now one other thing: We must try to be *dan lekafzechus* — to judge each other favorably. Shifra, when you fell asleep on the bus, Devory naturally wanted to move so as not to wake you. Also, you must admit, it's pretty boring to sit near a sleeping person. That's why she went to sit near Malky. Then, all day long, it seemed to her that you were enjoying yourself with your new friends. She didn't even know why you were upset.

"It's so very important to talk things over with each other when we feel hurt. We mustn't jump to conclusions. Do you understand?"

Both girls quietly nodded.

"Sometimes we build things up in our minds," continued Shani. "We imagine things as much worse than they are, and small things seem to turn into big, horrible events that upset us much more than they should. We make mountains out of molehills."

Shifra and Devory jumped at her words.

"That's just what my father says!"

"That's just what your father says!" The two girls looked shyly at each other. Then they both smiled.

Shani hugged the two girls. The warmth of their smiles almost turned the evening into a sunny day, and the cool night air was momentarily forgotten. "I think we're all going to have a great summer together, don't you?" she asked as the three stood up.

Shifra nodded. "We sure are."

And Devory added, "Thanks for everything, Shani."

Then the two girls winked at each other and followed Shani inside.

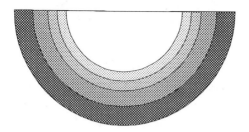

The Russians

Talia Hendler

We're from a different country
So foreign to your own
We're from a country and a land
That's virtually unknown

Our language you don't understand
Nor our mentalities
And yet you make kind overtures
You try so hard to please

You've welcomed us into your homes
You've set us up, and yet
Although you look at us as Jews
We're still "the Soviets"

"I live in Brooklyn and teach Russian high-school students. I began writing stories and poems in third grade. I was born in Moscow and moved to America when I was five. Today, *baruch Hashem*, I am the proud parent of a beautiful baby girl." — TALIA HENDLER

When we lived back in Russia
We were always labeled "Yid"
But now, within her school, my child
Is called "that Russian kid!"

Back there we were doctors and engineers
Back there was identity
Now we're just mere immigrants
Who were forced to run, to flee

You've shown us your Shabboses
Your *simchah* and your soul
You've given us education for free
Teaching Torah was your goal

And yet I'm still "that Russian"
Instead of being a Jew
And so I beg you, understand
We're just the same as you!

LONG AGO & FAR AWAY

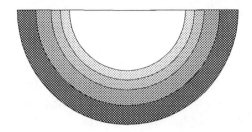

The Shoemaker of Shaarei Chessed

Sarah Berkovits

I f you ever come across a place where the streets ring with joy, where there are signs of poverty everywhere, where people are eking out a meager living yet every face beams with contentment, serenity, and inner calm, you will know that you have hit upon the historic Jerusalem quarter known as Shaarei Chessed.

Friday night and Shabbos afternoon in the tiny back streets of Shaarei Chessed, you will encounter the quaintest, cutest, sweetest, *"bechaintest"* little children playing, all of them speaking Yiddish just like wise, bearded, old men. Big

"I started telling stories from about age six or seven, first to myself and then to my siblings — both captive audiences — and I've never really stopped. I might say I'm blessed with the gift of storytelling. I keep audiences of all ages spellbound, because I speak directly from the heart. I have read a couple of my stories on the radio, and I occasionally entertain senior citizens through my storytelling. When I am deeply touched by a person, I feel compelled to write about him/her. My dream is to go back to my roots and write about my great-grandmother, Rebbetzen Sheindel Wesel, whom I love, though I was not privileged to know her. Her soul, her essence, her being was truly great. I'd like to share her greatness with the world." — SARAH BERKOVITS

four-year-olds, holding hands with less big three-year-olds, holding hands with two-year-olds and wheeling carriages with one-year-olds inside is a common sight. Strolling past the houses and tumbledown huts huddled together as if for security, you may come across an unobtrusive little shack sandwiched in between two *shtiblach* where men and women have been coming to pray for generations.

Perhaps you have passed this street many a time without ever noticing the shack. You may even pray in these *shtiblach* but remain oblivious to its existence. Nothing distinguishes its few tin walls from all the other structures of its kind in the vicinity. Should you have passed by of late, you probably found the place locked up and without any sign of life. But occasionally the door is ajar, you may even hear the tap-tapping of a hammer at work.

Inside, on a broken-down stool surrounded by leather scraps and their pungent smell sits a wizened, unshaven old man bent double with age but hard at work. He wears a corset and a white apron, and his whole demeanor bespeaks the trials and tribulations of life. For years, he has been repairing the shoes of all the feet in the district.

With materials and labor so costly, finding the money for shoe-repair bills in families with anywhere from six to eighteen children can be quite a challenge. There is hardly enough money to feed all these kids let alone clothe them. But children do have a way of wearing down their shoes, and shoes with holes in them mean sick kids — especially in the rainy winter season — and sick kids mean doctors' bills and, in the final analysis, shoe-repair bills are cheaper and more desirable than doctors' bills.

So this old shoemaker is kept busier than his failing strength and ailing health permit.

How did I meet him? One day, I noticed that my shoes

were badly worn at the heel. I happened to be walking by the shack. The door was open to let in daylight and a bit of warmth from the winter sun. Surprised that I had never noticed the shack, and finding it hard to resist an open door, I peered in and caught my first glimpse of him sitting there, bent over his work. When he looked up, I saw he had sparkling, blue eyes and the kind, serene expression of a man at peace with the world.

"Can you mend my shoes while I wait?" I asked, and he nodded.

As I watched him working, I was struck by the pains he was taking. This was no slapdash job. Whatever he charged, he was giving me my money's worth.

"How much do I owe you?" I asked when the shoes were ready.

"One lira fifty."

I thought I hadn't heard him correctly. Why, even the Arabs in the Old City, who were cheaper than most shoemakers, were taking two lira fifty, and elsewhere I had paid four and five liras. But one lira fifty was all he wanted. I paid him and went home.

It was Friday and my mother was in the kitchen cooking for Shabbos. I told her what had happened and how bad I felt that the shoemaker had taken so little money.

"I feel I should take him a cake," I said. But I was afraid it would embarrass him, so I never did.

On my way to and from the school where I was teaching, I frequently passed the shack and saw the shoemaker. Often he would be hobbling across the street with a piece of dry bread and a glass of tea. More than once, as I passed by, he would call out to me: "What time is it?" I don't think he ever owned a watch, for who had money for such luxuries?

After the Yom Kippur War came the devaluation of the

lira. Prices rose daily. I took in another pair of shoes and picked them up weeks later.

"How much?" I asked.

"One lira seventy-five."

I couldn't believe it. Prices everywhere were sky-high. The material alone must have cost him that. I gave him more — he wouldn't take it. Finally, he accepted two liras.

"Everything is so expensive these days, life is hard," he said. "How can I take more?"

A short while later, I paid fifteen liras to have my boots reheeled, in a place down the road.

"Fifteen liras!" I exclaimed incredulously when the man told me the price.

"Everything is so expensive these days. How can I take less?"

After that, the shack remained closed for a long time, and for weeks I did not see the shoemaker. Then, one day, I spied him walking across the street. He was very bent over, his head closer and closer to the ground. I was filled with sadness and almost horror, for here was a man half in his grave. But in a flash, my sadness passed, for here, I realized, was a man *already* in heaven!

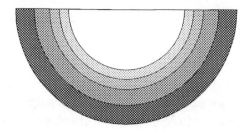

The Jews of Mashad, Persia

Tzvia Ehrlich-Klein
with Nehama Consuela Nahmoud

Mother, Mother!" cried little Nissim from the far corner of the courtyard. "Mother, Mother!" Rocks fell all around him. There were shouts in Persian and sounds of feet running along the street on the other side of the five-foot wall that surrounded his house.

"Nissim, Nissim!" called his mother frantically. "Where are you?"

"Mother, Mother!"

"Quick! Get into the house! Hurry. Leave your ball.

TZVIA EHRLICH-KLEIN is the author of *A Children's Treasury of Sephardic Tales* and *Happy Hints — Hints for a Successful Aliya*, editor of *To Dwell in the Palace*, and the "Family Fun" page of the *Jewish Press*. She invites all children to submit puzzles, poems, games, homonyms, stories, recipes, etc., to her at the *Jewish Press* for inclusion in the "Family Fun" page (include your name, school, and grade).

It was NEHAMA CONSUELA NAHMOUD, her historical consultant, who made Tzvia Ehrlich-Klein aware of the rich heritage of Sephardim.

Come *on!*" she screamed as she dragged him by the hand into the house. "Fast! There is no time. Close the shutters, Sarah," she yelled at Nissim's older sister while bolting the back door behind herself. "Go through the whole house, and check every door and window to see that it is closed and locked. Hurry!" she cried as rocks banged against the stone walls of the house.

Suddenly, there was a loud banging on the front door. "Mazal, Mazal, let me in. Mazal, hurry."

"It's Grandma," yelled Nissim to his mother. "Grandma is here."

"Get away from the window!" shouted Nissim's mother. "Quick! Stand behind the door as I open it, and get ready to push it closed if the Muslims try to force their way in."

"I can't believe it!" gasped Grandma, her shawl falling to the floor as she helped Mother rebolt the front door. "Gangs are roaming the streets, throwing rocks at every Jewish home and trying to burn some down. They're screaming, '*Yahud! Yahud* [Jew]!' My father came to Mashad eighty-six years ago with the first Jews that the Sultan allowed to settle in this city — and I've never seen such a thing like this in all my life! It can't be the Sultan's government that is behind this. The people themselves are just going wild."[1]

"Where is Grandpa, Grandma? Father hasn't returned from morning prayers yet."

"When Grandpa heard the shouting, he rushed back to the *beit knesset*. The men are going to try to hide the *sifrei Torah* in a safe place. *Be'ezrat HaShem*, they were in time."

"Here come Father and Grandpa," called Nissim. "They're running down the alleys towards the back of the house."

"What are you doing near that window?" yelled Nissim's mother. "Move away from there! Come and help me open the back door, Sarah. *Bar minan!* I hope they are all right. It sounds like the mob has moved off down the street."

"*Baruch HaShem*, we made it home safely," said Nissim's father after the back door was closed and bolted behind them. "Get Grandpa some tea," he added as he sank down onto the cushions on the floor. "We have been running the whole way, from the synagogue to the mosque and then back here."

"To the mosque?" exclaimed Nissim's grandmother.

"Did you hide the Torah scrolls?" asked Nissim.

"Nissim," said his mother, moving him into a more comfortable position on her lap. "One minute, let Father and Grandpa catch their breath. Then they will tell us everything. Thank you for bringing the tea, Sarah."

"Yes, we got all the Torah scrolls and books out of the synagogue, just minutes before the Moslem gangs came charging through the front doors. They broke all the windows and tore up the benches. Then they tried to burn the synagogue down," said Grandpa. "Ovadia stayed behind to watch and warn us if they tried following us. He said they didn't even seem to realize the *sefarim* were gone."

"It was Ovadia's idea," said Father. "We were gathering up the books, wondering what had got into the Moslems. Yazdi said to talk later. Now we had to decide where to hide the *sifrei Torah*. Somewhere safe, where the Moslem gangs would not look. Ovadia turns around, looks Yazdi straight in the eye, and says, 'Let's put our *sefarim* in the safest place there is right now. A place the Moslems would never think to look...the basement of the mosque!' So that is what we did."

Minutes later, there was a banging on the door.

"Open up! We come as representatives of the Imam [religious head of the city's Moslems]. He asks all Jewish leaders in Mashad to come to an emergency meeting with him in the mosque. He has sent an armed guard along to protect you from the gangs."

Within minutes, Nissim's grandfather found himself standing in the middle of Mashad's main mosque with the other Hakhamim of the city. They looked around at the lavish decorations. They had never been in a mosque before.

The Imam looked down at the rabbis. "I've called you here this morning," he began, "to try to help you. We do not agree with this rampant raving of the faithful. But we must return order to the city. Therefore, to protect you, I am offering to convert all of you. My assistants have already counted thirty-two Jews dead from this rioting. Let's stop it now. Otherwise it could go on for days, until all of you are killed. Please think about it."

Two hours later, Nissim's grandfather returned to the expectant family. The Hakhamim had decided what the Jewish community should do. "We are basing ourselves on the Rambam's letter on apostasy," announced Nissim's grandfather. "A vote was taken by all the rabbis in Mashad. It is definitely a matter of *pikuach nefesh* [danger to life]. Also, since we have no other choice, and because the Moslems do not allow statues in their mosques or anywhere else, so they are not technically idol worshippers, we agreed that, for the sake of saving Jewish lives, we would pretend to convert."

"Grandpa!" gasped everyone in the room.

"Let me finish," he said. "We will act like Moslems on the outside, but we will keep the Torah secretly. Father and I have to return now to Ovadia's house. We have to finish planning a system for minyanim three times a day in basements and attics. And we have to figure out how to be converted this afternoon in the least forbidden way. Maybe we can think of an idea. And there is also kashrut to worry about — the *shochet* will be under especially heavy surveillance. May the Almighty give us strength and wisdom and help us."

"Amen," everyone responded, looking fearfully at each other.

After Father and Grandfather left for Ovadia's house, Mother gathered the children around her and explained, "Everything, God willing, will be all right. We will just have to work harder than ever to keep HaShem's mitzvot and to do His will. We are going to have to act like Moslems on the outside, for a while, but inside, secretly, we will keep the laws of HaShem and all the mitzvot. But we can't let the Moslems know that we are really still Jews."

Soon Nissim was walking in a long line of Jews, clutching his father's hand. Behind him walked his mother and sisters, and behind them, his grandparents and older brother. In front of him walked David, Nissim's best friend, also holding his father's hand tightly. But Nissim didn't nudge David or even call out to him. In fact, Nissim couldn't take his eyes off the long line of Moslem men lining both sides of the dirt street. They stood there like soldiers, silently watching, their dark eyes flashing. Some still held clubs in their hands. They were standing and staring, watching and waiting, as the long procession of Jews slowly walked down the middle of the road towards the city's main mosque. Nissim shuddered and clutched his father's hand even tighter.

To get rid of the fear, Nissim thought about what his father had told him to do when they got to the mosque. As *Muslimin Jedidin* (new Moslems) they would have to say "Allah is one, and Muhammed is his prophet," out loud. But instead of saying "Muhammed," Nissim and all the Jewish people were going to mumble "Moussa" instead (Moussa is Moshe Rabbeinu).

The line of Jews started filing into the mosque. The

Imam called each Jew forward. He pointed to one and said, "From now on your name will be Nassr-ed-Din." Then he pointed to a different Jew and said, "From now on your name will be Hassan..." A scribe holding a large, red book stood next to the Imam. In this book, each Jew's new name was recorded.

Soon it was Nissim's father's turn. "From now on your name will be Achmad," said the mother. "Your wife will be called Johara."

As Nissim stepped forward, he was told, "From now on your name will be Oma." His grandfather was named Mullah Abd al-Aziz, and his grandmother, Jamilha.

By the time all the Jews in Mashad had received their new names, the Imam's men had dispersed the Moslem mob outside.

As the "new Moslems" filed out of the mosque, Nassr-ed-Din (Ovadia) whispered to Nissim's father, "A problem has come up about where to have the *talmud Torah*. We're meeting fifteen minutes early for *minchah*. Don't forget, it's in Sa'adia's attic."

"*Si-ha-tu-shalom*," whispered Nissim's father out of the side of his mouth as he kept his eyes on the carpeted floor. "*Si-ha-tu-shalom*. Go in peace."

Slowly the weeks passed, and the Jewish community of Mashad learned how to live as secret Jews. In the morning, all the Jewish children had to go to Moslem Koran school. But in the afternoon, they all went to the *talmud Torah* in Mullah (Rabbi) Aklar's basement.

Every market day, Nissim's mother went with the other Jewish women of Mashad to the Moslem butcher's stall in the city's outdoor market. There they spent hours bargaining along with the Moslem women, trying to get a lower price from the Moslem butcher for the "choice" pieces of meat.

Later, making sure they weren't being followed, these Jewish women would go the poor section of town and give away their nonkosher meat to the poor Moslems there. Sometimes, they just threw the nonkosher meat to the many hungry dogs that roamed the side streets of Mashad.

As evening came, these Jewish women hurried through the streets of Mashad. They were dressed like Moslem women: Their faces were covered by thick, white veils, and they wore long, billowing, black dresses that reached to the ground. Looking quickly to the left and right, these women ran to the *shochet* with a chicken hidden under their skirts. The *shochet* would be punished severely if he was caught. So, slowly, the Jews of Mashad got used to eating only chicken. It is much easier to hide a chicken than a whole sheep!

The women grew accustomed to lighting their Shabbos oil candles in their basements and wearing fancy Shabbat clothing on Fridays, too, so the Persian Moslems would not suspect they were dressing up for Shabbat.

Yet Shabbat was somehow still Shabbat. The whole family sat together on the floor on beautifully colored Persian rugs. Piles of thick, round pita bread, covered with an elegant cloth, lay on a big, ornate, brass Shabbat tray in the middle of the eating area. Places were set for the whole family with fancy plates and large, silver spoons. Soon Father would return from praying in Avshalom's attic and make Kiddush. And, as always, the family would talk about the laws of Shabbat and how to keep them while pretending not to...

"Remember," cautioned Nissim's father, "I have to keep the store open tomorrow even though it's Shabbat. But most of the time I won't be there. Nissim, as the youngest of the family, it will be your job to try not to sell anything, since it is forbidden to buy or sell on Shabbat. Your brother and I will be at the *beit knesset* most of the day. If a customer comes into the store during Shabbat, say that your father had to go away for an hour or so, but he will be back. Tell the man, 'But if the kind gentleman wants to be sure, maybe it is better for him to come back early tomorrow.' If you have seen the customer before and already used that line on him, just tell him a price three times what the rug really costs. That should stop anyone from buying, and we therefore will not desecrate Shabbat by selling or buying anything that day."

But some things were harder to get used to...

"Father, Father, get up," called Nissim as he rubbed his eyes. "Hurry, Father, it is already 3:30 in the morning! It is time to get up, or you will be late for the mosque. The muezzin already finished called everyone to prayer."

Parting the beaded curtain of his bedroom, Nissim's father came out into the hallway. "Thank you for waking me, Nissim," he said "We are lucky you are an early riser! A person can't get a decent night's sleep around here anymore. Look how dark it is outside! Check that Rahamim is awake. Then go straight back to bed."

As Nissim's father and older brother hurried along the dirty streets towards the mosque, they smiled unobtrusively at the other Jews they met on the way. Suddenly, they heard a whispering behind them...

"Don't turn around! Were you told about the *rav*? He heard that the authorities are watching his house. So besides *minchah*, the *minyan vatikin* will also be at my house this week. See you later."

Soon after Rahamim returned home from the mosque, he went to the still-sleeping Nissim and started shaking him. "Wake up, Nissim," he said. "It's time to go to morning prayers."

"I'm still tired," Nissim yawned. "Can't I sleep a little longer?"

"Get up, sleepyhead," answered his brother. "I've been

out for hours already. You are lucky you are too little to have to go to the mosque. Try being all dressed at 3:30 every morning! Come on, Nissim. Hurry, or we will be late for the minyan. Enough talking."

Soon all the men in the house were walking quickly towards Sa'adia Eliahu's house. As they walked, no one said a word. The gray, predawn light gave everything an eerie look.

Entering the courtyard of Mullah Eliahu's house, Nissim saw Mrs. Eliahu in the far corner of the cobblestone courtyard. She was carrying a huge, metal washtub. As she filled it with hot water, she winked at Nissim.

Nissim thought the Hakhamim were very smart to have the secret minyan in Mrs. Eliahu's house. She and her husband had thirteen children, *ben porat Yosef* (*bli ayin hara*), so she had a lot of clothing to wash every morning before sunrise. By the time the last of the Jewish men had tiptoed upstairs into her attic, Mrs. Eliahu was busily washing her family's clothing in the metal tub.

A sudden noise made Mrs. Eliahu stop and look up. There stood Abu Bakr, from the Imam's office.

Forcing a big smile onto her face as she wiped her soapy hands on her apron, she said, "Salaam aleikum [*shalom aleichem*], Abu Bakr. I hope the Imam is well. What brings you to our humble home this morning?"

"Nothing in particular," answered the Imam's assistant as he looked around the deserted courtyard. "Nothing in particular."

Suddenly Abu Bakr screamed, "Look out!" as he jumped backwards.

"Oh, my," exclaimed Mrs. Eliahu. "My washtub! Oh, no! Please excuse me! How clumsy of me! My clothes are going everywhere. Please help me pick them up. Oh, I am so sorry.

Look, your robes have gotten all wet from the soapy wash water. How clumsy of me to have knocked over my washtub. Now I will have to do my clothes all over again. But of course, that doesn't interest you, Abu Bakr. Would you be so kind as to hand me that shirt over there by the bushes? I would appreciate it greatly. What a mess. How very clumsy of me."

Meanwhile, in Mrs. Eliahu's attic, Nissim's father had heard the loud clanging when the big, metal washtub fell onto the cobblestones of the courtyard below.

"Hurry," he said. "I heard the signal. Mrs. Eliahu has dropped her laundry tub! Someone must be spying downstairs! Quick! Over the roofs! You all know your routes. See you at Mullah Mordekhai's house for *minchah*, God willing. Hurry now. Move fast!"

With that, everyone scurried out of the windows and onto the roof. They had all practiced many times and knew exactly where to go.

Below, in the courtyard, Mrs. Eliahu could not stall the Imam's man any longer. He pushed her aside and began climbing the steps to her attic. Slowly, Mrs. Eliahu bent down to finish picking up her laundry. There was nothing else she could do. She silently began saying the *tehillim* of David...

As he neared the attic, Abu Bakr quickened his pace. "Something peculiar is going on here," he thought.

Soon he was at the attic door. He opened it gently and looked inside. The room was a normal, empty attic with several windows open wide to the roofs beyond. Abu Bakr turned to leave. It was obviously a mistake. There was nothing wrong here. Just as he was about to close the attic door, however, he noticed a book on the floor. Picking it up, he saw that it was written in Hebrew. Aha! Something had been going on here!

Abu Bakr quickly went downstairs and called for Sa'adia

Eliahu. He was arrested and dragged off to the main mosque.

Telling her oldest child to watch the younger ones, Mrs. Eliyahu rushed out of the courtyard. She ran from house to house, trying to get some idea of what was going to happen to her husband, and how the other hidden Jews were going to try to free him. Soon it was time for praying at the mosque again, so Mrs. Eliahu returned home. There was nothing more she could find out now, and she still had thirteen children to feed.

As she entered her courtyard, she was shocked to see her husband walking out of their house towards her. And there was no armed guard around.

"What happened to you?" she exclaimed. *"Baruch HaShem, you are all right! Baruch HaShem!"*

"Shh! Careful!" whispered her husband, beckoning her into their home. "I only have a minute, because the muezzin has already finished calling to go to the mosque."

"What happened to you? I was so worried! What punishment did they give you for having a siddur in the house?" asked his wife.

"I have to sit for one week solid in the mosque, all day long, reading and rereading the Koran. When I finish it, I have to begin over again. But I can come home for lunch and dinner and to sleep, *baruch HaShem.*"

*   *   *

A few months later, the Imam himself made a very important announcement in the central mosque. The yearly hajj (pilgrimage to Mecca) was being organized from Mashad for the Moslem faithful. The Imam was pleased to announce that there would be a caravan leaving Mashad in two weeks for the pilgrimage. Every Moslem who wanted to strengthen his faith was to make the long and expensive trip to Saudia Arabia. Of course, all new Moslems who could afford to go would want to reserve a place early.

"Mazal! Mazal!" Nissim's father shouted as he ran into his house. "Mazal! Quickly! Gather all the children in my study. I have wonderful news for everyone. We are going on the hajj!"

"What is so wonderful about that?" retorted Nissim's mother.

"You'll see..." answered Father.

"Can I drive my own camel?" asked Nissim. "Are Grandma and Grandpa coming? Will we be gone a long time? Can I choose my own tent?"

"We'll discuss all those details when the whole family is together," answered Father. "You will just have to wait, little one."

And so, on the appointed day, Nissim and his entire family left Mashad on their pilgrimage. It was a long and hard trip. And many times Nissim was glad he didn't have his very own camel to drive!

After they were in Mecca for a few days, Nissim's father told the Imam (who had also come) that he was going to continue his religious pilgrimage and go the additional expense of taking his family to visit the Mosque of Omar in Jerusalem. The Imam was impressed to see how seriously Nissim's father took his religious duties. He therefore gave the entire family a special blessing for a safe trip to Jerusalem and a speedy return home to Mashad.

Nissim and his family arrived in Jerusalem. They went directly to the Bukharan Quarter,[2] where Nissim's mother, Mazal, had an aunt and some cousins. And that evening, the entire family went to the Kotel for *arvit* prayers. There, they gave thanks that they had arrived home—to their real home—safely...

Notes

1. One day in 1839, a Moslem doctor prescribed a cure for the wounded arm of his patient — a Jewish woman. He told her to soak her arm in the blood of a dead dog. The Jewish woman paid a Moslem urchin to kill a dog and bring the blood to her. Afterwards they argued about the price of the medicine. The little boy ran off, telling everyone that the Jews were insulting Islam by calling a dog "Hussein," the name of a Moslem notable being publicly mourned that day. Within minutes, a pogrom had started — the first in the eighty-six-year history of Jewish settlement in Mashad.

2. By 1957, over 1,000 Mashadi Jews were living in Jerusalem, mostly in the Bukharan Quarter. Today, there are only a handful of Marrano families still in Mashad.

Bibliography

1. Galante, A. *Marranes Iraneens*. Istanbul, 1935.
2. Stillman, N. *Jews in Arab Lands*. Philadelphia: Jewish Publication Society, 1979.

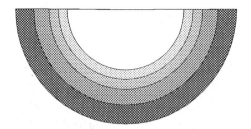

The Yooden Savannah

Gershon Kranzler

Shortly after the Dutch took possession of Brazil in 1624, a group of Jews left Amsterdam to settle in this strange land far to the West. Among them were Moses and Gracia Elazari. They bought an old, dilapidated plantation near the city of San Mandano, where many Sephardic Jews had settled. They called their plantation El Eden, and in ten years of unceasing labor they succeeded in turning the place into a veritable paradise which bore rich harvests and repaid the hard work invested in it many times over. The mansion was restored to its original beauty, and fifty clean, new huts housed the scores of Negroes who did the heavy labor on the plantation.

The Elazaris' happiness reached its height when their marriage was blessed with the birth of a boy, whom they called Joseph. From the very beginning he was the apple of their eye, adored not only by his parents but by the black and white servants.

Mammy, Donna Gracia's personal maid, took care of the

This article is reprinted from *The Golden Shoes* with the permission of Feldheim Publishers.

boy from the moment he was born and taught him the kind of practical knowledge that a wise, life-hardened Negro woman had to have in order to survive. Under her care, and surrounded by the love and luxury which his parents could afford to give him, Joseph Elazari grew up to be a most handsome, healthy and well-mannered boy who knew as much as any Jewish child — and more.

Naturally, he had the very best examples in his own parents. Don Moses and Donna Gracia were not at all affected by their hard-earned wealth. They were never conceited or haughty, unlike so many others in their position, nor did they squander money on all sorts of foolish luxuries. Nor did they ever allow any ill-treatment of their slaves, which was customary among plantation owners.

Why, even Don Moses' own brother, Abraham, who owned the adjoining estate, had assumed the lordly attitudes of the native landowners. To him, Negroes were like dumb cattle, not human beings. The only thing he abolished was the brutal floggings that the plantation supervisors used to administer for the slightest reason. Otherwise, Don Abraham was not at all concerned with his slaves. He lived a solitary life in his mansion, surrounded by the splendor and luxury that his rich plantation afforded him.

Not so the gentle Don Moses and Donna Gracia. They had deep, personal regard for each and every one of their slaves and tried to make their working conditions at El Eden as pleasant as possible. Don Moses even made it his business, like our forefather Abraham, to teach his slaves true knowledge of God. He had them observe the laws of the Torah concerning the conduct of servants of a Jewish master. And, with the help of his wife, he changed the whole atmosphere of El Eden into one of harmony and happiness, even among his lowliest of slaves. Naturally, the workers greatly appreciated this kindness, and they would gladly have given their lives for their masters.

As a matter of fact, when the humane treatment of the servants at El Eden became known, other plantation owners began to grumble and complain that Don Moses was responsible for making the slaves of the entire country lazy and rebellious, and that the blame would be his if trouble came — as it was bound to, they said, if he continued to spoil his workers in such a foolish manner. Yet, despite all the complaints and threats, Don Moses and Donna Gracia Elazari did not change. They were convinced that the love and kindness they showed others could only bear good fruit.

When trouble did come to El Eden, it did not originate among its slaves. On the contrary, it came from the plantation owners, who could no longer bear to see the success of the farming and breeding at El Eden. Full of envy and hatred, they did not blame themselves for their own poor results; rather, they blamed Don Moses for making their slaves lazy. But as long as the brave DeJoong governed the land, they would not dare undertake anything against El Eden, for the govenor would have punished them severely for doing anything illegal. When Dutch rule began to falter, however, and it became obvious that the Portuguese would soon be back, the plantation owners lost no time in punishing the Jew from Amsterdam for his unheard-of treatment of his slaves.

One of Don Abraham Elazari's friends warned him that his and his brother's plantations would soon be raided by their competitors. Not a man to be frightened by threats, Don Abraham took counsel with his brother, and they decided to stay on and see it through. Their combined servants would be enough, they felt, to withstand any attack by their neighbors.

The only thing Don Moses insisted on was that his wife take their six-year-old son Joseph to the security of her sister's house in the city of San Mandano. Unhappily, Donna Gracia realized that her husband was right. She and Joseph would be safer in the house of her sister Rachel and her brother-in-law, the well-to-do goldsmith and rabbi, Don Samuel d'Acosta.

With the greatest reluctance, Donna Gracia made the necessary preparations. It was as if an inner voice told her that once she and her son departed from El Eden and Don Moses, they would never see each other again. With a heavy heart, they finally set out for San Mandano, protected by a troop of Don Moses' strongest and most loyal servants. Don Moses would have taken his beloved wife and child to the city himself if not for the alarming news about the impending attack. He did go along with them as far as he could and then returned, unashamed of the tears that flowed from his eyes.

Mammy was most helpful to her mistress and young Joseph on the wearying, three-day journey. She knew all the tricks of jungle life and of protecting oneself against the strong heat. Thanks to her efficient management, the trip went as smoothly and as comfortably as circumstances permitted.

What Mammy did not know was that the enemy planters had hired spies to watch what was going on around El Eden. When they discovered that Donna Gracia was taking her son to San Mandano, they hired a band of outlaws to murder them along the way.

But the outlaws did not count on Mammy's alertness. They were still far from the clearing where Donna Gracia's party had decided to spend the night when Mammy's suspicions were aroused, and she warned Don Moses' servants. In the brief battle that followed, the murderers were successfully turned back, but a stray bullet severely wounded Donna Gracia.

Although she still had strength enough to complete the trip to San Mandano, Donna Gracia died in her sister's arms — at about the same time that her beloved El Eden was burned to the ground. Abraham Elazari's slaves had turned against their master and joined the enemy planters. Don Moses' servants did not yield an inch as long as they had one bullet left, but they and their master were easily outnumbered by their attackers.

Thus, before he had really enjoyed life, Joseph Elazari was an orphan at the age of six. Fortunately, his uncle and aunt, Don Samuel d'Acosta and Donna Rachel, who had no children of their own, loved him as if he had been born to them, and they gave him all that their considerable wealth and learning could provide. They permitted Mammy to stay with them and take care of her young master. A private teacher instructed Joseph in Hebrew and secular studies, and he grew to be as fine a young Jewish student as any boy with his wealthy background.

But this relatively happy phase of Joseph Elazari's life did not last long. A few short years after tragedy had struck El Eden, the Portuguese reclaimed Brazil from the Dutch. The Jewish colonies that had flourished during the thirty-year reign of the Netherlands collapsed. The Jewish immigrants, most of whom had been — like the Elazaris — descendants of Spanish and Portuguese Sephardim, were now forced to give up their promising careers and sell their estates and other possessions at a fraction of their value. Again they had to look for countries that would offer them refuge.

Don Samuel and Donna Rachel d'Acosta joined a group of their friends who were sailing to Dutch Guiana. Of course, they were taking Joseph Elazari with them — but they didn't quite know what to do with Mammy. They would have gladly taken her along, too, but Don Samuel, like all the rest, had to sell all his precious belongings at a ridiculously low price. It was simply a question of not being able to afford Mammy's passage to Dutch Guiana and, after their arrival, not being able to afford a maid for Joseph altogether.

However, they needn't have worried. A few days before they were to leave, Mammy came to Don Samuel and said quite firmly, "Honored master, I know that you have not enough left to pay for my board and passage. Do not worry. During the years you have permitted me to stay with young Joseph, I have been washing and mending for other people in my spare time, and I have managed to save enough for my own passage. Once we reach our destination, I promise that you shall not have to give my support a single thought. As long as I may be near Joseph, I shall take care of myself."

Naturally, no one was happier than Joseph Elazari, now a handsome and studious boy of ten. For Mammy was his only bond with the precious memories of his beloved parents and the paradise of El Eden.

After many weeks of troubled, nerve-wracking traveling, the d'Acostas, Joseph and Mammy arrived in Surinam. Again, on the boat, Mammy proved herself a most valuable helper, and many a time not only her own people but the other refugees from Brazil blessed her and thanked the Almighty for sending this wise woman to ease their plight.

The d'Acostas moved on to Paramaribo, the capital of the Dutch Guianas, and Don Samuel became the first leader of the Jewish community they founded there. Under his guidance, a simple synagogue was built, and soon afterwards a schoolhouse was added. There Joseph Elazari spent the next few years studying day and night, until, at the tender age of fifteen, he received *semichah* from Rabbi Gimlah, the spiritual head of the Jews of Surinam.

Joseph had no intention of becoming a congregational rabbi. He entered his uncle's goldsmith shop as an apprentice, and in a few years he'd mastered his craft to a degree that astounded even Don Samuel d'Acosta, who was no mean craftsman himself. Soon Don Samuel declared that there was nothing more he could teach young Joseph, and he made the young man a full partner in the prospering business.

One evening, upon returning home from the shop, Joseph found Mammy waiting for him. It was quite obvious that she had not come to take care of his laundry. She seemed to want to have a talk with him.

"What is it, Mammy? What is on your mind?" Joseph Elazari was a little puzzled, for he could not remember Mammy ever wanting anything from him.

"My young master," the by now gray-haired woman said, "I have been thinking about this for many months and years. It is no sudden whim of mine, and I beg of you to take me seriously: I want to become a Jew like you. Pray, teach me all the things I have to know to become a member of your faith."

Joseph was rather taken aback by this request. He did not want to hurt the feelings of good old Mammy. Yet he could foresee a great many difficulties arising from such a step by this Negro woman. Joseph consulted his master, Rabbi Gimlah of Surinam, who was also very reluctant about the whole matter, and he tried very hard to dissuade Mammy from this step. But when she persisted and proved to him that it was true conviction that had moved her to seek the Jewish religion, because she had come to like and admire it during her many years with the Elazaris and the d'Acostas, he found no legal excuse for refusing her request.

Despite her age and lack of formal education, Mammy had no difficulty learning the fundamentals of Judaism. She already knew so many of the customs and laws, and she grasped the basic ideas and principles so easily, that Joseph Elazari was constantly amazed. After a few months of study, Mammy was accepted into the Jewish community.

This step by Joseph Elazari's former nursemaid had many consequences. Mammy was something of a leader among the numerous Negro servants in Paramaribo. They respected her experience, knowledge, and wisdom, and they often sought her advice on many a problem. Therefore, when Mammy became a Jewess and began to live according to Jewish laws and customs, they wanted to know what it was all about. In her simple yet effective way, she explained what she had learned from Joseph Elazari, and it did not take long before many of her friends wanted to accept the Jewish religion as Mammy had done.

Mammy's admittance into the Jewish community had caused some astonishment and even some dissatisfaction and resentment. But when close to a hundred of Mammy's eager disciples requested to be taken into the Jewish fold, the community council objected violently — despite the pleas of Rabbi Gimlah and Joseph Elazari to consider the requests without bias.

"If they really mean it," shouted councilor, "let them emigrate to different countries in small groups, so the native population will not find fault and make us suffer for it. I think we all have had enough of being driven from place to place, and we do not care to provoke more trouble."

Mammy had guessed how the council would feel, and she was ready for it when Joseph Elazari conveyed the decision to her.

"Well, my dear master," said the kindly old lady, "you do not have to be so sad about it. As a matter of fact, I had thought that the councilors would object to taking so many of my friends into the community. But, if you are willing, you can help us find a way out.

"You see, one of my people discovered a small, uninhabited island off the coast of Surinam. I have already been there and looked it over myself. At the moment, it is rather dreary and fruitless. But I am convinced that with good care and hard work, it can be made into fertile soil. My friends and I are willing to work hard to make a decent living for ourselves. However, we need a man like you to come with us and direct us."

It did not take Joseph Elazari long to make up his mind. Convinced of Mammy's sound judgment and of the skills and willingness of her large group of friends, he undertook to carry out her plan. And especially now that he had succeeded in winning the favor of Rabbi Gimlah's daughter to be his wife, he found this a wonderful opportunity to start out on his own in his new married life.

Thus began one of the strangest chapters in Jewish history. Under Joseph Elazari's capable leadership and with the effective help of Mammy, the little island (which they called El Eden in memory of their old home) changed from a barren, deserted piece of land into a fertile, well-developed community. The Negroes were used to hard work. They cleared the ground of its jungle growth and tilled the soil patiently. Joseph Elazari designed beautiful jewelry, and he taught many of the women the basic skills of his craft. Thus, they produced rings, bracelets, lockets, and brooches in large quantities at reasonable prices. Other members of the community took the jewelry all over the Guianas and nearby islands and returned with handsome profits for the people of

El Eden. They shared all they earned and possessed, and soon they were able to build solid, well-furnished homes instead of the primitive huts that had been their shelter for the first few years.

In the beginning, the people of Paramaribo were somewhat hostile towards the Jews of El Eden, which they called the "Yooden Savannah." But when they saw the excellent products of their industry, their attitude changed. New immigrants were invited to settle on the island, and many of them married Negro women who had embraced the Jewish faith. Joseph Elazari remained the head of the growing community until his death, when his oldest son succeeded him.

It is not known how long the Jewish community of El Eden, or "Yooden Savannah," existed. But fifty years after Joseph Elazari and Mammy moved to the island, more than a hundred Jewish children attended the school at El Eden — children from marriages between Negro women and Jewish immigrants from Holland, Portugal, and Brazil. Beyond that, there are no records of the strange Jewish community of "Yooden Savannah."

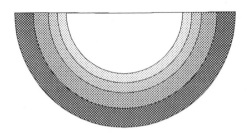

A Piece of Lace

Lena Spitzer

James Scrivener faced a problem. The master of his English class had set them an interesting holiday task. "Search out your family roots," he had said, "and write an essay on how your family came to settle where it is now."

The master made all manner of helpful suggestions about where to start such a search: parish records, town halls, registries, and books on surnames. His schoolfellows were very enthusiastic, but James was a bit perplexed. No one had suggested how a Jewish boy might go about this task. Ignorant of Judaism though he was, James knew his roots were not likely to be found in church registries! But James enjoyed a challenge, and this certainly looked as if it was going to be a good one.

When he returned home to Guildford for the winter holidays, James broached the subject with his father. After all, Geoffrey Scrivener was a successful solicitor and was probably used to searching through documents.

"Well, son, I know your great-grandpa Henry founded a

If you want to read about LENA SPITZER, turn to page 75.

lace factory in Nottingham, which was one of the first places to produce lace on machines," he said slowly. "But that's about all I know."

"What about Great-Aunt Ida?" Mrs. Scrivener interrupted.

She and her husband were first cousins, and she was the one who kept up with their assorted near and far relations. She turned to James.

"Your great-aunt Ida will know more. Why don't you ask her? That'll start you off."

Mr. Scrivener smiled. The Scriveners had been a prosperous family for several generations now. He and his brothers were all involved in respected professions, and he had great hopes that his son James would, in time, join him in a brilliant legal career. Whatever James discovers about the family, thought his father with confidence, he will have every reason to be proud of his ancestry!

So it was that James found himself sitting in one of Great-Aunt Ida's enormous armchairs on a Sunday afternoon.

"Well, I remember the factory in Nottingham," she began. "Lace was made there by machine, you know. The first factory in Britain to do that, we were," she continued proudly. "I always liked the handmade lace better, myself. I used to love watching the women's hands flashing about, threading the cotton round the bobbins, which had been set into patterns on a cushion. The ladies' movements were so flowing and precise. Their speed and dexterity is an art which is now all but lost," she sighed.

"Each lace-maker had her own set of bobbins," she continued, "and very proud of them she was, too! The bobbin heads were made of pearl, ivory, and glass and were wonderfully decorated! Ah, the handmade lace," she sighed again.

"Let me show you something, James," she said suddenly.

James watched as Great-Aunt Ida pattered over to an antique cabinet and unlocked it. She brought out a glass frame, and James leaned forward to examine it as she set it on the table before him. Inside the glass was a piece of exquisite, handmade lace; creamy gold with age, it was elaborately patterned with birds and flowers, and in the center was a beautiful, eight-branched menorah.

"Now that," said Great-Aunt Ida, "is a work of art. Don't you agree, James?"

James's finger tentatively traced the menorah. "Quite a Jewish symbol, isn't it, Aunt?"

"More than just a symbol, James," she said dryly. "I'm afraid it has come to that in our generation, hasn't it? Yet I can still remember seeing a glowing menorah on the window-sill of my grandfather's house while we sat round the table and played some game... Chanukah, I believe..." her voice trailed off.

"Was this lace made in Nottingham, Aunt?" asked James.

"No, no. This piece is much older. I was told that it has been in the family for hundreds of years! They gave it to me because I am so fond of old lace. But I am sorry, I don't know its origins. I do know, though, that it was in the family long before the Nottingham factory opened."

"Where did the family come from before Nottingham, Aunt?" asked James, leaning forward in his chair.

Great-Aunt Ida laughed. "Oh, James, that is going back a long, long time! Three or four generations of Scriveners lived in Nottingham, so you are asking me to have a very long memory!"

She sat quietly for a moment. "I think I was once told that the family originated from the West Country — Devon or Cornwall or suchlike..."

James was pleased with his progress, but he was determined to find out more. He questioned, nagged, telephoned, and wrote to every member of his family, until he had exhausted every avenue of inquiry. But though they had filled in information about the later history of the family, no one knew anything of its origins.

Later that week, Mr. Scrivener announced that he had to travel to Plymouth for four days to attend the Crown Court there for a case he was working on. He invited James to come with him. James was delighted and planned to make the most of this opportunity. Maybe Great-Aunt Ida's hunch had been right? Maybe the family had originated in Devon?

While his father was occupied at Court, James planned to visit some towns and villages in the area. It was cold, but the air was clear and fresh and James enjoyed the views from the bus. He watched the progress of the narrow winding rivers as their icy waters splashed their way over the rocks and boulders in their path and flowed onward in determined fashion under old, stone, arched bridges.

He stopped off at Totnes and Newton Abbott to explore and then set off again for Honiton, a town famous for lace-making. Walking through the main street of this little market town, he spotted the Museum of Lace. He soon found himself inside, surrounded by glass cases showing lace shawls, tablecloths, and baby gowns from bygone days.

His heart leaped when he saw it. There was no mistaking the detailed pattern of birds and flowers and that intricate menorah in its center. It was identical to the piece of lace Great-Aunt Ida had shown him. The card beneath it read:

SAMPLE FROM THE TEXTILE HOUSE OF JACOB SOFER
EXETER AND HONITON 1760

A strange excitement filled him; he had to find out more about the origins of this delicate lace sample. Approaching the lady curator, he asked her if she had any further information about "The Textile House of Jacob Sofer."

"Our records only tell us that many lace samples originated from that house," she said, smiling. "It was a thriving business, operating mainly from Exeter, with interests in Honiton, where much of the lace was made." She looked at James. "If it's Sofer himself you are interested in," she said, "I believe he was a Jew. It is possible that the old synagogue in Exeter may have records of him and may be able to help you further."

James thanked her and quickly boarded the first bus to Exeter. The chase was on!

When the bus arrived in Exeter, James asked for directions to the oldest part of town. In Synagogue Place, off a street strangely named Mary Arches, and dwarfed by some tall, modern buildings, James found the old synagogue.

It was Mr. Poplack, the *shammas*, who opened the large doors and listened to James's story.

"Sofer...the name rings a bell," said the friendly, round-faced *shammas*. "Well, the records will soon show. I used to read them sometimes. Jolly interesting they are, too!"

He led James to a small office, pulled out several ancient, leather-bound books, and quickly riffled through them.

"Ah, yes, here we are then!" he exclaimed triumphantly. "It seems that Reb Yaakov Elya HaSofer came to Exeter in 1750 from Ghent — that's in Belgium nowadays, I think. He traded in lace and textiles, and by all accounts he was a very rich man. Seems he was truly a pious Orthodox Jew who cared greatly for the community. He helped found this synagogue and a Hebrew school for the children, where he taught. Hmm. It says here that part of his diary and business records is locked in the safe. I could open that for you. Are you interested?" He looked up at James and smiled. "Do you think you have found an ancestor?" he teased. "You haven't even told me your name."

"Oh, I'm James Scrivener, from Guildford."

Mr. Poplack's eyes widened. "Scrivener, you say? And your great-aunt says that the lace has been in your family for generations? Well, well..."

James stared at the little man.

"Do you understand any Hebrew or Yiddish or know anything about Jewish names, son?" asked Mr. Pollack.

James shook his head.

"Well," began Mr. Pollack, "a *sofer* is a scribe, and the name Sofer often indicated the profession of its bearer. Reb Yaakov Elya was a *sofer*, and in fact, he wrote a Torah scroll here. Often the name was converted to the popular 'Schreiber' in Europe, which means the same, or, in your case, to Scrivener, a more English-sounding version."

James gasped. He knew now that he would not leave the synagogue until he had read every detail about his respected ancestor.

So James settled himself in Mr. Poplack's small office, and the old diary of Reb Yaakov Elya took him on a journey through time, way back into the world of eighteenth-century trade and commerce. James learned about the prices lace could fetch in London and Plymouth and the dangerous and tedious journeys of many months that Yaakov Elya would undertake back to Europe to trade in Bruges and Ghent. But the boy also learned about the great faith of the man who left his wife, Esther, and his children on countless occasions, knowing that the ways of his household would not change during his absence. James learned of Yaakov Elya's great generosity, not only to the shul and the community but to the countless orphans who passed through his house to be brought up alongside his own children. On the days that trade and commerce took up all his time, his candles would burn until daybreak as he learned Torah through the night.

This was no journal of a hard-core capitalist who lived for his ledger. The beautiful, old handwriting — faded and barely legible in parts — was difficult to decipher, as Old English intermingled with foreign words. Yet it still bore a purely factual account of Reb Yaakov Elya's life. No self-praise, no pride, but every deed recorded a unique trust in Hashem and great care and effort in the performance of His mitzvos.

As James turned the pages, an old document slipped out of the crumbling diary. The illuminated script seemed to have been presented to Reb Yaakov Elya on some public occasion. James could barely make out the words, and some of it was in Hebrew, but the last section was more legible:

> *...and for all the goodness and generosity that has come from your hand, the community prays for ever-lasting blessing on your house. May Hashem grant you righteous and upstanding children who fear Heaven, love their fellow Jews, and remain faithful to the ways of the Torah forevermore...*

James sat looking at this paragraph for a long time. He felt that a silent rebuke had come down the generations and echoed round him in the quiet, little office. True, his father and grandfather had been generous to Jewish institutions, but "faithful to the ways of the Torah"? He certainly knew very little about it. His family lived too far from the local cheder for a small boy to go by himself. His father had taught him the blessings for his bar mitzvah, but after that, his studies at the famous school he attended had been far more important than learning about his religion.

James thought about Aunt Ida and her distant memory of a menorah on a windowsill. Staring out at the darkening sky, he couldn't help feeling that his family had let Reb Yaakov Elya HaSofer down.

Mr. Poplack returned and was amazed to find James still sitting at the old desk. Apologizing profusely for having stayed so long, the young man prepared to go.

"No, wait a moment, son. It's raining heavily outside, we have an evening service starting very soon, and we need a minyan. Chanukah begins tonight, and we shall light our old menorah. Come and join us. It's a mitzvah!"

"Chanukah!" James started. He was too embarrassed to admit that he could not read much Hebrew and had no idea what a minyan was. The word "mitzvah" jogged something in his memory, though — it was a good thing to do for your soul, and his was certainly in need of some nourishment.

Mr. Poplack looked at the boy in front on him, a borrowed yarmulke on his young head, and sensed his hesitancy.

"Don't worry," he whispered. "I'll tell you when to say amen!"

The chandeliers in the old shul were now lit up, and the polished wood on the carved *aron kodesh* reflected their glow. The shul looked cared-for, and a very homey atmosphere prevailed in this long-forgotten corner of the Jewish world. Some eight men were settled in their places, and it did not look as if more would come on such a wet night.

"I said we'd need you to be a tenth for our minyan, James," Mr. Poplack whispered.

James beamed. He was a Jewish man, and this synagogue needed him for a service! Yet he knew that he felt compelled to stay for the sake of Reb Yaakov Elya.

And so it was that for the first time in his life, James

Scrivener saw a menorah being lit on Chanukah. As the little flame faltered at first and then grew and burned steadily, James knew a small flame had been rekindled within him, too.

Walking back through the rain to the bus stop, James stopped to look at the ancient, half-timbered houses that still stood near Synagogue Place. He wondered if Reb Yaakov Elya and Esther had brought up their children in a house like these. Had Esther sat for hours at these bow-fronted windows, rocking a cradle and waiting for her husband to return? Was it she who had held a cushion on her lap, skillfully threading and knotting cotton between the fragile bobbins to create the exquisite lace menorah that had begun his search?

The bus drew up, and James got on it. Looking back through the window, he knew that it would be a long time before he'd forget his family in Exeter. What had started as an assignment had become a quest, and it was not over yet...

*   *   *

"Where's James?" Mr. Scrivener asked from behind his newspaper.

"Some session of sorts at the synagogue," his wife answered, "called Project SEED or something. Young men come up from London, apparently every week, and learn with some local lads and older men as well. James never misses a session. He's become very friendly with one young man and has been learning a lot about Judaism these days. I really don't know what set him off."

"Well, it can only be a good thing for the boy," mused her husband. "He never went to cheder like I did, so he can catch up a bit now. It's a fine thing for a Jewish man to read

Hebrew, you know, follow the services, and perhaps make a seder. My grandfather could do all that..."

The newspaper jerked suddenly.

"As long as he doesn't neglect his studies!" Sudden alarm jarred his complacency.

"He works hard, Geoffrey," his wife assured him calmly. "Look at the time and effort he put into that family-history project. Even his headmaster commended his essay. It was so well done, and we discovered so much from it, too. He's a good boy, Geoffrey. He won't let us down."

Anne Scrivener was right. Two years later, James passed all his examinations with flying colors.

"Well, James," Geoffrey addressed his son, "we are very proud of your results. Now it's just a matter of packing your case, and a Cambridge education is yours."

"Father, I wanted to talk to you about that," began James. "I wish to defer Cambridge for a year and do something else. I — "

"Postpone a Cambridge education, James? Are you mad?" his father thundered. "Why, it's a privilege given only to a select few. Who knows? You may not get a second chance! What do you want to do in this precious year, anyway?"

"I wish to study at a yeshiva in Jerusalem, Father," James answered calmly. "It's something that has been growing inside me for a few years now. Please try to understand."

"Understand? All I understand, James, is that we've given you the finest education parents can provide, and you owe it to your mother and me not to throw your opportunities away!" Geoffrey Scrivener's voice was cold and more controlled now. He turned his back on James and faced the window.

James was silent, and then he said something his father would never forget:

"Yes, I owe my parents a lot, and I am truly thankful."

James said quietly. "But I have another debt to pay — to an ancestor who made it his life's work to educate Jewish children. Somewhere down the years, his own children lost direction, but I feel a debt of honor to go back and seek the education he so dearly wanted us to have. This education, too, is a privilege given only to a select few!"

Geoffrey Scrivener looked at his son in amazement. He opened his mouth to say something and then shut it again. His thoughts were in turmoil; he was tense and angry. But then another feeling began to work its way above the rest — a feeling of pride.

*   *   *

It was winter, but the day was sunny and warm when Geoffrey and Anne Scrivener landed at Ben-Gurion Airport. It took a long time to get through customs with all their packages, but they finally emerged, elated and exhausted, to meet a very excited son.

Geoffrey Scrivener embraced James and took a long look at the bearded young man and brand-new father.

"The bris will be on time," he told them excitedly.

"So we're just in time," smiled Anne Scrivener.

The bris took place early the next morning. James's Jerusalem flat was crowded with friends and neighbors. Anne Scrivener wiped away a tear when she heard the *mohel* announce the name of her new grandson:

"*Veyikarei shemo beYisrael* Yaakov Eliyahu ben Yonasan!"

At the *seudah*, Geoffrey Scrivener rose to speak. The room hushed as he began.

"Today is the first day of Chanukah, the time when the house of Hashem was rededicated in holiness. James always tells me that it was on the first night of Chanukah, years ago, in a small shul in Exeter, that he started on the return road which led to his rededicating our own home to holiness.

"May this infant, Yaakov Eliyahu, whose bris we celebrate today and whose life has already been dedicated to Torah, grow to be a true and worthy descendant of Reb Yaakov Elya HaSofer of Exeter!"

All those present echoed a resounding "Amen!"

NO
COINCIDENCE

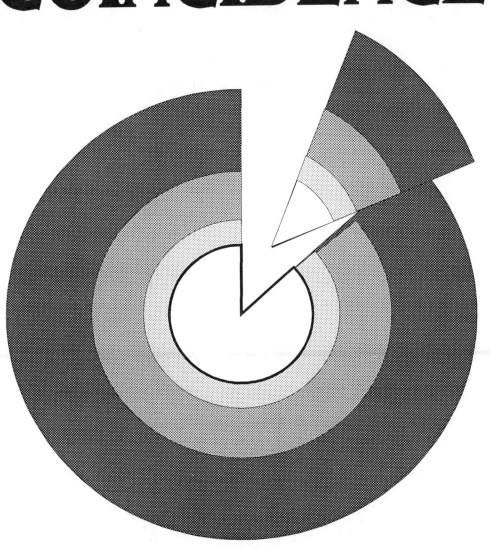

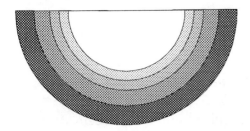

Shabbat in the Desert -
A True Story

Batia Elnadav

Uncle Al Azar is a big-hearted man with a ready laugh and well-timed joke. We all enjoy having him around, and if there's one thing he loves, it's an audience for his stories. We kids always look forward to his visits. He never fails to arrive well equipped with a new story and a reservoir full of jokes.

This particular visit, however, was special. My oldest sister, Leah, and her husband, David, had just come in from Eretz Yisrael for the first time since they were married three months before. Uncle Al hadn't made it to the wedding and had met David only once. Now my uncle delighted in his fresh audience.

He looks forward to new audiences, because, as he says, "You can tell 'em anything, and they'll be too polite to contradict you. My stories are always true...for the most part, anyway — what's a story without *some* stretching? These fellows are the only ones who wouldn't dare question what I

BATIA ELNADAV is a Sephardic Beit Yaakov high school student living in the Flatbush section of Brooklyn.

say! Not like this crew here!" He'd smile and throw a grin and a wink our way, as if to say, "But you guys are still the greatest!"

That night, Uncle Al outdid himself. It seemed to me that he overwhelmed poor David, a shy fellow who hung on Al's every word.

"I've been in quite a few sticky situations in my time," Uncle Al began, "but nothing comes close to the time I was stuck in the desert over Shabbat. And then a lion came and — nah, you wouldn't believe me if I told you *that* one! I really was stuck in a desert, though. Jackson, Mississippi, may as well be one as far as Judaism is concerned. The 'natives' there probably think that Jews are wild creatures with horns, the kind you see in the zoo...

*   *   *

...I knew a Thursday afternoon appointment with Mr. Gibson was too close to Shabbat. That's one of the disadvantages of being a salesman. You've got to plan your schedule to accommodate others. Mr. Gibson, as his little secretary told me over the phone, and over the sound of gum-cracking, had no other available appointments. So Thursday afternoon it had to be. I booked a seat on the first flight back to La Guardia Friday morning.

Thursday noon found me checking into the local Motel Six to freshen up before my appointment with Mr. Gibson. As I unlocked the door to my room, the telephone rang. Mr. Gibson's secretary, young as she sounded, must have been very efficient to have tracked me down so fast. The news she had for me was not good.

"Mistah Ayzah?" she crackled into the phone. Between the gum, the static, and the accent, I had a hard time figuring out what she was telling me. "Ah'm sahrray, an emurgensay's cuhm up, ayand Mistah Gibson cayen't mak his mettin' with ya tiday."

By the time what she'd told me actually registered, I had another appointment with this character Gibson for "Joo-lah," whenever that was. The only thing I was sure of was that I'd come down south for no reason.

I thanked the girl and dialed Delta Airlines. Three hours and about a dozen telephone calls later (I averaged twelve minutes and thirty-eight seconds on hold per call, listening to what some people call music), I was ready to quit. All flights to New York that night and the next morning had been canceled due to "suhm-im up thayeh cahlled a blizzahd. Sahrray, suhr, cayen't help ya' ennay further!" Even Amtrak had stopped its regular express to Grand Central.

Finally, I made one last call, to Brooklyn. I spoke to Carole and the kids, told 'em I couldn't make it home for Shabbat. Believe it or not, Carole's response was, "Next time, *I'll* go on the business trip! It's my turn for a vacation from this crazy house!" Funny. There I was, miles away, wishing I could be at home with my family, and my wife wanted to switch places with me.

The next morning, Friday, I checked out of the motel and into a more comfortable room. I wasn't paying for it, so why save money at the expense of my happiness? If I couldn't be in the relative comfort of my home, I could at least spend Shabbat in surroundings with more than a bed and a lamp. Maybe I could even have a chair to sit down on!

I opened the door to my new room, shoved my suitcase onto the bed, and made a beeline for the lobby. Once outside, I ran, following my instincts, towards where local traffic was going. Sure enough, I found an A & P about two blocks away from my hotel.

What wouldn't I have done to have Carole and her keen shopper's sense with me? I found myself looking for tuna fish in the pet foods section, cookies in the dairy aisle, and bread in the fresh produce department! For the first time in my life, I regretted not having gained more experience at home by shopping for Carole.

I managed to find some Stella D'Oro cookies and a couple of cans of tuna. In addition, I picked up some apples and hoped this would get me through Shabbat. Then, with Shabbat so early, I rushed back to the hotel to shower and unpack. Of course, I forgot which direction I had come from and wasted another precious thirty minutes finding the hotel.

Candlelighting was in about forty-five minutes. I quickly showered and dressed. Then, with another half an hour left, I proceeded to unpack my belongings. I put my sample catalogue, my wallet, and my tefillin in the top drawer of the old, worn mahogany bureau, my siddur and tallit on top. The toothbrush went next to the hairbrush, and the toothpaste — whoops — forgot it this time!

Then I shook out my shirts. I'd conveniently forgotten to bring an iron — or even some hangers to prevent those crisp, white shirts from getting creased. In my opinion, they still looked pretty much okay, though what Carole would say would be a different story! I refolded them as best as I could and opened the second drawer to put them in, then shut it suddenly, dropping the shirts. I picked them up, dusted them off, and inserted them into the bottom drawer with shaking hands. There, at least, nothing was playing tricks on my imagination.

Gingerly, cautiously, I reopened the middle drawer to see if it all was still there — and shut it again in disbelief. I walked over to the sink in the corner of the room and splashed cold water on my face. Strangely, I felt just as wide-awake as before. I pinched myself hard, and, satisfied that I wasn't dreaming, looked into the middle drawer again, taking stock of its contents.

There, as though waiting for me to come along and make use of them, sat a pair of traveling candlesticks, complete with candles and matches (courtesy of Holiday Inn), a siddur, a *chumash*, even a mishnah! And the food! I touched the stuff to make sure it was real. This was no plastic kosher airline meal. There were three *challot*, proudly bearing a paper label reading Korn's Bakery, a bottle of Kedem Malaga wine (*mevushal*, of course), a jar of gefilte fish, and even a bag of salted pumpkin seeds, a popular Syrian Jewish snack.

I couldn't understand how this "care package" had gotten into the middle drawer of my hotel room. Hadn't room service cleaned the room before I checked in? For once, I was thankful to have gotten a room that wasn't thoroughly cleaned. Wow, I thought, this is real *hashgachah pratit* happening to an average guy like me!

I looked at the stuff again, this time certain it was real. Yes, this was truly happening. It was not just a mirage. It was an oasis in the middle of the Mississippi desert for a lonely, Jewish traveler. Someone somewhere was watching over Al Azar and making sure he wasn't entirely miserable on that Shabbat he spent far away from home...

*　　　　*　　　　*

Uncle Al sat back and took a deep breath. "Whew," he said. "Telling a story really takes all I've got!" He chuckled as he passed his plate for a refill. "After Shabbat, I took the first available flight back home, and that was the end of that!"

"Oh, no, it wasn't," my usually quiet brother-in-law spoke up. "You didn't mention the rest of the things in the drawer."

Uncle Al looked up in surprise. "How would *you* know what was there? And would you care to share your knowledge with the rest of us?" he added with a bit of suspicion.

This was his story, after all, and he wasn't used to people outdoing him, especially strangers. (Notice how David went from being a welcome addition to the family, to a "newcomer" once Uncle Al felt his storytelling throne was being usurped!)

"Well," said David as he leaned back (we all leaned forward, including Uncle Al), "in addition to what you mentioned in that memorable middle drawer, there were: a black, unlabeled tallit bag, a white tablecloth, a box of animal crackers, and an extra blue, velvet *kippah*."

Uncle Al's eyes nearly popped out. "How did you *know*?" he exclaimed.

"Well, this is what happened to my father when he was on a business trip in the 'desert.' (Funny, he referred to it as a *midbar*, too.) Anyway, he had to see a client in Jackson. He got there right on schedule Tuesday morning, and he booked a Wednesday-morning flight back to New York.

"On Tuesday night, he was gripped by sudden, severe stomach pain. He was rushed to the nearest hospital for an emergency removal of his appendix. With a lot of begging and arm-twisting, he managed to be discharged Thursday afternoon and caught the last flight back home that night. He went straight to the airport from the hospital, as he had all his belongings with him, except for the Shabbat travel kit he always brought along in case he had to spend Shabbat away from home. Somehow, it had been overlooked in the rush to the hospital. Isn't it amazing how you managed to be the next occupant of his room, so you would have some *oneg* that Shabbat?"

For once, we all agreed, someone had topped Uncle Al.

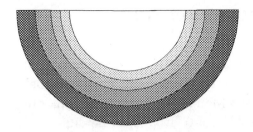

Menashe and the Bird

Yaacov Dovid Shulman

Menashe lived at the edge of town in a big, two-story house. Outside his second-floor bedroom window was a big field that was full of yellow and red flowers in the summer, and filled with white, clean snow in the wintertime. Far beyond the field was another town named Barton, but Menashe couldn't see that far.

Menashe had a bird that he kept in a cage. It was a small, gray bird that didn't look handsome, but it could sing a hundred different songs. Menashe liked to hear it sing. He liked to give it birdseed and water in two little dishes, and a piece of white chalk to scratch its claws and beak on.

But Menashe also liked to poke the bird with a stick. Then the bird would squawk and flap its wings and fly

YAACOV DOVID SHULMAN is the author of *The Maharal of Prague* and *Pathway to Jerusalem*, a translation of Rabbi Ovadiah of Bartenura's travel letters.

Rabbi Shulman was born in Paris and moved to New York as a boy.

He says: "When visiting friends for Shabbos, I thought of this story and told it to their children. Soon afterwards, I wrote it down so I wouldn't forget it and could show it to others."

around the cage, trying to get away from Menashe's stick. But it never could, because the cage was small, and Menashe's stick was long. Sometimes Menashe's parents caught him poking at the bird and told him to stop it, so he did — but only for a few days. And then he would start all over again.

One day, when Menashe was giving the bird its water, his brother, Ezra, called him from downstairs, "Menashe, we're going to play softball."

"I'm coming," Menashe shouted back. He quickly shut the bird cage and ran downstairs to play with Ezra and their friends in the field.

But Menashe hadn't closed the cage door all the way. After a few minutes, the bird noticed that the door wasn't shut in place. It pushed against the door, and the door moved. It pushed a little more, and the door swung completely open. After a few seconds, the bird hopped out. It hadn't been out of a cage for almost its entire life, and it wasn't used to the feeling. It flapped its wings and flew over to the window. Below in the field, it saw the boys playing baseball.

"What should I do?" the bird thought. "The window is open, and I can fly out to my freedom. I'll get to fly, to find a wife and raise my own chicks."

The bird hopped back and forth on the sill. "Yes, that's true, but if I stay here, I don't have to migrate every year. I don't have to worry about finding food, about dangerous animals, or about snakes eating my eggs."

The bird stood on the window sill for many minutes, unable to make up his mind. But at last it decided: "It would be an adventure to fly away, but it's safer to stay here after all."

Just then, the bird looked down and saw Menashe going up to bat. Menashe stepped up to home plate, swinging a bat back and forth, getting its feel.

"Menashe and his stick," thought the bird, and a bitter feeling filled him. "No. I don't want to ever be poked again by Menashe and his stick — even if it means having to find my own food, to look out for other animals, to migrate a thousand miles twice a year, and to fight off snakes that want to eat my eggs."

So, with a last look at the room and the cage where it had spent such a long time, the bird flapped its wings and flew out over the field where the boys were playing softball. At that moment, Menashe hit a high pop fly to right field. His eyes followed the ball, and over the ball he saw a bird flying. But he didn't know that the bird flying higher than his ball, far out into the field and away from his big house at the edge of town, was his own.

When Menashe came back to his room and saw the cage door and window open and the bird missing, he knew that the bird had flown away. At first he blamed Ezra, but he finally had to admit that it was his own fault. Menashe was sad that he didn't have the bird any more. But after a few weeks, he forgot about it. For a while, the cage stayed in his room. Then in April, when he was cleaning for Pesach, he decided to throw it out. And soon after, he never thought about the bird anymore.

A few years passed, and Menashe turned thirteen. He became bar mitzvah. Now he was learning Torah in a *mesivta*. A few more years passed — now Menashe was seventeen years old, and he already had a mustache and a few hairs on his cheeks. Then he turned eighteen, and he went into a *beis midrash* far from his parents, in a big city where many Jews lived. When he was twenty-two years old, Menashe met a young woman named Chaya Sarah, and they decided to get married. After their wedding, Menashe learned in a *kollel* for three years, and then he began working as an accountant.

Meanwhile, he started having children — seven in all: three boys and four girls, and he and Chaya Sarah loved them all.

The years passed, and his children grew. Eventually they also married, and when Menashe was fifty-six years old, he became a grandfather. Then he turned sixty. His beard was gray, and he always wore a scarf when he went out in the country. When he was sixty-five, Menashe stopped working as an accountant, and instead he spent all his time in the *beis midrash*, just as he had when he had been young. Throughout his life, Menashe had given charity and helped other people, and now that he had more time, he made helping other people part of his daily schedule.

Menashe was a very good father and a very good grandfather, too. He helped his children and grandchildren whenever he could. And when Menashe was eighty-six years old, he became a great-grandfather. More years passed. Menashe's wife, Chaya Sarah, passed away, and he went to live with his oldest daughter and her family.

One day, when Menashe was ninety-one years old, he felt too weak to get up. His son-in-law called the doctor. The doctor brought Menashe to the hospital, but they couldn't help him. With his children at his side, Menashe passed away.

When Menashe died, his soul passed out of his body and rose from the earth. Soon it came to a courtroom, where three judges sat to decide what would happen to it.

Menashe stood before the judges. A clerk stood up and called out. "Witness for the defense!" One by one, all the angels that had been made by Menashe's good deeds came before the judges.

The first witness stepped forward and said, "Menashe put on tefillin every day; he prayed in a minyan, and he always answered amen to Kaddish. He never talked in the synagogue or pushed aside anyone else who was praying."

The next witness said, "Menashe gave between ten and twenty percent of what he earned to charity. He also helped people in other ways. He gave people rides in his car. He brought food to people who were sick at home. He visited sick people in the hospital and prayed for them. He was always honest with everyone, Jew and gentile."

Another witness stepped up. "Menashe never stopped learning Torah, even when he was raising a family and making a living. He always made sure that his own children would learn Torah. And when he retired, he spent his time in the *beis midrash* every day."

Then another witness spoke. "Menashe always treated his wife and children with respect. He always let them know that he loved them and thought a great deal of them."

The angels said so many nice things that Menashe grew embarrassed.

When they finished their testimony, the clerk stood up and called out: "Witnesses for the prosecution!" Menashe trembled. These were the witnesses who would tell all the bad things he had done. And now they came up, one by one. They told the court about when he had said angry things to his wife and children; they told about when he read the *N.Y. Post* instead of learning Torah; about when he didn't invite a certain Jew to his house for a Shabbos meal because he had believed some gossip about him.

One after another, the witnesses came forward and testified until Menashe cried in shame and regret.

After the last witness had spoken, the judges murmured together. Finally, the chief judge announced, "Menashe ben Reuven, we have examined the witnesses' testimony, and our verdict is that you may go to Gan Eden."

"Thank you! Oh, thank you!" Menashe said, lifting his

eyes. But something flew between him and the judges and landed on the floor between them. It was a bird.

"Who are you?" cried the chief judge. "What are you doing here in this court of law?"

"I am a witness that no one called," the bird declared, "but I wish to testify, too — *against* Menashe ben Reuven."

"I-I don't know who this bird is!" protested Menashe.

"You don't know me?" cried the bird. "Maybe after your long life of treating people so well, you've forgotten a humble little animal like me, whom you didn't treat so well — whom you poked with a stick until my feathers fell out and my heart beat so hard that I thought I would faint. Oh, Mr. Menashe ben Reuven, don't you remember any of that? Don't you remember all the pain you caused me? You treated everyone else so nicely. Everyone else is so happy with you. But, Mr. Menashe ben Reuven, don't you remember how you treated me?" The bird turned to the judges. "Doesn't anyone want to hear how this wonderful father and grandfather and great-grandfather treated me, a simple bird, a helpless creature whom Hashem placed on Earth?"

"Oh yes, I remember," said Menashe. "Now I remember you. But that was so long ago. I was just a little boy — just a very little boy."

" 'A little boy,' he says," the bird laughed. "But you weren't too little to hurt me, were you?"

Menashe turned to the judges. "I was just a little boy. I didn't know I was causing him so much pain."

The judges leaned over and talked to each other. Then the chief judge leaned forward to Menashe. "It is true that you were just a little boy. But causing animals pain is a very bad thing — especially since you did it for fun. This is our decision: To cleanse yourself, you must spend three days in Gehinnom."

Menashe felt weak. Three days in Gehinnom! He broke out in a sweat. The bird snickered.

Then, from the back of the courtyard, a large man with a long, white beard strode up to the judges. The old man held up his hand. "Wait, Your Honors."

"Yes?" said the chief judge. "What is your name, and what is your testimony?"

"My name is Mordechai Sheppard. I have come to testify on behalf of Menashe. Know, Your Honor, that my life and the lives of thousands of other people were saved because Menashe poked that bird with a stick."

Menashe stood silently. He had never seen this man before. What on earth — or in heaven — did he mean?

"Explain yourself," the judge commanded.

"Yes, Your Honor. When Menashe was a small boy, I was the sexton of the synagogue in a border town called Barton. In those days, the neighboring country's army used to raid our border villages, and one summer they laid siege to Barton. We had enough men to hold them off, but we couldn't get food or drink, and they had cut off our communications to the outside world. We held them off day after day, but we knew we would soon have to give in — and then they would enter the town and kill us all.

"We were very near the end of our rations, and one day, as some of us sat in the synagogue reciting Psalms, I stepped out to get smelling salts for an old man who had fainted. I saw a bird on the ground in front of the synagogue. I was carrying a damp towel to rub the man's brow, and I quickly threw it over the bird. I had an idea how we could use it. I wrote a message asking for help, tied it to the bird's leg, and then threw the bird into the air. It flapped its wings and flew off. It was a chance in a million, and I thought we would never hear anything from it again. I thought that we were lost.

"But I was wrong. The next morning, we saw hundreds of soldiers marching to our town — our soldiers! I never saw a happier sight. Within two days, they fought off the enemy and saved our lives.

"Later, we learned that they had in fact learned about us from the message I had tied to the bird's leg.

"And that bird," the man pointed his finger, "is the very one Menashe poked with his stick. So you see, because Menashe poked this bird, all our lives were saved."

"Yes," said the three judges, and they put their heads together and talked. Then they looked up, and the chief judge spoke. "Menashe, we have determined that you do not have to go to Gehinnom."

"Thank you so much," breathed Menashe. He turned to the tall man. "And thank you so — "

"Wait a second," interrupted the bird. "I flew away to Barton because Menashe poked me, but he didn't mean to help anyone. He meant only to hurt me. Even though all those people's lives were saved, he can't get the credit for that. It isn't fair!"

The chief judge said, "Please do not interrupt. We have taken into account the bird's testimony. It is true that because of you, Menashe, thousands of lives were saved. But the bird is right. You didn't mean to save those lives; you meant only to poke the bird. As a result, you created a flaw in your soul that you must correct. Therefore, before entering Gan Eden, you must return to earth — as a bird — and correct what you have spoiled."

"Wait a minute, Your Honor!" cried Menashe, but suddenly the courtroom disappeared.

A moment later, Menashe found himself floating in a round room. It was very warm and comfortable. Although he was in the middle of a thick liquid, he didn't have any trouble breathing. To the contrary, it was very pleasant.

From day to day, Menashe felt himself getting bigger and stronger. Finally, one day, he banged his head against the side of his room. Again and again he banged against the wall, until it cracked open. A strong, white light broke in on him together with a rush of cool air.

"Where am I?" Menashe cried, but only a thin peep came out. Menashe realized, "I was in an egg, and now I've just hatched. I'm a baby bird." Menashe opened his mouth and cried. His mother — a handsome nighthawk — stuck some food in his mouth, and he swallowed it greedily. He felt better, and he slept.

Each day, Menashe grew bigger. He fought with his brothers and sisters to be the first to eat, and a few weeks later, he took his first steps out of the nest. A couple of days after that, he made his first short flight. He practiced day after day, until he could fly from branch to branch, then from tree to tree, and until he could soar high in the air, riding the air currents and swooping through the sky.

By now Menashe was grown up, and he left his parents' nest. Menashe was always trying to think of how he could fix himself so he could get to Gan Eden. But he couldn't think of a thing. After all, what could he do as a bird? Could he give charity? Where would he get the money, and to whom would he give it? Could he put on tefillin? Nonsense! How could he get a pair of tefillin his size? And who ever heard of a bird putting on tefillin? He tried going to a *beis midrash* to listen to the people learn Torah and answer amen to their prayers, but they chased him away.

"Wait!" Menashe called. "You don't understand. I'm not a bird. I'm Menashe — Menashe!" But instead of speaking, he could only chirp.

When Menashe cried out, the people listened to him and

said to one another, "Listen to how beautifully that bird sings."

"Who cares about beautiful songs?" Menashe would cry. "Listen — I'm Menashe. Can't you help me?" But no one understood anything he said.

Bitter and disappointed, Menashe left the people and made his home in a large poplar tree next to an old house. In the house lived a young Torah scholar and his nine-year-old son, Avner. The man's wife had died when she was very young, and now the man was raising Avner by himself.

Menashe paid little attention to them. He was bitter — bitter and silent. He had been sent back to earth to suffer as a bird — and there was nothing he could do to help himself get back to Gan Eden. Day by day, Menashe sat in his nest, leaving only to find food, growing more and more bitter, feeling sorrier and sorrier for himself.

Once in a while, he saw a doctor with a thick, black bag come to the Torah scholar's house and examine Avner. He noticed Avner getting paler and thinner. Soon, Avner spent almost all his time lying in bed. One day, Avner and his father left the house in a taxi. Menashe heard Avner's father tell the taxi driver to go to the hospital. In the evening, Avner's father came back home alone. Menashe heard him crying in the house.

A few weeks later, Avner returned. Now he lay in bed the whole day, and his father stayed home and took care of him.

But Menashe hardly noticed. He was so disappointed and depressed that he hardly noticed anything at all.

And so things continued for weeks and then months.

Then, one day, Menashe had a thought. "Look," he told himself, "I was sent back to earth to fix myself. Ha! How can I fix myself as a bird? There's no way! But that doesn't mean I have to stop serving Hashem. It doesn't mean I have to sink into this black depression. You know what? Everyone says I sing beautiful songs. So let me sing beautiful songs to Hashem, even if it can't fix me. So what? At least I'll be serving Hashem as best I can."

So Menashe began singing. At first his voice was rough, because he hadn't sung for months. And besides, he was still depressed. His songs were very moody. But after a few days, Menashe started to cheer up. His songs to Hashem were like prayers, and he sang them with all his heart. He sang all sorts of songs: songs of longing, songs of joy at being healthy and able to find food and swoop through the air, songs of loneliness and unhappiness, and songs of bitterness that turned into songs of happiness.

Meanwhile, Avner was very sick. The doctors didn't think he would live more than a few months. That was why they had sent him home: They had thought it would be more comfortable for Avner to spend his last few months on earth in his house rather than in a hospital.

Avner lay in bed hopeless, bored, and tired. One day, he heard a bird singing outside his window. The sound bothered him, and he wished the bird would go away. But the bird kept singing, and it sang every day from then on. Soon, Avner found himself listening to the bird's beautiful, wonderful song. It almost never repeated itself, and it was almost always full of hope and love and happiness and meaning. It filled Avner with joy and the will to live. As the days passed, he felt the bird's song enter his flesh and bones and give him strength and health. Avner started to get well.

Little by little, he grew stronger; little by little, he grew healthier. One morning, he got out of bed, sat down next to the window, and looked at the bird singing so joyfully outside his window.

When Avner's father came in to bring him breakfast, he

was shocked. "Avner, what are you doing out of bed? You'll make yourself worse!"

"No, Father," answered Avner. "I'm feeling so much better. Please let me sit up."

Avner's father rushed over and kissed him, then ran downstairs and called the doctor. A few hours later, the doctor came and examined Avner.

"It's a miracle!" he said. "Avner is getting well. He's tired from lying in bed so long, but his disease is gone. I just can't understand it."

"I'll tell you how I got well," said Avner. He walked over to the window and pointed up at the singing bird. "Every day, when I listened to that bird, I felt better. That bird gave me back my health."

That bird was, of course, Menashe. When Menashe heard this, he was filled with joy and gratitude to Hashem that even as a bird he could do some good in this world: He had helped a poor boy, a Torah scholar's son, to become cured of a terrible disease.

Menashe was so happy that he began to sing as never before. The whole night he sang songs of happiness and thanks to Hashem, until he wore himself out and slipped off into sleep.

The next morning, Avner's father said to his son, "Let's go out and hang up a carton of food for your bird to eat. That's how we'll thank him for saving your life."

They didn't have any birdseed in the house, so Avner crumbled up some bread and put it in a milk carton. He and his father walked out of the house and under the branches of the poplar tree.

"That's funny," said Avner's father. "I don't hear him singing now."

"He was singing all night," said Avner. "Maybe he's tired." Then he pointed. "Look, Father! The poor bird!"

There on the ground lay Menashe, unmoving.

Avner's father bent over the bird. "I'm afraid we can't thank him, Avner," he said. "He is no longer alive."

"He's dead?" said Avner. "But he saved my life. He sang for days and days, and he healed me. And now, is that his reward, that he should die? Father, is that right? Is that fair?"

Avner's father put his arm around the boy.

"Avner," he said, "everything Hashem does is full of wisdom. We see only part of the story. We don't know the greater picture. But we have to have faith that even when we don't understand it, everything Hashem does is for the best."

At that moment, freed of its imprisonment in the body of the bird, Menashe's soul was entering Gan Eden. And as he entered, Menashe sang a song of thanks to Hashem.

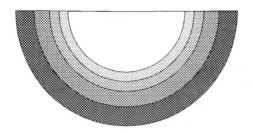

The Identity Crisis

Talia Hendler

ave you ever seen a blue sky? I don't mean an ordinary blue sky with clouds flitting around, I mean a bright, glorious, blue sky, clear and vibrant, with not a cloud on all its majestic horizon! If you've never been in Eretz Yisrael, then you shouldn't be taken in by imitations. There is absolutely no blue sky like a Yerushalayim one. What makes me such an expert? Nothing, really, except that I have been in Eretz Yisrael for three days, and I just can't get enough of it.

Here I am, going on and on about blue skies without even properly introducing myself. Hi! My name is Avigail Stern. I'm thirteen years old (thirteen-and-a-half, really). I have wavy, dark brown hair (permed, if the truth be known) and hazel eyes, and I'm petite and thin. I hate when people call me short and skinny. "Petite and thin" sounds so much nicer, don't you think?

As I mentioned, I've been in Eretz Yisrael for three days (plus six hours and twenty-two minutes, to be exact). I mean to savor every single second in the Holy Land. My sister (she's

If you want to read about TALIA HENDLER, turn to page 190.

eighteen) is in B.J.J. Seminary, and my parents decided that instead of making her come visit us (a *yeridah*), we would all be *oleh* and visit her in Yerushalayim. So, here I am, a mere speck beneath the vast Yerushalayim blue.

This was going to be a great day. I could feel it! My neighbors, the Slomianskys, came from Monsey yesterday, and they had a package for my sister from her best friend, Riki. Anyway, the exciting part was that my parents, after much pleading and convincing, allowed me to go pick up the package all by myself — provided, of course, that I didn't get into any trouble. This included not taking solitary walks through the Moslem Quarter, getting on a bus to Hevron, and other such brilliant ideas.

The Slomianskys were staying at the Chaim Hotel, on Rechov King George. I had to take a #2 bus to the fourth stop on Rechov King George, then walk down the street, and to my left would be the hotel. Sounds pretty simple to me, but somehow, whenever I get involved, nothing is ever simple!

After the long bus ride, I found myself standing at the hotel entrance. The Chaim is definitely not the nicest hotel in Yerushalayim. It's pretty small as hotels go, and, for some strange reason, it always smells like fish.

I asked the receptionist which room the Slomianskys were staying in. She looked down to see where the noise was coming from (being petite, I didn't reach the top of her tall desk). When she located the source of the disturbance (me), I could see her deciding whether or not she would deign to acknowledge my existence. I don't know what *zechus* I had, but, *baruch Hashem*, she decided in my favor. "Room 242" was her terse reply. No "Thank you" or "Have a nice day" — that was reserved for paying customers!

Wait a minute, didn't we learn in school about the mitzvah of being *dan lekaf zechus*? This was a perfect opportunity to put it into practice. Maybe she had had a long night, or maybe someone was sick (*chas veshalom*). With that in mind, I gave her a hearty *"Todah rabbah"* and one of my brightest smiles. Miracle of miracles, she actually smiled back! Being *dan lekaf zechus* really does work wonders, I thought to myself as I ascended the stairs. Room 242 was the third room from the staircase. I knocked lightly on the Slomianskys' door, happily anticipating their surprise at seeing me here all by myself.

Well, they were surprised, all right, but not half as surprised as I was, because the person who opened the door was definitely not Mr. Slomiansky!

"Oh, excuse me," I stammered. "I'm afraid I have the wrong room."

The man standing at the door looked down kindly at me (he was about six feet tall, so when I say he looked down, I mean he looked down!). "Who are you looking for?" he asked me.

"Mrs. Slomiansky," I answered.

"Well, then, you haven't got the wrong room at all. I'll get her for you in a jiffy."

Now I was really confused! What was Mrs. Slomiansky doing with this strange man?

I heard a woman's footsteps approaching. "Yes, I'm Mrs. Slomiansky," said a woman I had never seen in my life. "What can I do for you?"

"Well, you're not the Mrs. Slomiansky I know," I said, feeling very foolish.

"I hope you find whoever it is you're looking for," said the mysterious Mrs. Slomiansky. With that, she closed the door, and I heard the lock turning on the other side.

Very perplexed, I walked down the stairs. Maybe there were two Slomianskys staying at the hotel, I thought. I'll have to bother the receptionist again, I'm afraid. Slomiansky is not exactly a common name, but you never know.

I approached the desk with some trepidation. Clearing my voice and standing on my tippy toes, so that my forehead and eyes were visible, I said, "Ah, *selichah* (excuse me), but is there another Slomiansky staying at this hotel?"

"*Lo.*"

Okay, here goes another one!

"Ah, *selichah*, is there another Slomiansky booked in this hotel who hasn't arrived yet?"

"*Lo.*" Looking down and seeing how dejected I was, she smiled at me and said, "*Al tid'agi* (don't worry)."

I love *Yidden*, don't you?

Walking out of the hotel, I turned the whole thing over in my mind. What could this possibly mean? My parents had told me the Slomianskys were staying at the Chaim Hotel. There were Slomianskys listed in the hotel, but they were total strangers to me. Maybe they were impersonating my neighbors. Maybe my neighbors had been kidnapped or... Oh, stop being silly, I chided myself. I'm sure I just misunderstood which hotel they were staying at. Or perhaps they had planned to stay at the Chaim and changed their minds at the last minute.

Trying to persuade myself that there was nothing to worry about, I walked to the bus stop, oblivious to all the people and shops surrounding me. Questions and thoughts were confusedly revolving in my mind, preventing me from concentrating on the scenery. I got on the bus, plopped down in the nearest seat, and sank into my own reverie. Staring out the window, I kept on thinking about what could have happened to the Slomianskys.

All of a sudden, I saw them, my Slomianskys, walking down the street. In my excitement, I let out a shriek! Think-

ing that someone had gotten hurt, the bus driver brought the
bus screeching to a halt. *"Mah karah? Mah haba'ayah?"* he
shouted to the back of the bus. I ran to the front, panting
excitedly, and told him I just had to get off. Fearing that I
must be sick or something, he opened the door and let me out.
(That in itself was a miracle, because bus drivers usually
refuse to deviate from their schedules, no matter what!)

Running in the direction that I'd seen my neighbors, I
sent up a silent prayer that they shouldn't have disappeared
into some store or taxi cab. Please, Hashem, let me find them.
I'll give two dollars to *tzedakah*, I promised. I'll give three
doll —

There they were, up ahead, on the other side of the
street! Running as fast as my little legs could carry me,
huffing and puffing, I was finally able to call out to them:
"Mrs. Slomiansky! Mr. Slomiansky! Wait up! It's me —
Avigail!"

By now I had attracted the attention of many passersby,
who were looking at me pityingly. ("Those strange *Ameri-
cayot*, always in such a hurry!")

When my neighbors realized who it was, they stopped
and waited for me to catch up to them. After a few minutes
of hugs and kisses, I was finally able to ask them where they
were staying.

"At the Chaim Hotel, Avigail. Didn't your parents
know?" was their surprised answer.

Ignoring the question, I asked, "Room 242?"

"Yes, that sounds about right. What do you think,
Moshe?"

Mrs. Slomiansky's husband thought for a second and
then said, "Yes, that's right, room 242. It's very close to the
stairs."

"Well, then," I burst out, "there are people in your room

right now who claim to be Mr. and Mrs. Slomiansky, and I've never seen them in my life!"

At first they thought I was just joking, but after I told them the whole story, I could see they were a little worried, too.

"Let's check it out," Mr. Slomiansky suggested.

We were a rather quiet group as we proceeded down the busy, colorful street. As we got near the hotel, I felt a nervous, tingling sensation down my spine. What if it was some group of robbers or terrorists pretending to be Jews? What if they tried to hurt us or pretend that they were the real Slomianskys and that my Slomianskys were the impostors?

This was turning out to be quite an adventure. I remembered the promise I had made earlier this morning not to get myself into trouble. Well, this doesn't count, I said to myself. After all, I'm just trying to pick up a package. It's not my fault that trouble seems to follow me around!

As we neared the receptionist, for the first time in my life, I was glad I couldn't reach the desk. Somehow, I was sure she wouldn't be happy to see me.

"*Selichah*, is there another Slomiansky staying here at the hotel?" asked Moshe Slomiansky.

I could have told him the answer to that one myself. Did he think I was dumb or something?

"*Lo*, Adon Slomiansky. May I help you with anything?"

Why do taller people get so much more respect?

"No, thank you. We'll just go up to our room now."

I wondered how the meeting between the real Slomianskys and the imposters would work out.

We all climbed the stairs and started walking down the hall. As we approached the third door, I could hear my heart thumping wildly. Then we passed the third door.

"Wait a minute," I cried! "You've passed it!"

"That's not room 242, that's room 240. The zero is a little unclear — that's why you must have mistaken it for a two."

"But I don't understand. The receptionist said there were no other Slomianskys staying at the hotel, but when that man answered the door, he said Mrs. Slomiansky was there."

"You must have mistaken the name — maybe it was another long name with an *S*, and since you were looking for Slomiansky, you thought that's what he said," Moshe Slomiansky suggested, trying to hold back the smile forming on his lips.

Blushing, I said in the steadiest voice I could muster, "I am sure he said Slomiansky!"

Seeing that I was getting upset, he tried to explain to me that there are very few Slomianskys in America:

"We're all related, you see, so I can't imagine who it could possibly be. In fact, there is only one Slomiansky that we haven't kept in touch with. When my brother was *niftar*, we somehow lost track of his wife. She has just disappeared! You know, I haven't seen or heard from her for over twenty years!"

Just as we finished speaking, the lady from room 240 (not 242) walked out into the hall. "Moshe!" she exclaimed. "Is it really you?"

"Chana! I can't believe my eyes!"

Within minutes, my Mrs. Slomiansky and the other Mrs. Slomiansky were hugging and kissing each other, everybody was speaking at the same time, and we were all making a great ruckus. It wasn't until much later, when everybody had calmed down, that the whole story came out.

Moshe's brother, Chana's husband, had been *niftar* many years before, and his wife's name was now Green. But when I had mistakenly knocked on her door and asked her husband for Mrs. Slomiansky, he had thought that I must be someone who had known her before she had married him. That's why they weren't listed under the name Slomiansky — because her new husband's name was Green!

Then everybody started hugging and kissing me.

"Could you imagine, Avigail? If you hadn't knocked on the wrong door [which turned out to be the right door as far as everyone was concerned], we might never have met! We could have stayed one door away from each other for the whole week without even knowing it! What *hashgachah pratis* this is. This is a perfect example of Hashem taking good care of us. Sometimes, we do things that we think are wrong, but they are in reality for the best. *Gam zu letovah.*"

"Yes," Chana Green (formerly Slomiansky) added, "especially since if you hadn't knocked, you would never have seen us, because we're leaving tomorrow!"

They all began to walk towards the (real) Slomianskys' room to catch up on each other's lives. I was about to say goodbye, when all of a sudden, the whole reason for my being there suddenly popped into my mind. I had gotten so involved in the Slomiansky mystery that I had almost forgotten!

"Mr. Slomiansky, I know this is not a good time to bother you — but do you have a package for my sister?"

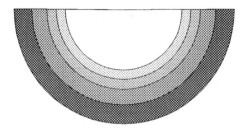

The Dream

Miriam Deutsch

Mimi was a dreamer. She lived in the exciting world of imagination. There were so many things to invent and create in her own little world. In reality, Mimi's life was confined to the limits of a seven-year-old. But in her mind it was very different.

It was morning. Time to get ready for school. Mimi sat at the edge of her bed and began putting on her navy blue tights. She managed to reach one toe without twisting the tights. Suddenly she saw it. She was a princess with pink, silken tights, and her shoes were woven of gold with glittering, diamond buckles. One foot in and one foot out, Mimi sat

---

"I have always enjoyed writing. When I was in high school, I kept a journal, which did a lot to help me develop my writing skills.

" 'The Dream' happened to me in real life.

"After I submitted this story to Targum Press, I didn't hear from them for quite a while, so I forgot all about it. A few months later, I was contacted by a family in difficult financial straits. They were $6,000 short of buying a desperately needed, two-room apartment. On their behalf, I raised the missing funds. Gratified that I'd accomplished my mission, I phoned the family to tell them the good news. No sooner did I hang up the phone than it rang again. It was Targum Press, informing me that my 'Dream' would come true, not only as a chance to help a poor family but as a story in this anthology." — MIRIAM DEUTSCH

seeing things only she could see.

Then her mother's voice called from the kitchen: "Mimi dear, the school bus will be here in fifteen minutes..."

With a jerk of her head, Mimi quickly continued pulling on her plain, woolen tights.

Mimi sat at her little, wooden desk in the second grade. Her fingers traced the patterns carved into the desk top. She tried to erase some of the old grime with the tip of her pink eraser. Hmm... "Rachel" was spelled out on the desk top, encircled with a heart. Now who was Rachel? Was she tall or short? Did she have long, blonde tresses or short, black curls? And where was she now? Perhaps she was already in eighth grade...

"Mimi." Her teacher's voice pierced her dreamland. "Mimi, will you please concentrate?"

Mimi sat on the floor, playing Monopoly with her brother. She had just bought the railroad. Playing piece in hand, she froze in her spot, rooted in dreamland. She was a railroad conductor. Cap pulled down low over her eyes, she stared ahead at the winding tracks. They were traveling down the mountainside now, faster and faster...

Mimi's brother grabbed her long, brown ponytail and pulled. "Mimi, it's your turn — where are you?"

Suppertime was not bad for dreaming. Despite the noise around her, she could enter her own little world. Along with the soup, chicken, and potatoes, she digested so many interesting trimmings.

But her favorite time was bedtime. Bedtime meant dreaming with no rude interruptions. Mimi looked under her pillow and breathed a sigh of relief. Her new, pink pajamas were there. She had been afraid they would be in the wash, and she would have to wear her old, blue ones, with the holes in the toe.

Mimi loved her pink pajamas. The top had pink cuffs

and rows and rows of pink and purple flowers on a white background. The pants were solid pink. They were soft and smooth and had no pulls or stains. She pulled on her pajamas and went to brush her teeth.

Mimi squeezed toothpaste onto her green toothbrush and smelled it. Mmm...it smelled like mint. Quickly, she brushed her teeth and rinsed her mouth. Dragging a step stool over to the sink, she climbed up and took a look in the mirror. Mimi smiled at her reflection. Big, brown eyes fringed with dark brown lashes smiled back. There was still some toothpaste on her chin. Squeezing her eyes tightly shut, she rubbed white soap on her cheeks. Then she splashed cold water onto her face.

Mimi padded down the hall to the kitchen. Her mother was at the sink, washing the supper dishes. Mimi sneaked up behind her and gave her a big hug around her waist. Her mother turned around and wiped her sudsy hands on her apron. Then she gave Mimi a big kiss and a hug.

"Goodnight, my *maidelah!*" she said. "Sleep well."

Mimi glowed; there was nothing like Mommy's goodnight hug.

Next Mimi went into the dining room, where her father was sitting, bent over his *sefarim*. He hummed a soft tune as he learned, filling the room with warmth. Mimi approached and stood at his elbow until she caught his eye. He smiled and nodded at her to begin. Mimi covered her eyes with her right hand and recited, "*Shema Yisrael...*" When she finished, her father leaned over and kissed the top of her head.

"Goodnight, Mimi," he said.

Mimi smiled her shiny smile and padded back down the hall to her bedroom. Later, Dini would come sleep in her room, but right now Mimi had the place to herself...and it was time to arrange all her adopted children. Out came the small dolls from the dollhouse in the corner. Those went between her pillow and the wall. Next came the three big dolls from the doll carriage; these she put under her covers, their heads against the wall. Then came the stuffed animals from the shelf. One, two, three, four, five — rabbit, chick, elephant, and two teddy bears all sat at the foot of her bed.

Mimi climbed carefully into bed. She spread the quilt over all her friends and leaned back on her pillows. Suddenly, she sat up and jumped out of bed. She had forgotten the tin soldier and the clown from the dresser top. How lonely and cold they must be! She quickly tucked them in and once again settled down under her covers.

Everyone was sheltered for the night. Now Mimi could relax. It was time to dream. As usual, she opted for her favorite dream. She closed her eyes and began.

They were a very poor family with many children. They all lived together in one cold, damp room. The children were hungry and sad. They didn't have much to eat, and they had no toys at all. Their clothes were ugly and torn. Their mother was very unhappy to see her children suffering.

Mimi sighed, and a little tear escaped from under her lashes. Oh, it was so sad to think of those hungry, cold children! And the sweet little baby, who had no toys!

But then one day, the whole family went to visit their cousins far away. And that's when Mrs. Mimi stepped in. Her painters painted the family's apartment a nice, bright color. Her handyman fixed the roof and put in warm radiators. She stocked the kitchen with all kinds of delicious food. The closets she filled with pretty, new clothing. On the shelves she placed books, toys, and games.

Mimi smiled sleepily. It was such a lovely dream.

She covered each bed with nice, soft, warm quilts.

The family came home. How surprised and happy they

were! The children squealed with delight as they discovered all the nice things Mrs. Mimi had left for them. The mother...

Mimi was sleeping, a smile still on her face.

*　　　　*　　　　*

Mimi sat on the bus and dreamily stared off into space. She found herself dreaming very often these days, almost like she used to when she was a little girl.

It had been many years since second grade. In the interim, Mimi had discovered that dreaming was not a very productive pastime. There was so much to focus on and accomplish that she was left with very little time for dreaming. She still had her trips to imagination land here and there, but generally she concentrated on getting things done.

Now, however, it was different. Mimi was a *kallah*, and there were just so many exciting things to dream about. A wedding, a husband, a new life — all the busy plans were mixed with dreams.

Mimi checked the slip of paper she had tucked into her pocketbook. "1467 56th St." was the address of the basement apartment she was to look at today.

She walked slowly up the block, checking the house numbers as she passed. 1465, 1467 — here it was. The house was old and gray. It had wide, cluttered porches and a dilapidated front yard. That was funny — she had thought the landlady had said it was a new house.

Mimi walked up the steps, crossed the porch, and knocked on the front door. There was no answer. "If I'm not home, the present tenant will show you around. Just knock on the basement door," the landlady had said.

Mimi retraced her steps and walked up the drive. The side door stood ajar, and she entered. She descended a rickety flight of steps to the basement. There was a lot of noise behind the finger-marked door, and it took a while for her knock to be answered. Finally, a little boy pulled open the door and stared at her with big, round eyes. Behind him, a bunch of little children peeked out.

"Is your mommy home?" Mimi asked hesitantly. Could this possibly be the wrong address? she thought to herself.

The little gang of kids disappeared into the next room. Mimi took a step forward and surveyed the room. She was in a kind of combination hall and kitchen. The kitchen cabinets hung from their hinges, the kitchen sink was piled with dirty dishes, and the faucet dripped steadily. The paint was peeling off the walls, and the brown linoleum was riddled with holes. A table surrounded by rickety chairs took up most of the space in the small room.

There were two rooms off the kitchen, and Mimi could see into the first one. Crowded into it were a crib, four beds, and a dresser. The small window cast very little light onto the airless room.

A tired-looking woman in a faded housecoat emerged from the second room, holding a crying toddler in her arms. The kids trooped behind her.

"Yes?" she said stiffly, embarrassment written all over her face.

"I'm sorry," said Mimi. "I was given this address to see an apartment for rent."

"You must be looking for 1468, right across the street. There's an apartment for rent there," the woman said.

"Thank you," said Mimi with a compassionate glance at the children's faded, outdated clothing. "I'm sorry to have bothered you." She quickly backed out the door.

Mimi crossed the street and rang the bell at 1468 in a daze. She couldn't believe people lived in such poverty.

The landlady showed her around the basement. It was new and nicely furnished, and Mimi should have been delighted.

The landlady took a look at Mimi's face and asked, "What's the matter? Don't you like it?"

"Oh, I'm really sorry," Mimi stammered. "I was thinking about something else. I must ask you something," she continued. "Do you know the family who lives in the basement across the street?" Mimi couldn't conceal the horror in her tone.

"You must be referring to the Newman family in the old house opposite," the landlady answered.

Mimi explained how she had come to knock on the wrong door. "Isn't anything being done to help them?" she asked.

The landlady shrugged. "I know, it is an awful situation, but what can be done? The father isn't well, and the mother can't work. They don't seem to have any relatives. So who is going to pay their bills? Yes, it's terrible, but what can be done?"

Mimi took leave of the lady, promising to let her know whether or not she would take the apartment. All the way home, the phrase kept on repeating itself in her mind like a tuneless song. "But what can be done? But what can be done?"

That night, before Mimi went to bed, she opened the closet where she stored her growing pile of acquisitions for her new home. She unloaded her day's purchases onto the shelves: another set of monogrammed towels, a fluffy, pink and red bathroom rug, and a tablecloth. She surveyed the shelves for a moment, but somehow the usual pleasure wasn't there. Before her appeared the dilapidated basement apartment and its inhabitants. She quickly shut the closet door.

"But what can be done?" Then and there, Mimi decided that something *would* be done.

It took a lot of time, effort, and courage. Mimi discussed the problem with her father. He did some research. She threw a party for her high school class and spoke about the family's plight. She asked each girl to pledge a monthly sum. For some reason her cheeks burned, and she felt like a charity case herself. But she shrugged off the feeling and persevered.

Next, an apartment had to be found for them. Mimi's hand trembled as she signed her name on the lease.

Then a connection had to be established with the family. Mimi's father found someone to talk to them. Somehow they were convinced, after signing some phony papers, that the government would pay their rent in a new apartment and provide them with a monthly stipend.

The big day was moving day. Between the blinds of her new basement apartment, Mimi peered at the van across the street. A pitiful amount of furniture was placed in the van as the children watched. Mimi's eyes filled with tears as she thought of the sunny, warm apartment they were moving to.

She finished straightening up her apartment. Her wedding was in just a week now, and she wanted to bring over her things the next day. As she locked her door that day, she met the landlady in the hall.

"Do you remember that family you asked me about?" the landlady said. "Well, I have happy news for you. They are moving to a new apartment today."

"Really?" Mimi said. "That's so nice."

"Yes, their financial situation seems to have improved."

In bed that night, Mimi suddenly remembered "the dream." She smiled sleepily. It was such a lovely dream.

The family came home. How surprised and happy they were! The children squealed with delight as they discovered all the nice things Mrs. Mimi had left for them. The mother...

Mimi was sleeping, a smile still on her face.

IN GOOD TASTE

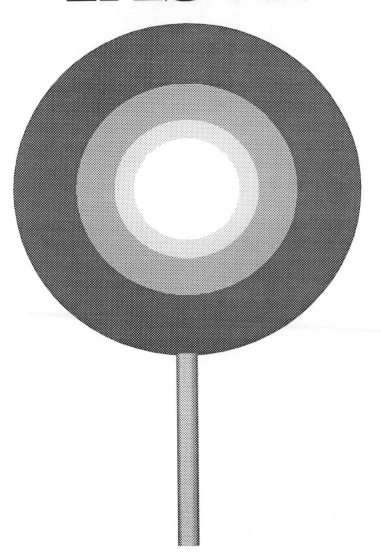

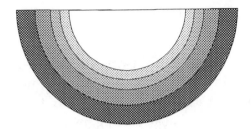

Sugar Twins

Esther Van Handel

David," said Mrs. Flink to her husband, "we've got to do something about the twins."

"What's wrong with Rifka and Shifra?" asked Professor Flink. "They're very sweet girls."

"That's exactly what's wrong. They're too sweet. They must be made of sugar, since they eat so much of it. They're always nibbling cookies, cake, candy, gum, chocolate bars, peppermint sticks, lollipops, or ice cream. But when they come to the table for a meal, they have no appetite."

"Then why do you give them so many sweets?"

"Aside from Dina's cookies, I don't give them so many. But their friends have plenty, and there's always some around."

"Hmm," said Professor Flink thoughtfully. "Sounds serious. This calls for drastic measures."

"What did you have in mind?" asked Mrs. Flink in alarm.

"A trip to Tante Zeesel," Professor Flink said gravely.

If you want to read about ESTHER VAN HANDEL, turn to page 103. "Sugar Twins" is an excerpt from her forthcoming book, *Flink Family Adventures*.

The first day of winter vacation, the twins packed their suitcases, and Professor Flink drove them up to the snow-covered mountains. Traveling a newly shoveled path, they arrived at a red brick house with smoke curling up from the chimney and icicles dangling from the window frames. Tante Zeesel must have been watching for them, for the door opened even before they had a chance to knock.

After the twins took turns kissing Tante Zeesel's plump, red cheeks, they detected a tantalizing aroma wafting from the kitchen: chocolate cake baking. "Mmm," they sighed happily.

Tante Zeesel invited her guests to sit down in the dining room. She wheeled out a serving cart laden with good things: hot chocolate with whipped cream floating on top, lemon cookies, and luscious white cake with orange icing — all homemade, of course.

After a while, Professor Flink said, "It's time for me to head back to the city. Girls, will you be okay here for a week? You won't get homesick now, will you?"

"Oh, no," said Rifka quickly.

"I'm sure we're going to enjoy every minute here," said Shifra.

Tante Zeesel and the girls walked Professor Flink to his car and waved goodbye as he drove off down the lane. Then the twins noticed the blanket of pure, white snow on Tante Zeesel's huge lawn.

"It looks just like sugar," said Rifka.

"What a snowman you could make!" said Shifra.

"Go right ahead," said Tante Zeesel.

Rifka rolled a huge ball of snow for the base. Shifra rolled two smaller ones, one for the middle of the snowman and one for his head. Tante Zeesel gave them an old hat and scarf to keep Mr. Snow warm and colored buttons to serve as his eyes, nose, and mouth. The twins surveyed their handiwork with pride. Mr. Snow looked quite respectable.

"He needs a house to live in," said Rifka.

"Let's build him an igloo," said Shifra.

Then they piled up snow to make three walls and an entrance. They brought a flattened carton from the house to serve as the roof and covered it with more snow.

"It looks just like the igloos in books," said Rifka.

"Do you think it's warm inside?" asked Shifra.

"Let's find out," said Rifka.

She crawled inside, and Shifra followed.

"It's toasty as can be," said Rifka in amazement. "The only thing that's missing is food."

"I'm so hungry, I could eat a whole steak and a few salads and five baked potatoes," said Shifra. "Let's go see what Tante Zeesel is serving for supper."

They hurried back to the house, took off their coats and boots, and sat down at the table.

"What an unusual meat loaf, Tante Zeesel," said Rifka. "It looks just like chocolate cake."

"It *is* chocolate cake," said Tante Zeesel.

"This place is truly heavenly," said Shifra with a dreamy sigh as she began to cut the cake.

"You may take more from the serving plate when you're finished," said Tante Zeesel.

"Thank you so much," murmured Rifka in disbelief.

After supper, as they sat before the cozy fire crackling in the fireplace, the twins made up a little poem, which they read to Tante Zeesel.

What, ho,
The snow,
Pure and white,

A real delight.
Zillions of flakes,
With zillions of shapes,
What ho,
The snow.

That night, the twins covered themselves with patchwork quilts made by Tante Zeesel. They dreamed about a snowman made of sugar, which you could bite into whenever you wanted, and houses made of peppermint sticks...

The next day, the girls helped Tante Zeesel dust and vacuum the house. They saw a teddy bear sewn by Tante Zeesel that was as big as they were. In the garage, they found something even more interesting: a sled.

Tante Zeesel noticed the twins' eyes light up. "Would you like to ride it?" she asked.

The girls nodded happily. After bundling up in warm sweaters, ski jackets, boots, gloves, and scarves, they pulled the sled up the hill. Then they took turns sliding down, squealing with glee as they went. As soon as they reached the bottom, they climbed right back up to the top.

By the time the girls came inside, their freckled cheeks were red as tomatoes, and snowflakes adorned their freckled noses and their hoods. Their fingers were cold despite their warm gloves, and their appetite was as big as only cold fresh air could make it.

When they came into the kitchen, a stunning sight greeted their eyes — a bright yellow and white lemon meringue pie. Tante Zeesel watched with a smile as the girls polished off the whole pie and then downed a quart of strawberry ice cream for dessert. The twins had never been so happy in their lives. They were so full that when Tante Zeesel offered them sourballs as a snack, the girls declined.

The next morning, they went to the closet and took out their pleated, wool skirts. But when the twins put them on, the buttons refused to close.

"These skirts must have shrunk at the dry cleaner's," said Rifka.

"It's a good thing we have others," said Shifra.

They took out their plaid skirts. The zippers rose half-way and then came to a sudden stop.

"We must have taken Miri's skirts by mistake," said Rifka.

Finally, they donned the skirts with elastic waists that they had worn the day before. Today, the skirts were uncomfortably tight. This time, the twins couldn't think of any excuses. They looked in the mirror.

"Let's face the facts," sighed Rifka. "We're getting a little plump."

"We'd better go on a diet," said Shifra. "Starting this minute, I won't have more than two helpings of ice cream for dessert."

During the night, a fresh blanket of snow fell. The twins could hardly wait to bundle up and go out. They offered to shovel the walk. Tante Zeesel gratefully accepted.

The girls took the big shovel and took turns scraping the paved path and scooping up little hills of white crystals. The work warmed the twins up. Only their fingertips and toes felt cold. "Come and see, Tante Zeesel," they called. "Now you have a path to walk on."

Tante Zeesel inspected the path and smiled her approval. "That was some job," she said. "You must have worked up quite an appetite. Come in; it's time for lunch."

The twins could hardly wait to get into the kitchen. There on the table was a huge cherry pie.

To tell the truth, the girls were a little disappointed.

They were getting tired of sweets and would have preferred meat and potatoes. After one portion of pie, Rifka began to feel slightly nauseous, and Shifra's stomach began to ache.

"Is it my imagination," wondered Rifka, "or do my teeth hurt?"

The twins put down their forks. "Thank you very much, Tante Zeesel," they said. "We've had enough."

The next day, when the girls came down for breakfast and saw strawberry shortcake waiting for them on the table, they burst into tears.

"Whatever is the matter?" asked Tante Zeesel as she patted their heads. "Do you feel all right? Are you a little homesick?"

"I'm just fine," said Rifka.

"Only, er, is there anything else to eat?" asked Shifra.

"Why, of course," said Tante Zeesel. "Would you prefer sugar cookies or perhaps honey cake?"

The twins sobbed even louder.

"Oh, dear," exclaimed Tante Zeesel. "Shall I call the doctor, girls?"

"No," said Rifka. "We would just like some food."

"Real food," explained Shifra. "Not sugar."

By now the girls were almost hysterical. "I can't stand these sweet things anymore. They're making us fat and nauseous," wailed Rifka.

"And ruining our teeth," cried Shifra. "We want healthy food that will make us strong."

Tante Zeesel quickly prepared a steaming bowl of wheat cereal and served it with milk. The twins dried their eyes.

While they ate, Tante Zeesel slipped out of the kitchen and quietly phoned Mrs. Flink. "Mission accomplished," she reported.

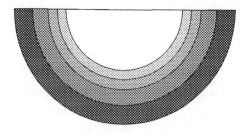

Falafel Is a Funny Food

Shoshana Lepon

Falafel is a funny food
But few will find it filling;
For many fail to figure
How to keep it all from spilling.

Perhaps the problem is the pita,
Falafel's pocket-bread,
That causes me to fill it full
And still remain unfed.

I'm posed with a predicament
For which I had not planned;
To hold a pita properly
I need an extra hand.

SHOSHANA LEPON lives in Jerusalem with her family. She is the author of *No Greater Treasure: Stories of Extraordinary Women from the Talmud and Midrash* and the children's books *The Ten Tests of Abraham, The Ten Plagues of Egypt, Joseph the Dreamer, Noah and the Rainbow, Torah Rhymes and Riddles*, and *Hillel Builds a House*.

Two hands to keep the pita bread
From splitting at the base,
And one to wipe the techina sauce
That's oozing down my face.

Tomatoes, cabbage, falafel balls,
Hot pickles and French fries;
If any makes it to my mouth
I'm taken by surprise.

More frequently I feel falafel
Falling on my feet;
I'm sorely tempted to surrender
And admit defeat.

But people have the power
To protest this painful plight;
Should we forgo our favorite food
And not put up a fight?

So unite, falafel fellows!
Our demands are overdue;
Let pita bakers hear our cry:
"Stop skimping on the glue!"

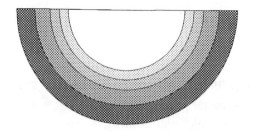

Your Loss, Our Gain

Bracha Steinberg

Don't put that piece of *challah* in your mouth," my mother said to me in a matter-of-fact tone of voice from the other end of the Shabbos table.

I looked down at what was in my hand and then, realizing my mistake, put it back on the *challah* board. You see, it would have been my second piece (I wasn't even aware that I had reached for it), and I was on a strict diet.

It all started two weeks ago.

"Chani," my mother had said, "come sit down with me in the kitchen. There's something I want to talk to you about."

So I sat down at our rectangular, butcher-block table and waited with some curiosity. My mother came in, a tall, thin, and elegant woman in her early forties. She untied her brightly colored terry cloth apron, smoothed her *sheitel*, and sat down.

"As you know," she began, "your bat mitzvah is about three months away. We'd like to make you a party to cele-

---

BRACHA STEINBERG is an editor at Feldheim Publishers and the author of *What About Me?* She is a graduate of Stern College and New York University.

She says: "I've been battling my weight since grade school!"

brate, but we thought we'd let you choose what kind you want. If you like, we can make a party in the house for your class. Nothing elaborate — some pizza, falafel, maybe a few knishes. Or we can have a *melaveh malkah* at the Keter Plaza for our friends, and you can invite a few of yours."

"The Keter Plaza! Wow!" I said.

"It would be very fancy," my mother continued, "with a buffet spread of everything they have to offer, and we'd even buy you a dressy bat mitzvah outfit, if..."

"If what?" I asked.

"If you can lose twenty pounds by then," she finished, looking directly into my eyes.

My mouth dropped open, and my cheeks began to burn.

Twenty pounds? My parents had never said anything about my weight before. Neither had my three brothers and three sisters. Sure, they were all tall and thin with straight, brown hair, while I was short and (okay, I admit it) plump, with frizzy, blond hair, but it was something we all cheerfully accepted as perfectly normal.

I guess I like to eat more than they do. I take seconds and thirds of just about everything my mom puts on the table. She's a great cook. And dessert? Forget it! I've never met a cookie or a piece of cake I could refuse.

I knew I looked different from them, but nobody had ever said anything about it to me. I was the only one who ever joked about it from time to time.

Now I felt really hurt. I blinked back some tears. Had everyone been talking about me behind my back? I thought they loved me the way I was.

"Twenty pounds is a lot," I said to my mother. "How can I ever lose that much?"

My mother smiled warmly at me. "I thought we'd ask Dr. Feingold to suggest a diet for you," she replied.

"Can you at least give me some time to think about it?" I asked, my voice cracking. There was a lump forming in my throat.

"Certainly," my mother answered. Studying my face, she looked a little worried. "Chani," she continued, "the choice is yours. Whatever you decide is fine with us. This is just to encourage you to do something we think you already want to do. You're always joking about your weight. We thought that now would be a good time to help you along."

"Yeah, well, I'll let you know in a couple of days if I want to be helped," I replied absently. I was already imagining how I would tell my best friend, Sara, about all this.

The next day I found her in the school cafeteria. It was lunchtime, and Sara was sitting at our usual table on the side. We liked sitting there because it gave us the best view of everything that was going on.

"What's for lunch today, Chani?" Sara inquired, brushing her too-long, blond bangs out of her eyes. She got a kick out of the lunches I brought — maybe because I packed them myself.

Sara's fish-stick sandwich, sliced tomato, and bag of potato chips lay untouched before her. "Let the feast begin!" she said, beckoning me to sit next to her.

Sara was as short as I was, but that's where our resemblance ended. She was trim and wiry, and even her hair was thin and wispy. But we had something very basic in common — we both loved to eat!

Only too happy to accept her invitation, I plopped down in the chair nearest her and opened my lunch bag. "Here we have two strawberry-and-whipped-cream sandwiches (Boy, was I glad my mother hadn't come into the kitchen when I was making those!), a bag of corn chips, three chocolate-frosted cupcakes, and a banana. What's mine is yours," I announced, tossing it all onto the table. "Take!"

"That's what I love about your lunches, Chani," Sara said, reaching for the corn chips. "You're always so careful to include both fruit *and* vegetables!"

I looked my lunch over and replied, straight-faced, "Hey, it's important to eat healthy."

Then I told her about the deal my mother had offered me.

"The Keter Plaza!" she exclaimed. "That's *the* hotel right now! You're so lucky!"

"Yeah, well who needs it?" I replied. "A party at home would be just fine. Besides, I wouldn't want to make the other girls jealous."

"But everybody knows your father is the best heart surgeon in town. Everyone loves him! I'm certain no one would think twice about him celebrating his youngest daughter's bat mitzvah in a nice hotel. He's earned it."

"And I'm the one who's going to have to pay for it," I grumbled.

"True," she said, "but look at it this way: It's only for three months. After that, you get a new outfit and a great party — and then you're free to eat as you please."

"I guess so," I said, and together we finished what was to be my last creative lunch.

The next afternoon, my mother took me to see Dr. Feingold, a balding, middle-aged man with a twinkle in his eye and a friendly smile. He measured my height and weight, and checked my blood pressure. Then he reviewed my medical history and asked a few questions.

Finally, he said, "Chana, you're in good health, and you should be able to lose weight if you follow the diet I'm going to give you. But in order to succeed you've got to *want* to do it. Otherwise, you're going to cheat every time you get the chance."

I thought for a moment. This diet was my mother's idea — but then I had to admit: I wanted it, too. I really was tired of joking about my rolls of fat. And after all, as it says in *Pirkei Avos*: "If not now, when?"

"It's what I want, Doctor, and I'll try very hard," I said sincerely.

My mother squeezed my hand.

"Well then," Dr. Feingold continued, "here's a diet I prescribe for girls your age. Your mother will explain it to you. But remember, if you cheat, you won't lose. It's as simple as that."

Dr. Feingold told me to stop by his office once a week to weigh in and have my pulse and blood pressure checked. He also suggested that I keep a diary of my thoughts and feelings while dieting. He told me to bring it along whenever I came to his office; it would remind me if there was anything I wanted to ask him.

When we got home, Mom gave me my instructions: I was to eat only what she put on my plate, she would prepare me one snack a day, and I could eat all the fruits and vegetables I wanted. (That'll be the day!)

*   *   *

MY DIARY

Week 1:

I've never thought about food so much in my life! What my mother gives me on my plate and in my lunch bag is about one-third of what I'm used to eating. I think about cake and cookies all the time. My stomach rumbles from morning till night. Why did I agree to this? It's all my mother's fault.

Week 2:

I lost two pounds last week! Not bad for all that suffering! I guess I'll stick with it a little longer and see what happens.

Sara says she'll be glad when this whole thing is over. She says I've been moody and snapping at her — especially when she's eating potato chips. I told her that if she'd only eat a few of my carrot and celery sticks, she'd know exactly how I feel. But she turned me down.

Week 3:

I lost only one pound last week. Dr. Feingold said a pound a week is good. I finally got up the courage to really talk to him. I told him how I daydream about hot-fudge sundaes and three helpings of cholent (in separate dreams, of course!). I also told him how I sometimes want to quit. It's so hard now. I love eating, but now I don't get to spend enough time doing it for it to be fun anymore. And lately I have so much free time on my hands — no more noshing all afternoon. Dr. Feingold suggested that I find a hobby or something to keep myself occupied.

*   *   *

One day I came home from school, and my mother handed me my snack: a white, frothy drink that tasted like a watered-down milk shake.

"We're so proud of you, Chani," she said warmly. "We know you're really trying. I hope you don't mind when I remind you not to eat this or that."

In fact, I resented it very much, though I knew I shouldn't. She was only trying to help, and she was, because often I absently reached for a cookie or a second helping of something. I guess it made me feel better to be angry at someone else rather than at myself. After all, wasn't it my overeating that had gotten me into this mess in the first place?

"No, I don't really mind," I replied. "But this dieting business is a pain. I mean, I can't figure out what to do all afternoon if I can't nosh."

My mother considered this problem a minute and then said, "I think you need something besides food to fill up your time. I'm sure our neighbor Mrs. Charney would be happy to teach you how to sew. But I think it might be even better for you to find a *chessed* project."

"*Chessed?*" I repeated.

"Yes, as in helping people," my mother dryly replied. That's her sense of humor. Well, I guess it was something to think about.

For days I racked my brain, trying to come up with a project to keep myself busy. Our school has a fundraising committee to support its two pet *tzedakahs*, but asking people for donations didn't appeal to me. We also have a *bikkur cholim* club, but whenever I visited kids I didn't know, I never could think of what to say. So I decided I had to come up with something all my own.

Then one day after school, I spotted Luba, one of the Russian girls who had joined our class last year. She was standing in the front hallway of the building, waiting for her best friend, Nadia. Luba's school uniform looked fairly new, but her coat looked very secondhand, and her shoes were probably from Russia. She was openly studying all the girls as they walked by. I was planning to hurry past, to escape her stare, when I got an idea.

"How's it going, Luba?" I walked over to her and asked.

"Is good," she replied, glancing shyly at me.

"Tell me, are you able to understand the teachers in class?"

"Some," she said, nervously looking down the hall again for Nadia. "We learn some English before we come."

"Listen, Luba," I said, "I just happen to have a lot of free time right now, so if you need any help with math or history or *dikduk*, I'd be happy to go over it with you after school whenever you want."

Luba's gaze suddenly snapped away from down the hall and fixed on me. "Really?"

"Yes," I replied.

"Nadia, too?" she asked. "We here only one year and is still hard."

"Sure. Here comes Nadia now. Let's call our mothers, and if it's okay with them, we can go to the public library and use a study room there."

Luba explained my offer to Nadia in rapid Russian. We all phoned home, and then we started walking. We felt uncomfortable together, and no one spoke.

I wondered if I could handle this. Why had I never thought to do this before? Because they're so foreign-looking, and they're always chattering away to each other in Russian, I decided. And how would I act if I were suddenly uprooted and set down in the middle of a school in Russia? I puzzled. Uck, I didn't even want to think about that.

So we walked along, staring at our feet a lot. But once we got inside one of the library's tiny study rooms and closed the door, things changed.

When I asked Luba if she understood what was going on in math, she immediately started impersonating Mrs. Waters, our teacher. Then Nadia joined in, and I couldn't decide who was funnier, I was laughing so hard. That broke the ice.

From then on, we went to the library every day after school. I explained any homework they couldn't figure out, and before tests I reviewed all the material with them and asked them questions I thought the teachers might ask.

*   *   *

MY DIARY

Week 5:

I've lost about five pounds already. Sara thinks she sees a difference! She also says I'm not grouchy anymore, so she's going to keep eating lunch with me.

I told her about Luba and Nadia. I wanted her to know that even though they seem so different at first glance, they're really very nice. Sara says she's going to make an effort now to get to know them.

*   *   *

I'm not sure exactly how it happened, but Luba, Nadia, and I began to tell each other more about ourselves in that little study room.

"I never know what I not have in Russia till I come here," Luba said.

"Same for me," Nadia chimed in. "Here you can say what you think and not be afraid. Here you can be Jew in the open. Here there is food in the stores."

I began to like them more and more. One day, I finally confessed my deep, dark secret.

"Listen, there's something I just have to tell you. The idea to tutor you only came to me when I was trying to think of a way to keep busy in the afternoons so I wouldn't eat. You see, I'm on this big diet, and I've lost seven pounds so far. I hope you're not angry with me. I'm so glad we're studying together, no matter the reason why we started."

Luba and Nadia glanced at each other and were quiet for a minute.

Uh-oh, I thought.

Then Luba said, "It no matter. Your loss, our gain!"

Both girls broke into peals of laughter.

A few days later, Mrs. Rubin, our principal, called me in to see her. Of course, I had no idea why, and I began to worry.

I knocked on her door and walked in.

"Chana," she greeted me, "how good to see you. I've heard what a beautiful job you're doing with Luba and Nadia. Their teachers tell me that the girls are getting higher marks now, and they've even begun participating in class. How wonderfully selfless of you to devote your afternoons to helping them!"

I couldn't tell her that I hadn't been selfless at all — just the opposite! Besides, I really enjoyed being with Luba and Nadia. Hearing them talk about life here has helped me see things a lot differently. Suddenly, I felt *lucky* being able to keep Shabbos, and even building a sukkah in our backyard without having to be afraid. I had never even thought about these things before!

"That brings me to the reason I called you in here," Mrs. Rubin continued, drawing my thoughts back into the room. "I'd like you to head up our new tutorial program for our Russian students. You would be in charge of matching our foreign students with suitable tutors. You would also have to stay in touch with each pair to make sure there were no problems. It's a big responsibility, but I know you can handle it."

Wow, I thought, that won't leave me a single minute free at night. I'll constantly have to be on the phone, checking on things. Well, maybe that's not so bad. It'll keep my mind off snacking.

I accepted the job. Then I walked back to class, proud as could be.

*　　　　*　　　　*

MY DIARY

Week 8:

It's hard for me to find time to write! I've lost nine pounds so far. It's going more slowly than I thought. I told my parents that at the rate I'm losing, I probably won't reach twenty pounds in time for my bat mitzvah. They said that's okay, as long as I keep up the good work.

Meanwhile, food is no longer my favorite pastime. I'm much more interested in my different projects now.

I've paired up sixteen girls and have made only two mismatches so far. Each member of the two pairs called me privately to tell me that they really didn't feel comfortable with their study partner. So I decided to switch one member from each pair and now they're getting along great!

Week 10:

I've lost eleven pounds and feel terrific! I have so much more energy now, and the girls at school are starting to compliment me. And I've been invited to a formal meeting with my parents after supper to plan my bat mitzvah cele-bration.

*　　　　*　　　　*

"The Keter Plaza has an opening in another three weeks," my mother began as we sat down at the kitchen table. "I

thought you'd like to hear what we're going to serve at your
melaveh malkah."

"But I haven't reached my weight goal yet," I protested.
"I still have nine pounds to go, and the rate I'm losing, it'll
take me another two months."

"You're probably right," my mother replied. "But we see
how beautifully you're keeping to your diet, so we thought
we'd go ahead with your celebration. For appetizers, we're
going to have yummy mushroom blintzes, spicy potato knishes,
and golden fish nuggets with the chef's special hot sauce. And
wait till you hear about the main courses! Of course, we'll
have to start shopping for your bat mitzvah dress right
away..."

"Hold everything," I said, raising the palm of my hand.
"I don't feel right about this fancy *melaveh malkah*. I know
Abba's a big doctor around here, so everyone will say it's okay,
but I still feel funny about it. I'd rather do something that
will mean a whole lot more to me."

My parents glanced at each other, my father arching an
eyebrow, and then they looked back at me expectantly.

"I'll stay on my diet until I lose the full twenty pounds,"
I began hesitantly. "And for my bat mitzvah...I'd like a simple
party in the house for all my friends *and* all the girls in my
tutorial program. They could use the chance to get together
socially and get to know each other better. And whatever food
you serve will be just fine. That kind of stuff doesn't interest
me so much anymore. Well, what do you say?"

My mother and father stared open-mouthed at each
other for a full thirty seconds.

"We say...we're awfully proud to be your parents," my
mother whispered, wiping a tear from her eye.

My father nodded in agreement.

*   *   *

MY DIARY

Week 21:

Mazel tov! I made it! I've dropped twenty pounds, and I look pretty good. (I don't want to brag *too* much!)

I've decided to keep up this diary, even though I've reached my goal. It helps me sort out my thoughts, and I like being able to look back and read what I was doing and thinking before.

I'll be seeing Dr. Feingold once a month from now on. He's going to give me some guidelines for staying at this weight. I certainly don't want to gain all those pounds back!

I'm so glad he's my doctor. He's really been understanding whenever I asked him anything. I don't think I could have done it without him.

And my mother...well, she was right. Losing weight was something I truly wanted to do. I just needed some encouragement. I think I'll go thank her after I finish writing this.

I get compliments at school almost every day — on my losing weight and on the tutorial program. And why not? I've worked hard at both. And I've never felt better about myself!

TARGUM PRESS proudly presents
the winners of its
KIDS' KOSHER COOKING CONTEST

And the Winner Is...

Decisions, decisions. So many difficult decisions went into putting this anthology together. Undoubtedly one of the toughest was choosing the tastiest and most original concoctions from among the dozens of scrumptious recipes that *Kids' Kosher Cookbook* readers entered in our Kids' Kosher Cooking Contest.

The Targum Press taster-testers spent hours debating texture, taste, originality, and clarity of instruction — smacking their lips and rubbing their tummies all the way.

For statistic lovers: 25% of the recipes, hailing from such far-flung reaches of the globe as Australia, England, and the U.S., were variations on Basya Knopfler's Rice Krispy/chocolate/peanut butter combination. About 87% of all recipes were desserts, and about 13% were main dishes. As for veggies, to tell the truth, there wasn't a single entry.

Congratulations to all the winners, and to all our readers, enjoy!

First Prize: Most Original

Mindy's Pie Surprise

Mindy B. Rothstein, age 12
Akiva Hebrew Day School
Southfield, Michigan

1 small onion, chopped
1 tablespoon margarine
4 potatoes, peeled and sliced
1/4 pound sliced corned beef
1/4 pound sliced bologna
1/4 pound sliced salami
1/4 cup matzo meal
1 cup parve cream
1 unbaked pie shell with top crust

Brown onion in margarine. Add potatoes and meat. Cook until potatoes are soft. Add matzo meal and parve cream. Place all ingredients in pie shell, top with crust and bake at 350° for 45-50 minutes until golden brown.

Second Prize: Most Original

Lunch Lickers

Esther Shira Gettinger, age 8
South Bend Hebrew Day School
South Bend, Indiana

1 9-ounce can tuna
4 tablespoons mayonnaise
4 eggs
1 teaspoon salt

1/4 teaspoon pepper
8 ice cream cones or cups
another 4 tablespoons mayonnaise
olives, pickle slices, cherry tomatoes, carrot curls,
crushed potato chips

can opener
mixing bowl
fork
scoop
teaspoons
egg pot

1. Open can of tuna and drain off liquid.
2. Place in bowl with 4 tablespoons mayonnaise, and mash well with fork. Set aside.
3. Place whole, uncracked eggs in pot. Fill with water. Bring to a boil. Lower heat, and simmer for 15 minutes. Pour out water. Rinse eggs with cold water, then peel.
4. Mix eggs with salt, pepper, and 4 tablespoons mayonnaise. Mash well with fork.
5. Place one scoop of tuna or egg mixture (or a scoop of each) into ice cream cones.
6. Top with dab of mayonnaise (like whipped cream).
7. Garnish with vegetable toppings or crushed chips.

First Prize: Tastiest

Chocolatey Peanut Chews

Basya Knopfler, age 14
Bais Yaakov Grammar School
London, England

1 cup crunchy peanut butter
1 cup sugar
1 cup Golden Syrup or corn syrup
5 cups Rice Krispies
3/4 cup chocolate chips

2 saucepans
cup
baking tray
wooden spoon
fork
knife

1. Boil peanut butter, sugar, and Golden Syrup or corn syrup in saucepan on low flame, stirring continuously with wooden spoon.
2. Remove saucepan from flame and stir in Rice Krispies.
3. Pour mixture onto tray, and flatten with wooden spoon.
4. Refrigerate tray until mixture sets.
5. Melt chocolate chips in saucepan on low flame.
6. Cut mixture into squares with knife.
7. Using fork, dip each square into melted chocolate.

Second Prize: Tastiest

Crunchy-Coated Chicken

Joshua Levy, age 10
Chabad of South Bay
Lomita, California

1 bag (6$^1/_2$ ounces) potato chips
2 teaspoons seasoned salt[*]
1 medium-large chicken, cut in pieces

rolling pin
roasting pan with cover

1. Using rolling pin, crush potato chips in bag.
2. Add seasoned salt to bag, and mix.
3. Rinse chicken pieces, and place one at a time in bag with potato chips. Shake bag until piece is coated.
4. Place chicken pieces in pan.
5. Pour any extra crushed potato chips over and under chicken.
6. Cover pan, and bake at 375° until done (approx. 1$^1/_4$ hours). For an even crunchier coating, uncover 15 minutes before chicken is done.

*Note: If barbecue-flavored potato chips are used, omit seasoned salt.

Yummy Applesauce Cake

Hadassah Machlis, age 10
Bais Brocha
Brooklyn, New York

4 cups flour
$2^1/_2$ cups applesauce or 6-7 apples, grated
$1^1/_2$ cups oil
$2^1/_2$ cups sugar
3 teaspoons baking soda
2 teaspoons cinnamon
4 eggs

Combine all ingredients, and mix well. Bake in 10" x 13" baking pan at 350° for 1 hour.

FAMILY CIRCLES

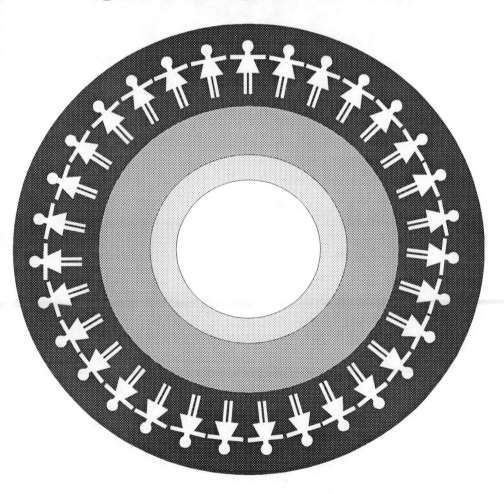

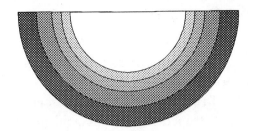

My Ima Loves to Write

Debby Garfunkel

My name is Yossi Miller, I'm six months old, and I have a story to tell. Let me begin by saying that I'm adorable. Everyone thinks so. People comment on my huge, blue eyes, rosy cheeks, and dainty little chin. I get so many compliments on my terrific personality, my charm, and how I already sit without wobbling and spit up only a small part of my milk.

I love it when we have Shabbos guests...naturally, they come only to see me. Perhaps I'll be executing a brilliant handstand or deftly shoving a pacifier into my ear. They pick me up, hug me, praise me, love me. And why shouldn't they? There's so much about me to love!

I still remember my bris (ouch). Okay, so it hurt, but what I cherish most was being surrounded by all of Abba's friends admiring me. After my ordeal, I was sharing some wine with my *zeidy*, and I overheard the *sandak* say how hard

---

"I grew up in Australia and began my writing career at around age five — with finger-paintings and splattered birthday-card poems for my family.

"Today, I live in Jerusalem with my husband and family." — DEBBY GARFUNKEL

it was to keep my strong, muscular legs down as I was kicking so vigorously. He clearly adored me, too!

At my *pidyon haben*, I at first felt like a bit of a *shmendrik* lying there on a cushion draped in all that gold and garlic, but soon I relaxed and began to enjoy all the oohs and aahs, the tickles and pinches, the praise and awe.

You can probably tell by now that I love attention. But I deserve it — I'm so wonderful!

However, as much as I love the attention of relatives, friends, neighbors, and even total strangers, there's one person whose attention I love more than anyone else's...that's right, you guessed it, my *ima*! It all began at my birth. I wasn't feeling so terrific that day...it's no picnic being born. But when I looked out from my linen straight-jacket, squinting into those harsh lights, I suddenly saw the most beautiful face in the world (apart from my own). At that moment, I decided that this face, this *ima* of mine, was my entire world. She would supply my every need. She would serve me every second of every day and all through the night. And enjoy it!

For the first few months after I arrived, she was doing quite nicely. I had a different scream for each specific request, and, clever little thing that my *ima* is, she learned what each scream meant very quickly. I can safely say that, what with all these different screams, I literally kept her on her toes round the clock. My *abba* helped, too, which was fun, but I felt it was more important to establish early on, by way of a specific scream, that I preferred Ima. *Abbas* are very nice, but they're not *imas*, are they?

So all in all, life was good. That is, until about a month ago, when disaster struck. I was lying on my tummy on the carpet, reading a fairly ordinary book about a talking *kneidel*, when I decided I was bored. So I screamed my bored scream, which always brings my *ima* galloping over with all sorts of toys, rattles, and assorted *chatchkes*, which she proceeds to bang and shake while making bizarre faces. It's all a bit silly, but I must admit I like it.

So there I was, screaming my bored scream, but this time there was no response. I tried again with more emphasis on the high notes, yet still nothing. Where on earth was she?

Time to investigate. I raised myself up on my hands and proceeded to slither (by the way, I slithered earlier — and faster — than any other baby this decade) over to where my *ima* was sitting at the living room table. Her face glowed as she stared, mesmerized, into her computer, her fingers lightly tapping the keyboard. This was a sight I beheld frequently. Too frequently.

You see, my *ima* loves to write.

I knew Ima was a writer. She wrote stories, articles, poetry, and such, but of course she stopped all that nonsense when I came along. But now, it seems, she feels a certain urge to return to her writing, and, God help me, she's writing a book.

I am not happy about this!

Before, when I screamed for a diaper change, I would get immediate service followed by tickles on the tummy, kisses on the cheeks, and pinches on the toes. Now I'm lucky to get changed!

Before, when I screamed for a feed, I would be offered a smorgasbord selection of mushy foods of every color and flavor followed by a choice of drinks in a cup or bottle. Now I seem to get cereal for every meal!

I could go on, but I think you get the picture.

Don't get me wrong, it's not like I don't understand her creative urges. When I tear books apart with my bare hands, drool on the new rug and then mush it in, and I bang for hours on the glass tabletop, that is all highly creative stuff. I'm not an unreasonable baby. It's not that I object to my *ima* taking some time off and having other interests. It's just that I think she should wait until I'm married and being looked after by my wife!

At a time like this, a baby needs friends, a kind soul to confide in. On my daily stroller ride, I looked out for my buddy Kovi. Sure enough, there he was, sitting in his stroller outside the fruit store, trying to pull apart the banana tree. I began to tell him of my *ima* woes, doubting that he would relate to my pain. To my amazement, though, he told me that his *ima* has creative urges, too! She loves to paint. He says she paints scenes of Yerushalayim.

"They're beautiful," he admitted, now attempting to kick over a barrel of kumquats. "But it distracts her from me. She used to stare at me all day long — whatever I did she found fascinating. She still stares, but now she's staring at those...those paintings." He gnawed resentfully on his teething ring.

Kovi told me that quite a few of our friends have the same problem. Shloimi's *ima* loves to do tapestries, and Moishe's *ima* loves to play piano. Malkie's *ima* loves to do pottery, while Surie's *ima* loves gardening. Chezkie's *ima* loves to bake fancy cakes, and Rachelli's *ima* loves to exercise. Tzippi's *ima* loves flower arranging, while Tuvie's *ima* loves to make miniature dollies. Baruch's *ima* loves to learn French, and Bracha's *ima* loves to swim. The list goes on and on. All these *imas* actually doing something other than *ima*-ing. *Unbelievable!*

And so the days passed. I learned to crawl (earlier than any other baby this century, by the way). I got my first tooth and a bigger diaper, and I figured out how to pull the telephone out of the wall. I'm well-fed, I'm warm, and I suck an Italian, orthodontic pacifier that cost a fortune.

As you can see, my life is full. There must be thousands of babies out there who would love to be in my bunny slippers. So why am I so miserable? Because, although I'm looked after and played with and respected by my peers, things just aren't the same. Because my *ima* loves to write. And when she writes, she's not one hundred percent there for me. *And she should be.*

One morning I awoke earlier than usual and decided I wanted to get up. So I screamed my Ima-come-and-get-me scream, which, without fail, ever since she started writing that book, has always brought her scampering in to greet me. Well, I was screaming away, waiting for her to appear, when I heard the click-click of a different footstep and...what? I couldn't believe it! She'd sent in her next-door neighbor, Chanie! What an insult! I screamed my I-don't-want-the-neighbor-I-want-Ima scream, but it did no good. With lots of clucking and cooing, Chanie picked me up, kissed my forehead, plopped me down, and proceeded to change my diaper. *How embarrassing!*

Things had gone far enough. I needed some *eitzah* from a worldly, mature point of view. I needed my rebbe. The next day, when Abba took me to the park, I found Rav Moishie at his favorite sandpit, scooping damp sand into a hot-pink pail.

"Rav Moishie!" I called out from my stroller.

"Ah, Yossi," he replied, furiously scooping.

"May I talk to you, Rav? I have a problem."

"Go ahead, I'm nearly done here."

I'm very attached to my rebbe. He's very old (nearly two and three-quarters), he's toilet-trained, and he has most of his teeth. But there doesn't seem to be any generation gap; he understands me perfectly.

"Well, it's about my *ima*...," I began.

"Uh-huh." Rav Moishie smiled knowingly. *Imas* were hot topics for *eitzah*.

I went on to describe the whole traumatic story. Rav Moishie listened quietly, every now and again spitting some sand out of his mouth. I finished and waited nervously for his response. What would he advise me to do? Leave home? But I wasn't even weaned yet. Who would blow my nose? Mash my banana? Clean my tooth?

My rebbe broke into my thoughts with a question.

"Tell me, Yossi, does your *ima* take care of you?"

"Yes, but..."

"Does she look after your needs?"

"Yes, but..."

"Would you say she is a basically good *ima*, a good person?"

"Of course she is, but..."

"Okay, so what is the real problem, Yossi? Maybe your *ima* spends time writing, but she's doing her job. You don't seem to lack anything."

"That's true, but..."

"Then why are you upset, really? Do you feel that maybe your *ima* doesn't love you? That maybe she's spending a bit less time with you because she doesn't enjoy being your *ima*? Could that be it, Yossi?"

Suddenly I tasted warm, wet salt in my mouth. I was crying! My rebbe had hit the nail on the head. (He had also hit the pail on his head by mistake.) I was worried Ima had stopped loving me, stopped enjoying my company. Deep down I feared that she loved her computer more than me, and I was deeply insecure about playing second fiddle to a late-model IBM laptop.

"I think you may be right, Reb Moishie," I whispered, hoping the guys on the slide hadn't seen me cry. "I am very worried about that."

"Okay," said Rav Moishie, shaking sand out of his ears.

"So now I want to teach you an idea I hope you'll always remember. My older brother taught it to me, and our older sister taught it to him, and my *abba* to her, and it goes all the way back to Har Sinai, which I believe had some great sand. The idea is called '*dan lekaf zechus.*' "

"That's quite a mouthful, Rebbe!" I exclaimed.

" '*Dan lekaf zechus*' means that we must always judge a good person favorably. We are so quick to judge others unfairly without really knowing all the details, and this mitzvah helps us remember not to be so hasty. In your case, you are assuming that just because your *ima* works at the computer, she loves it more than she loves you. You feel that she's neglecting you. But the mitzvah says to judge her favorably, give her the benefit of the doubt. That's what you must do, Yossi, and believe me, you'll see things differently. Now I'm late for my nap, and my nana's calling. Much *hatzlachah.*"

He's got to be kidding, I thought as I waved goodbye. How could I judge my *ima* favorably when she was so clearly wrong! On the other hand, this advice had come from none other than my wise and worldly rebbe. He'd been eating solids for over a year-and-a-half now — he knew about life! But this mitzvah was going to be a challenge, perhaps as challenging as giving up Cheerios for Pesach. I would have to go home and think in my playpen. Banging my giant, solar-powered clock rattle always gives me clarity.

Three days and much rattle-banging later, I had come up with eighty-seven sound "*dan lekaf zechus*" reasons to judge Ima favorably. They didn't come easily; after all, I was not in a generous frame of mind about this. But in spite of myself, I found favorable ideas popping into my head.

For instance, because of my fabulous energy and zest for life, my *ima* needs to relax a bit with her computer. And my brilliance overwhelms her, so she needs to unwind at the computer. And my tremendous cuteness so amazes her that she has to take a break from it with her computer. I just went on and on, listing my superb talents and realizing the drain they must be on her. It couldn't be simple being the *ima* of Yossi the Gaon!

So recently, I was sitting in my high chair having breakfast (cereal again) and working on my *"dan lekaf zechus"* reason number eighty-eight, when I happened to lean forward to grab a glob of oatmeal from Ima's spoon. Suddenly, I got a close-up of her computer screen, which, as usual, was on. I could see the title for the first time. (You may wonder how a six-month-old reads. Well, the credit must go to alphabet soup, which I eat and read regularly.) There it was, in bold lettering, "MY YOSSI"!

My *ima*'s book was about me! *Me!* I couldn't believe it! I had just spent the last three days racking my little brain to come up with reasons to give my *ima* the benefit of the doubt, when all the time the best reason was the real one! I felt my confidence oozing back after all those insecure weeks. This book would make me famous! Babies the world over would read about me and thrill to my adventures. I'd receive enormous mailbags of letters with requests for my autograph, my photo, used pacifiers. I'd be interviewed by all the leading Jewish papers. I'd be the hero of the sandpit!

Of course, all these fantasies paled in comparison to the wonderful feeling that my *ima* still loved me. Even though she loved to write, she was spending all these hours writing about me. From now on, I wouldn't scream or cry or make any demands on Ima. After all, she was working on a very important project!

The following week, I looked for Kovi at the fruit store and told him the good news. I also told him that we have to tell all our friends to judge their *imas* favorably. Because, even though they're not all writing books about us, no matter what they're doing — whether it's painting or tapestries, swimming or flower arranging, pottery or baking fancy cakes — no matter where they are or what they're involved in, a special place in their hearts is always reserved just for us!

Now you may wonder how a six-month-old came up with such a profound idea... Well, if the truth be known...I read it on page 57 of my *ima*'s book!

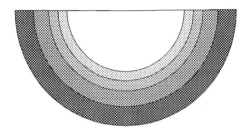

Life with Grandma

Fayge Pertzig

Once I shared a room with Grandma, or should I say Grandma shared a room with me. It wasn't at all like having a big sister or a little sister for a roommate. No comparison whatsoever.

There were no late-night whispers and giggles, no fighting over territory. There was no commiserating when life seemed unfair and no differences of opinion. It wasn't as if Grandma wanted pink bedspreads and I wanted yellow. It was nothing like that. And anyway, the room was already done up in blue, so there was nothing to talk about.

Grandma was different all around. She moved slowly and I moved quickly. I could remember *anything* (except at exam time), but Grandma's words could be so garbled that no one, not even I, could make sense of them.

Most often, Grandma sat planted in a rocker near the

FAYGE PERTZIG lives in the Judean Hills with her husband and children. She likes to sing, draw, write, and garden. But most of all, she likes to mother, which she finds the most challenging, rewarding job in this world.

She says about writing: "It helps me sort out my thoughts and view life from the right angle. Writing down an idea heightens my commitment to that idea."

doorway between the kitchen and the den. We could rarely sneak a dish of ice cream past without her motioning to "give me some of that." I always gave her some, but Mom would shoot a glance of disapproval at me.

Grandma snored awfully loud. In fact, she was once evicted from an apartment house as a result of the high volume. Sometimes I thought I would go out of my mind. But I didn't. It's a good thing we lived in a house. And it's a doubly good thing that I was Grandma's roommate. I'd never evict her.

How I loved Grandma! Words played hide-and-seek with her. They eluded her when she needed them, and she would chuckle. She just laughed to herself — a private joke, I guess. After all the years, all the work-worn years of living, a widow with three young sons. She's been a sharp, quick woman who knew her business as nobody did. After all that, she chuckled, while a kind of mist rose up in her fog-blue eyes.

I loved to kiss Grandma. Her skin was like velvet. When I hugged her, she laughed a little, and her face lit up. It was easier to kiss Grandma than anyone else. Yes, Grandma certainly appreciated me. And if she laughed, it was only at herself.

My heart melted when those "others" came to visit — the people from her old life, who knew her when. Some of them ignored her mainly, and others treated her like a baby. I agree it was a bad predicament to be in. They didn't understand Grandma as I did. She was in no-man's-land — an adult yet not an adult. She was of this world, yet she wasn't. Indeed, a tough position to be in.

My grandma was once a young girl. I have a photograph to prove it. She ran through the alleyways of the city with her friends and siblings as all children do. She married and chased after three active sons. And she brought them up good and proper.

But then Grandma's knees became arthritic and terribly stiff, so she needed a walker. Deep in the night I'd hear her arise from her bed in slow motion, first one foot, then the other, and heave herself up inch by inch onto the walker. Then, "click, shuffle-shuffle, click, shuffle-shuffle," she'd exit the room, take care of her needs, and return to bed. The process was painful, but she never called for help. She didn't want to bother anybody; she was her own person whenever she could be.

I have some theories. The first one concerns my relationship with Grandma. Sometimes, I felt misunderstood by the whole world, and so did Grandma. Maybe that's why we got on so well and why I loved her so dearly.

The second one concerns why Grandma's knees went and why her memory became fuzzy; why she had to come live with us. It was for me, so I could learn to love a different kind of Grandma — the "after" Grandma, very different from the "before." It was so I could watch my father show the ultimate respect for his mother, and so my mother could teach me a treasured lesson in kindness and sacrifice.

Maybe Grandma knew it, too. Is that why she chuckled? Wherever you are, Grandma, I know everything's set right now. (And I hope you forgive me for putting the coconut-covered marshmallow inside the back ashtray of your car on that hot, summer day. Yep, it was me.)

I want to hug you. But I'll just hug the memory of you. And I hope that, if need be, I'll be able to chuckle like you and accept things as they come — the good, the bad, and the in-between. No, I couldn't have had a better roommate.

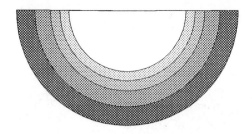

Follow Your Wonder

Yeshara Gold

Everyone told them they were so alike, but Rivka knew she wasn't anything like her older sister. Rivka was Rivka, Avigail was Avigail, and there wasn't any problem. Not until Aunt Malka came, that is. That's when Rivka started to wonder.

R ivka! Avigail!"
The girls were in the garden when they heard their aunt's persistent call.
Avigail had been busy gathering a rainbow of flowers for the kitchen table. Her little sister, Rivka, sat

---

"Even as a child, my family assumed I would become a writer. My own five children give me plenty of material to include in my books. *Hurry, Friday's a Short Day* and *Just a Week to Go* were about my son Rafi's activities here in Jerusalem.

"After a long and varied career as a writer, I developed an interest in fiber arts. My weaving, spinning, embroidery, sewing, and other crafts give me the opportunity to meet fascinating craftspeople around the world. To combine my interest in both writing and crafts, I am writing a fictional book for young readers that includes craft projects." — YESHARA GOLD

nestled in the trunk of an old oak tree, mud carelessly clinging to the hem of her skirt.

"Come on, Rivka," Avigail called as she quickly finished off her bouquet with an edge of blue asters.

Rivka didn't seem to hear. Her eyes were closed as she stroked the velvety petals of a rose against her cheek.

"Girls, girls!" called Aunt Malka through the back door. "Hurry up. We're going to the shoe store."

Rivka began to pick the rose petals from her lap, one by one.

"Why must you dilly-dally, Rikva? Sometimes you're as slow as molasses."

Rivka smiled at the thought of the molasses she had poured on her hot corn muffins that morning. She loved the taste of melted butter running into the thick, sweet goo.

Watching Avigail fill a vase with flowers and water, Aunt Malka said, "I just can't understand. On one hand, you girls are so alike with your red hair and hazel eyes. But I declare, you're as different as night and day!"

"We don't really look alike," said Rivka as she pushed the screen door open. "My hair is ginger, and Avigail's is more like strawberries. And our eyes aren't the same either — Avigail's are gray, but there are specks of green in mine," she tried to explain to her aunt.

"I declare, night and day," said the aunt, reaching for her car keys.

Rivka rode in the back seat, the rushing wind blowing her hair across her face.

"Get your head back into the car," Aunt Malka commanded.

Aunt Malka had been giving orders ever since she'd marched into their house three weeks before, after the sisters' baby brother was born. Their mother always seemed to be busy with the baby or resting.

Aunt Malka sure makes yummy muffins, thought Rivka to herself, but she doesn't make things fun like Ima.

"Look at all these shoes," Avigail sang as she sailed into the large store. "I want the blue ones with tassels. Oh, let me try on those black patent leathers." She rushed to the stalls offering her size.

Rivka's eyes wandered over the rows and rows of shoes. Up on the eighth shelf, a pair caught her eye. On tippy toes she reached up...almost...almost... Before she knew it, the whole rack of shoes had tumbled to the floor.

"Rivka!" Aunt Malka scolded her.

"I'll fix it, Auntie." Rivka stood on a chair and put all the pairs back except one, which she slipped on her feet. These are mine, she thought, even before she crossed the room to look into the mirror.

Avigail was still busy trying on shoes.

"Now, where is Rivka?" Aunt Malka asked the air. "Unless someone keeps an eye on that girl, she disappears."

Rivka didn't follow her feet so much as she followed her...wonder. She wondered about everything. Like what was behind that door, and what was beyond that, and...by that time, Rivka had vanished.

"So there you are," announced Aunt Malka when she finally found her niece sitting among boxes in a back room, chatting with a cleaning lady. "And just look at those shoes!"

"Yes, aren't they beautiful?" sighed Rivka, looking down at her feet. She didn't see the scuff marks that already marred the leather. She was too busy admiring the pink, yellow, green, and blue bows sewn on the front.

"Rivka," pleaded Avigail from across the store, "help me choose."

"Well, which do you like?" asked her younger sister.

"I like them all!" Avigail cried in despair. "The navy ones would go perfectly with my blue coat. And the black patent leathers would look so sweet with my pink Shabbos dress. The brown loafers I could put real pennies in. And did you see these white ones? Don't they look just like Ima's? Rikva, which should I pick?"

"Which ones fit?"

"They all fit," answered Avigail.

"I know they all fit your feet. But which ones fit you?"

"Oh, I don't know," said Avigail in frustration. "I guess I'll take the white ones that look like Ima's."

Rivka was the first out of the car. Racing through the house, she called out as she ran, "Ima, Ima, look at my shoes."

Resting on a lounge chair in the garden, Ima opened her eyes and smiled. "They're so pretty. I like all those different bows."

"Oh, the baby's up. May I hold him?" begged Rivka as she reached into the cradle.

Just then, Aunt Malka swung the screen door open. "What are you doing?" she demanded. "Put that baby down."

"It's fine, Malka. I'm right here," Ima said to calm her.

"Well, I'm not one to tell you what to do, sister dear, but that child is just too flighty to be trusted."

Rivka's eyes stung. She hid her face against the fluffy nape of her baby brother's neck.

"It's all right, Malka," Ima said softly.

"Well, I certainly can't understand your attitude. Come on, Avigail." Aunt Malka turned to the older girl. "You can at least make yourself useful and help me in the kitchen. I'm going to make cinnamon bread."

Ima was already dozing off. Rivka peered into her new brother's eyes.

"*You're* not useful," she whispered to him. "You keep Ima

up at night. And you are forever making a mess. Why does everyone love you so much?"

"He doesn't have to do anything for us to love him, dear," Ima murmured sleepily. "He just *is*. And so are you," she added as she held Rivka in her arms. "All you have to do is be yourself. And you do a fine job of that."

Rivka felt a moist kiss on her cheek where just moments ago it had been damp with tears. Carefully placing the baby back in the cradle, she walked to where the pink roses climbed up the lattices.

"A fine job...," Rivka repeated to herself as she gingerly pressed a thorn against her thumb. Over her shoulder, she watched Aunt Malka through the kitchen window, then glanced at her mother's sleeping face. How can two sisters be so different? she wondered.

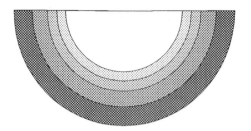

A Second Chance

Sheryl Prenzlau

My mother tells me life must go on. I know inside that she's right, but it's not really that simple. I guess for her it is a little different than it is for me. But I still don't think it's fair.

I suppose I should explain myself. My name is Shaina, and I'm thirteen years old. I live in a suburb of New York with my mother and two brothers. Our apartment is fairly small, on the second floor of a ten-year-old apartment building. We have a few Jewish neighbors, but we're really friendly with just two of them. The others are pretty nice to us, too, I guess — but then again, everyone tries to be nice to us. That's part of the problem.

Five years ago, my father passed away. It was really hard on us. One day at work he didn't feel well, and they took him to the hospital. It happened so fast. My mom rushed to the emergency room as soon as they called her, but by the time she got there, they told her he had had a massive heart attack, and they didn't think there was much they could do. My mother got to see him only for a few minutes, and I didn't

If you want to read about SHERYL PRENZLAU, turn to page 177.

get to see him at all. (That's how things are when you're a kid.) By the next morning, he was gone.

The rest of it is a blur to me now — the funeral, the *shivah*, the tons of visitors and all the relatives. Yanky and Chaim cried a lot. Of course, they were so little. I remember Chaim, only three, calling, "Abba, Abba!" every time any man walked in. It broke everyone's hearts. And Yanky, six-and-a-half at the time, saying Kaddish. There wasn't a dry eye in the house.

I had a real hard time, too. Being eight years old, I could understand much more than the boys, but I guess death is something even grownups have a tough time understanding. Mommy was really something, though. People kept commenting on how brave she was. I guess she knew she had to be strong for the rest of us.

After that, our life really changed. I guess people felt sorry for us. They invited us a lot on Shabbos. But my mom really likes to stay home. She says we kids should see what Shabbos is like at home and how it is to have guests of our own. Some of my friends don't know how to react, though, when my mom makes Kiddush. I guess it seems strange to them, but I've gotten used to it by now. And we've gotten a reputation at the local yeshivah as a great place to be invited to. After all, my mom's a great cook!

Sometimes people say the wrong things to us. Then they don't know how to undo their mistakes. I remember when my sixth-grade teacher kept insisting that both mothers and fathers had to come to some important meeting. Finally, my mom had to call her and explain. The next day she could hardly look at me.

And one time Chaim's rebbe gave out some papers and said that all the boys had to learn it with their fathers and then have them sign it. Chaim kept crying and wouldn't tell my mother what was bothering him. Finally, she'd made him tell her.

Since then, the boys have learned to handle it pretty well, and all our teachers are much more careful.

Anyway, I've just been talking about us kids. My mom is a different story. She's been pretty lonely, I guess, just having us at home to talk to. And she works so hard all day, she's always tired by the time she comes back. I think it must be very hard for her to be both parents to us.

Last year, she started going out on *shidduchim*. At first, it was a little strange for us. Every time one of her *shidduchim* came to pick her up, Chaim and Yanky would run and hide. Then they would giggle and peek to see what he looked like. The men that people set her up with always tried to be nice to us kids and talk about what we were learning in school. Some of them were okay, but I didn't like most of them.

Sometimes, after a *shidduch*, Mom would come in smiling, and sometimes she'd look kind of unhappy. Once I even saw her staring at my father's picture. I wonder what she was thinking.

To get back to what's happening these days, about three months ago, my mom was set up with this real nice guy. He brought some books and a ball for the boys and a nice bracelet for me. It's that new kind that all my friends are wearing. I wondered how he knew what a thirteen-year-old girl would like. He was real friendly, and instead of leaving the house with my mother — as most of her *shidduchim* do — he stayed in the kitchen with us, and we all baked a pizza together and ate it. It was really fun, and before we knew it, it was midnight, and he was leaving.

Then he began coming over more often, sometimes staying to visit with all of us and sometimes going out for a while with my mother. She seemed to change, too. She began smiling a lot and singing to herself when she thought no one was around.

Also, I noticed that she'd jump whenever the phone rang. She used to tell us to answer the phone, because she was too busy or whatever, but all of a sudden, she began running to the phone herself. And it was usually Dovid. (That's his name, by the way.) Soon, Chaim and Yanky began fighting over who would answer the phone, because they loved talking to Dovid, too. He always asked them riddles and things, and they really liked him.

Then things changed. One night last week, Dovid and my mother sat the three of us down in the living room. They said they had something very important to speak to us about. I guess I knew all along that things couldn't continue the way they were.

They began by saying they were considering getting married. My mom was almost crying when they said that. It was kind of funny, because she was sort of smiling at the same time. Then they told us that it was real important to them what we kids thought about the whole thing.

I figured I could basically handle their getting married. But then they dropped the bombshell!

I knew Dovid had lost his wife a few years before. My mother had mentioned that once. But I don't know why they never told us he had two kids of his own — a daughter who's thirteen and a son who's eight.

They told us that they hoped we'd all get along. And since Dovid and his kids lived in a big house in Monsey, they'd like us all to move there after the wedding! I would probably share a room with his daughter, Rochel, since we were almost the same age, and the boys could all share one room.

How many shocks do they expect us to take at once? It's

true that we all like Dovid a lot. But it's one thing to have him come over and visit with us once a week; it's quite another to move to some new place and live with him and these kids we never met!

Chaim and Yanky seem pretty pleased with the whole idea, but I'm not. I like where I live. I like my friends and the life we have. I guess it *would* be nicer to be like a complete family again, with a father (who makes Kiddush), etc. But how do they expect me to start switching schools right in the middle of eighth grade? I really want to graduate with my friends. And I was looking forward to going to high school with them next year.

Life just isn't fair! I know they asked how we kids feel, but it wasn't really a fair question. I mean, they'll probably go ahead with their plans no matter what I think! They seem to think that only their lives are involved here, but I'm expected to change everything, too.

I guess I *am* being a little selfish, though. You should see my mom's eyes sparkling these days. And she doesn't stop singing! She's really excited. And if anyone deserves a little happiness in her life, she does.

*   *   *

It's about a week later now, and things have really been changing quickly around here.

On Sunday, my mother, the three of us, and Dovid and his two kids spent the day together. I guess this was a real important meeting for all of us, because my mom even got permission to get Chaim and Yanky out of yeshivah early. She hardly ever does that. First we went to the pizza shop. It was a little awkward for a while, because I really didn't want to talk to Rochel. But she kept asking me questions and was so friendly that I finally had to behave myself and answer her. I wonder what she thought of me.

Chaim hit it off right away with Shloimy, but I saw Yanky staring at him a lot when he thought no one was looking. Shloimy looks a lot like his father. Maybe Yanky was seeing that in his face, too.

Mom and Dovid kept trying to make conversation with all of us. I guess it was hard for my mom. I could see that Rochel was acting a little strained with her. This must be weird for Dovid's kids, too.

After lunch, we all climbed into their old car and drove to Manhattan. It was a funny feeling to sit so crowded in a car. I guess I'm just not used to it. We spent the next few hours on this big ferry that circled the Statue of Liberty. My mom had told us that some day we'd get to visit the Statue, but I'd never pictured us going this way! I overheard an old lady tell mom and Dovid what a lovely family they had, and I was pretty surprised when my mom didn't explain our situation to her. She just looked at Dovid, and they both smiled and said, "Thank you."

Rochel is pretty nice, I guess, and Shloimy's not too bad, either, as eight-year-old boys go. After a while, Yanky started to warm up to him, and you'd have thought they'd known each other for years. I guess it was because Shloimy looks up to him. Shloimy kept asking Yanky questions and almost seemed in awe of his answers.

But then Chaim began fighting with Shloimy. I guess that's because they're the same age. I asked Chaim what was the matter, but he didn't want to tell me. It seemed to me, though, that he was a little jealous of the attention Shloimy was getting from my mom. Chaim's used to being the baby at home and doesn't usually have to share her too much.

The strange thing was that Dovid was really dividing

his time between everyone. I guess it was good that he'd had three months to get to know us. It's kind of unfair that my mom has spent only a couple of hours with his kids in the past few weeks. She has to make up for lost time.

Later on, after we'd climbed those million steps up to the top of old Liberty's torch, we went to a park. By then, the boys were happy to hit a few balls, and we ladies were glad to relax a little. The day had been fun, but I guess it was also a bit of a strain on us all.

Rochel and I got to talking.

Her story wasn't all that different from ours. After a long illness, her mother had died when Rochel was only six. They had a housekeeper to help them, and her aunt and uncle lived nearby. Her stories of the silly things people always mistakenly said sounded just like ours. Some of them even made us laugh.

I don't know how we started talking about it, but I might have asked her what she thought about the upcoming plans. I was pretty surprised when she said, "Well, I'm happy for them, but I don't really want to change *my* lifestyle. I mean, I have my own room, and I'm used to being the only woman around the house. I don't know if I can get used to four new people living with us and someone else telling me what to do all the time."

I couldn't believe it! Then I asked her how she thought *I* felt about moving, changing schools, and leaving my friends and my whole life. She told me she hadn't thought I'd feel like that at all. She'd thought I'd be thrilled!

I explained that she and Shloimy seemed pretty nice, and I really liked their father a lot, and my mom seemed so happy with him, but that didn't mean I was ready to change *my* whole life around!

We spent the rest of the time just talking about school,

not about the future, but I knew it was still on both our minds.
I planned to talk to my mom about it later.

The next part of the trip was really a surprise. I had
thought we'd start heading home around five, so I was
amazed when we went over a different bridge. Dovid announced that we were going somewhere special for supper,
but he wouldn't answer any more questions. Rochel's lips
were sealed, too. I had no idea we were going to Monsey.

Their house wasn't what I'd pictured at all. It was this
nice brick colonial surrounded by trees in the front and even
in the back. Inside, Rochel's aunt and uncle, Miriam and
Yitzchok, were waiting with their five kids. They all rushed
over to us at once, and the kids jumped on Dovid. He seemed
used to it, but I was surprised to see my mom lift up the
youngest. The baby, Shimmy, smiled at her, and she got a
kind of far-off look in her eyes. I really began to wonder what
she could be thinking...

The house was really nice! The kitchen was much bigger
than ours, and the dining room was tremendous. My mother
asked how many guests I thought could sit around the
dining-room table. I think that's what excited her most about
the house.

I looked around for Chaim and Yanky but couldn't find
them. Rochel said they were probably on the backyard swings,
so I looked out the window and saw them happily climbing
and swinging. Then she suggested that we join them, because
it sure smelled like the barbecue was ready.

Rochel's aunt and uncle seemed very nice and were so
friendly to all of us. I hadn't seen my mom enjoy herself so
much for a long time. I couldn't understand why Rochel kept
arguing with her, though. And over the silliest things. I guess
it's hard for Rochel to accept us, too.

Finally, by nine o'clock, everything was cleaned up, and

we began collecting all our things. Rochel and I went upstairs to get my sweater, and I couldn't help but notice how pretty her room was. There certainly was room for another bed in there. And I really *was* beginning to like her, I decided.

I took another quick look around the house and thanked them all before we went outside to the car. Rochel said she'd call in a few days to hear how I did on the test I'd told her about. The boys were in the middle of playing Monopoly, and the only way Dovid finally convinced them to stop was by agreeing to let them leave the game set up and continue next time. It was pretty late, and we were all tired by then.

The trip was a long one, and the two boys soon fell asleep. On the way, I closed my eyes and found myself somewhere between wakefulness and sleep. I could hear the soft murmuring of Dovid's and my mother's voices from the front seat, but I couldn't make out what they were saying. It was sort of comforting, though.

And as we drove the long way home, I realized how empty and quiet the car, and our lives, now seemed compared to the day we'd just spent. I think that's when I understood that even though we'd probably have plenty of problems at the beginning, together we'd be able to work things out.

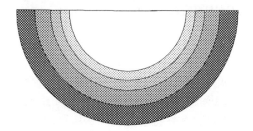

Banana Splits

Helena Jakubovics

Avi and Aviva Dingle were not the quietest children, but for the last half-hour they had waited patiently, their noses pressed up against the window. Suddenly, the twins turned around and began jumping. "Here comes Uncle Mendel! Here he comes!" they shouted.

Mrs. Dingle went to the window to look for herself, although she really didn't have to. She recognized the sound of the van lumbering down the block, as did probably the whole neighborhood. Uncle Mendel drove an old, yellow Dodge that wobbled more than rode and sounded something like a plane taking off. If that noise wasn't enough to grab everyone's attention, the car's large rainbow-colored sign, "MENDEL THE MAGICIAN," surely did.

Avi and Aviva had five uncles, but Mendel was their favorite by far. He always did tricks and told jokes.

Mendel stepped out of the van. His striped, blue tuxedo, red top hat, and white tie made him look like Uncle Sam.

HELENA JAKUBOVICS began writing and babysitting at the age of ten. Her experiences with both activities are combined to make this story.

Mrs. Dingle opened the front door.

"Is everything okay?" she asked. "You spoke so quickly on the phone that I could hardly understand you."

"Everything's fine," Mendel answered, "but I want to ask a favor. I need only a little more work with Harry before he's perfect for the act. In fact, I'm going to book a performance for us right now. But I can't take him along. Do you think you could watch him until I get back?"

Mrs. Dingle looked like she had suddenly gotten a toothache. "I...I don't know," she said. "I mean, the house. I wouldn't want it to be ruined. And I really don't know how to take care of Harry."

"Don't worry," Mendel replied. "Harry is a good boy, and I'll remind him to behave."

Avi and Aviva did not know who Harry was. And they had never answered for their mother before. But each of them was eager to help Uncle Mendel by babysitting.

"Couldn't we, please?" said Avi.

"I'll help," pleaded Aviva.

"There, you see? The children want to help, and we can't disappoint them. I'll go get him."

Harry was neatly dressed in a suit and tie. He held Mendel's hand as the two walked quietly towards the house. But the children had not expected to see a chimp, and after just one look at him they ran to hide.

"It'll be okay," Uncle Mendel reassured Mrs. Dingle. Then he covered his mouth. "Just be very careful not to say 'now,' because when Harry hears 'now,' he's trained to go into his act. 'Thank you,' is his cue that his act is over. He knows he has to stop then." He led Harry into the house and then left.

Harry sat down on a couch, crossed his legs, and began thumbing through a magazine.

The children cautiously moved closer, not taking their eyes off him.

"Are you afraid of Harry?" asked Avi.

"No," answered his sister.

"Then touch him."

"You first."

Avi studied him. Harry was compact and solid. "He looks so much like a person, so real."

"He is real," said Mrs. Dingle, herself fascinated by the chimp. "He's also very intelligent. He can count, build blocks, and understand things people tell him to do. He also can do a lot of tricks."

"Who taught him how to do all these things?" asked Aviva.

"Uncle Mendel," her mother replied.

"How?"

To Harry this sounded like "now"! He jumped off the couch, started to chatter, and raced around the room. He headed straight towards a wall, suddenly did a somersault, and then ran in the opposite direction.

Avi and Aviva took cover. Mrs. Dingle wanted to scream but couldn't find her voice. She hid her head in her apron.

Circling the room, Harry bumped into a table, sending a lamp crashing to the floor. Mrs. Dingle looked up to see the base in three large pieces. Harry became frightened by the noise and sped into the kitchen.

Mrs. Dingle's kitchen was small but very dear to her. She spent so much of her day cleaning it. It had newly polished, white, wooden cabinets, matching linoleum, and appliances neatly lined up along the countertops.

Harry jumped onto the table, landing with a thud atop a container of orange juice. Its contents spilled onto the floor.

Mrs. Dingle could not recall how to stop Harry. "No, no,"

she begged. But Harry ignored her pleas and did a few more somersaults.

Suddenly, Mrs. Dingle had an idea. "I'll capture him!" she said frantically, grabbing a long, heavy coat. Approaching Harry, she opened the coat and threw it as though it were a net.

Harry yelped and jumped into the air. He grabbed the light fixture and swung back and forth like a trapeze artist. Then he pulled a cabinet door open and hung from the top of it.

"Get off that!" Mrs. Dingle shouted, horrified by the squeaking of the hinge.

Mrs. Dingle always kept her cabinets very neat. The bottom shelves held the everyday dishes, and the good set, which she used only for special guests, was on top. She always took especially good care of that set.

Harry pulled out one of the good soup bowls and examined it. It didn't look very special to him, so he dropped it into the puddle of orange juice, splashing some onto the oven. Then he reached for another bowl. He didn't think any more of this one than he had of the first, so it crashed onto the table top. Harry must have liked the sound, because several more quickly followed. He giggled at his accomplishment.

As the stack of bowls ran down, Harry reached for the cups. These were lighter and much easier to fling. The first one flew across the room and hit the spice rack, filling the room with pepper.

A loud "achoo" echoed from Aviva, who had been taking in the whole scene from the kitchen doorway.

To Harry that must have sounded like "thank you," for he gently lowered himself from the cabinet door onto the top of the refrigerator, then down to the table, and finally onto a chair. There, he crossed his legs and held out his hand, waiting for a banana.

A lot happened in the months that followed. Avi and Aviva never again asked their mother to let them babysit. Uncle Mendel finally perfected his act and, pardon the expression, it became a smashing success — that is, until Harry realized he was the main attraction and went on to become a star in his own right. He was last heard from entertaining children all around the country.

It took nearly six months until Mrs. Dingle would even speak to Mendel again. During this time, he pulled off his greatest trick of all and became an accountant. He has agreed to prepare the Dingles' tax returns for free for the rest of his life.

Mrs. Dingle still enjoys keeping her house neat. But despite her best efforts, the linoleum still has an orange tinge to it. And these days, the good dishes don't cost much more than the everyday ones.

Mrs. Dingle just wants to put the whole episode behind her. She has company every week and has earned quite a reputation as a hostess. Even so, guests are advised never to ask for a banana.

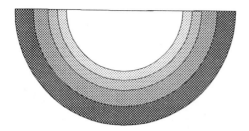

Keys to Love

Miriam Yellin

C ome, Josh. Let's go down to the basement," called
Abba.

"Coming, Abba!" yelled Josh.

Why is it always me? the second-grader fumed to
himself. Now that the new baby is here, everything has changed!
Ima's never available to play anymore. She's always feeding the
baby. The others are always pestering me to tie this shoe or
button that shirt. And the worst is, now we have to move. Move!
I've been living here for as long as I can remember. When Ima
had the twins, we didn't have to move. Not even when Moshe
came. But now we have a baby girl, and we have to move. I always
knew girls were trouble.

"What do we have to do down here?" asked Josh when
he'd caught up to his father.

"Well, Ima needs more clothes for the baby, and I want
to see what's down here for the move."

"I live in Israel with my family. Ever since I started babysitting, I've been
making up bedtime stories. I started a series of stories for my friend's
children, and she asked me, 'Why don't you write them down?' I have been
writing stories ever since. This is my first published story but hopefully
not my last." — MIRIAM YELLIN

"It's always 'for the baby'!" complained Josh.

"Now, Josh, that's not fair. We need your help, especially with little Avigail just coming home and us moving in less than a month..."

"I still don't see why we have to move. It's bad enough with the baby, but moving, too..."

"Josh, we discussed this before. Now come help me."

Abba pulled out his keys and unlocked the basement door. Josh had only been in the basement once, just after Moshe was born. His *abba* walked down the stairs and turned on the light. Josh was right behind him. There were boxes and crates and even an old, broken rocking chair. Josh wasn't so sorry he had to help anymore. There were a lot of interesting things to explore.

I bet there's a hidden treasure, he thought.

"I forgot where Ima said the box we need is. I'll be right back, Josh. You stay here." With that, Abba ran back upstairs.

Alone in the basement, Josh noticed that the boxes were marked. I bet I can find the clothes before Abba gets back, he decided.

Josh started reading the boxes. First he found the toys, but that wasn't what he was looking for. Finally, he found the clothes. BOYS, 2-3 YEARS OLD...12-18 MONTHS...

"Here it is," said Josh, not even realizing he had spoken out loud. The box said NEWBORN TO 8 MONTHS. The only problem was that it was on top of a high stack. Josh looked around for something to climb on. The rocking chair was no good, and he didn't trust the other boxes. At last, he spotted a crate that was easily accessible. It was very heavy, and Josh needed to rest after dragging it over. Once he was on top of the crate, getting the box was a cinch.

Now that that's done, let's explore, thought Josh. What's in the crate?

338 / EVERYTHING UNDER THE SUN

The side was marked P-I-C, but Josh couldn't figure it out. He found his father's toolbox and took out a hammer to pry open the crate. Inside were lots and lots of pictures.

Josh sat down to look through them. He loved pictures, old or new. There were photos of his grandparents and aunts and uncles and even some of him.

"What are you doing, Josh?" questioned Abba, having returned from upstairs.

"Oh, look, Abba, my baby pictures!" the boy exclaimed.

"Those aren't yours, I'm afraid."

"But it says my name on the back."

"Let me see." Abba examined the pictures. "Look at the date, Josh. That's my grandpa, Yehoshua Leib."

"Is that who I'm named after?" wondered Josh.

"Yes, it is. He was *niftar* when I was about seven years old."

"That's a year younger than I am now. Boy, am I glad all my grandparents are still alive."

"Yes, Josh, you're lucky. You even have a great-grandfather, don't forget — Ima's *zeide*."

"I remember... Who are the twins named after, anyway?"

"Well, let's see. Benjamin is after Ima's mother's father, and Yaakov is after my other grandfather."

"What about Moshe?"

"He's after your uncle and Moshe Rabbeinu."

"Why Moshe Rabbeinu?"

"He was born on Moshe Rabbeinu's *yahrzeit*."

"Oh. What about...Avigail?"

It was the first time Josh had said his sister's name. Normally she was "the baby." But talking about his family and whom everyone was named after, he'd suddenly realized something. Avigail was part of his family, too. And she had a name.

"She's named after Ima's great-grandmother," Abba replied. "And speaking of Avigail, I've got to find those clothes, and you have to clean up this mess."

"I found the box, Abba. It's over there."

"Well, then, I guess I'll help you put all these pictures away."

"Abba, what's in that old trunk?"

"The trunk! Well, let's finish this and go take a look."

Josh replaced the cover on the crate, and his father hammered it back down. Then they pulled the trunk into the middle of the room.

"This is a special trunk, Josh. You know that I'm the oldest in my family?"

"Yeah, Abba."

"Well, this was my special trunk. When I was growing up, my father worked in many different cities. We kept moving all the time. Usually, I shared a room with my brothers, but once all of us kids were in one room."

"All ten of you?" Josh asked, surprised.

"No. There were only six of us then. But this trunk was mine alone," continued Abba. "I could put anything I wanted in it — my baseball cards, my special books, even my shell collection."

"Just like mine?"

"Just like yours, Josh. Of course, my clothes had to go in there, too. One suit for Shabbos, two pairs of pants and four shirts for weekdays."

"Wow! What's in there now, Abba?"

"You know, I don't remember. Why don't we find out?"

Slowly, the lid of the trunk creaked open. It was an old trunk and had not been opened for a long time. Inside were some old clothes and books and a small, metal box.

"I didn't think I still had this," said Abba as he lifted out the box. He opened it up, then quickly shut it.

340 / *EVERYTHING UNDER THE SUN*

"What's in the box, Abba?" Josh was very curious.

"Well, remember I said we had to keep moving when I was little?"

"Yeah."

"I hated it as much as you do now. My *abba*, your *zeide*, used to take a picture of each house we lived in and make it into a key chain with a blank key attached. He would give me the key chain on the day we moved to a new place. I remember he always said, 'The picture is so you will remember the house and all the good times we had there. But the key is blank, not made to fit any door, because it isn't the key that made our house safe, it's the love we have for each other and for Hashem. As long as you remember that, you'll be okay. But before I give you the key, you must promise me never to have it made to fit any door, and to always remember the love that goes with it.'

"So that's what's in this box, Josh — keys and pictures of all the houses I lived in as a boy. If you promise me the same thing I promised my father, I will give you this box. And when we move, I'll give you a key and a picture of this house on a key chain, too."

Josh liked that — keys to remind him of the love he felt for his family. All of them, big and little. Even the new baby...Avigail.

"Oh, Abba, I promise!" he exclaimed.

Abba handed over the box with a tear in his eye, for he remembered how hard it had been to move when he was little and how much each key had helped. He hoped the keys would do the same thing for his son.

Josh took the box and ran upstairs to look through the keys. His *abba* slowly closed the trunk and followed, carrying the box of clothes for Avigail.

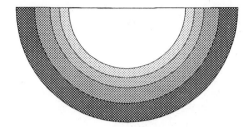

Son

Sheindel Weinbach

My son, you've had a busy day,
The minutes seem to fly away,
Why, just before it was still morning,
You woke up smiling, you woke up yawning,
And now the stars are in the sky,
You wonder where the time did fly.

Now stop and make a mental list,
Be sure there's nothing you have missed.
What kind of page will this day make?
Real? Full of mitzvos? Or somewhat fake?

Was this a day when you learned well?
You are the one to truly tell.
Did you tease your brother —
Or help your mother?
Did your day begin with a solid start?
Did you say *"Modeh Ani"* with all your heart?
When Mother called, were you a little lazy?

If you want to read about SHEINDEL WEINBACH, turn to page 46.

I know your memory is already hazy.
But now, at the end of a long, long day,
What do you have to show, to say
To the *malach* who comes to fetch your soul?

Will it be clear and pure and whole?
When today's page is placed in the eternal book,
Will you be ashamed or proud to look?
And the pages are all combined
On Rosh HaShanah, what will you find?

Before you sleep, my darling son,
Think back to all the things you've done.
Think back to all the things you've said,
Now that you're lying here in bed.

I know that you were a good boy,
You are my pride; you are my joy.
And if you sinned in any way,
Tomorrow is another day
To make amends, to make repair,
Through deed and word and then through prayer.

Now say Shema just for a starter,
And tomorrow you'll try a little harder.

Goodnight, my dear, and now sleep tight,
Tomorrow things will be all right.

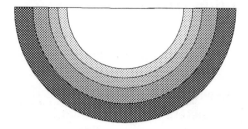

The Apple Tree

Deborah Guttentag

I t was hot and stuffy in the cupboard in which Aaron was hiding. He could feel the worn fur of his mother's coat, the rough tweed of his father's jacket, and a cluster of spikes and prickles that belonged to the umbrellas and brushes which populated the coat cupboard under the stairs.

When the light was on, you could see the names of Aaron's brothers and sisters inscribed over the pegs, which were used for anything but coats. Dustpan brushes and pans, odd bits of string, and even an old tie of his father's jostled for space in the disorder, and the coats were consigned to a couple of pegs on Aaron's right.

That was in the light.

But Aaron was in the dark. Quite dark it was, and he was hiding. He had difficulty seeing and great difficulty not being afraid, although he heard the voices of his mother and sister as they came down the stairs just above his head. He knew they were there, but they didn't know he knew. They

---

DEBORAH GUTTENTAG lives in Manchester, England, where her husband is the *rav* of the Whitefield Hebrew Congregation. Many stories she has written have developed from storytelling to her own children.

thought he was somewhere else, such as in bed or playing. Nobody expected him to be here.

But this was a test. He was testing them to see if they missed him, for among all his sisters and one brother, Aaron was sure he counted the least. If they did not miss him, he would run away. He was all prepared. He felt for the green, plastic bag that held everything he needed. Inside it were his dressing gown (pink, handed down from an older sister), his toothbrush, and ten pence — a lot of money.

His body tensed. They were coming his way. They were opening the cupboard door. Would they switch on the light? They did not. They did not need to. They could feel where everything was, despite the jumble. He crouched further down among the coats and held his breath, hoping nevertheless that they would see him. Maybe they would see the coats tremble. They did not. They found what they wanted and shut the cupboard door.

Darkness again, except for that crack of light from the hall. They were passing into the kitchen. Don't switch off the light, please! Darkness. Thick as Egypt. Let me out, let me out! He had not said those words. He could not speak. He was all alone. If he called, would they hear him? They were not far from him. He heard his father's footsteps passing by light and quick. He had flicked on the light. Don't switch it off, Daddy, not this time. But Aaron's father was economical. Aaron had learned that long ago. Would they never come?

That's the doorbell; his sister home from violin practice. Front door opening and closing. Hall light on. Ah, bliss, now the cupboard door opens. Come out now, now's your chance. Now that the light is on, you need have no fear. No creeping from darkness to darkness. Safety. The cupboard door shuts. Another chance lost.

He pushed against the door. It moved slightly. His sister

had been careless as usual. He could almost hear his father reprimanding her. Another push with Aaron's foot, and it was open. Funny how one kind of darkness could be so different from another. He had almost been strangled by the darkness of the hall cupboard, wrapped so tightly around him, but the blackness of the hall opening up from the door seemed like the yawning mouth of a monster that would swallow him up in its vastness.

Through the hall he crept, avoiding the umbrella stand and chest of drawers, which stuck out hugely like the monster's teeth. The plastic bag rustled against his leg. He shivered. Now for the difficult bit. The front door. The handle was very stiff; even his father had trouble with it sometimes. Stretch up. Grasp it firmly. Turn. Again. No. Again. And again. Aaron's wrist and fingers ached. He gritted his teeth. One last effort. Slowly, the handle turned.

He was out now. He stood for a moment at the open door, staring at the unlit path to the street. Here's your chance to turn back. He shook his head. No, he must go. If he gave in now, they would never know about his anger; they would continue to talk over him, through him, about him, but never to him. Quietly, he shut the door. Opening the rusty gate at the end of the garden path, he stood on the street. It stretched in front of him endlessly, longer than he had ever seen it, silent as the watching moon.

The streetlights cast orange beams along the road. The sky was a deep pool of black. He moved his eyes away from it. Down the street he went, bag in hand. He stopped a moment to check that all his belongings were there: dressing gown, toothbrush, ten pence.

He walked slowly, putting off leaving his own street. How many lampposts to go? One, two, three, four. He gasped. What was that by the third lamppost? It looked like a box.

He hurried towards it. It could be dangerous. It might contain a bomb. It could blow us all up. Not me, he remembered. I won't be here. But Mummy and Daddy, my sisters, and my brother. I must warn them. But that means returning home. He bent to look at the box more closely. It was soaking wet. He laughed out loud with relief. It couldn't be a bomb after all. Not in a soaking wet box.

He straightened himself, feeling braver. Time to march on now. He looked at the road again, wondering what lay beyond the fourth lamppost. The road looked very long. Standing there under the open sky, he became aware of the cold and of how unprotected he was. He had nothing with which to cover himself, and it was beginning to drizzle. He whimpered a little, not because he was afraid anymore, just sad that he was so alone in that long, cold street. He could be the only person in the world.

With a shock he realized there were noises in the street. Voices were shouting, car doors were banging, a woman seemed to be screaming — or was she crying? Quick as lightning, he crouched down and crawled towards the garden of one of the houses. Flopping down onto his stomach, he wormed his way along the garden to the back of the house, which was lit up by a source he could not identify. Heart pounding, he lay under a bush, waiting for the noises to cease.

Gradually, he became aware of his surroundings. The bush under which he lay was one of many that grew thickly around the garden. Nearby stood a tree whose branches overhung much of the lawn, and there seemed to be an extraordinary number of balls littered across it. On closer observation, he saw that they were not balls but apples.

Aaron was fascinated. He had ceased to be afraid, and his heart was now beating at a regular, comfortable pace; he was fascinated and at the same time disgusted at the profusion of apples on the lawn. They seemed to swarm all over the garden, as if it were infested with an ugly disease. The light that lit up the lawn was so bright that Aaron could see the color and shape of most of the apples. They were rotten. The lawn was riddled with rotten apples. But it was their number rather than their condition that revolted Aaron: The tree had somehow broken free of its normal restraints and was trespassing into foreign territory.

Now Aaron identified the source of the light. The moon was right above him, full and round — almost yellow, like the sun. For several minutes Aaron marveled at the flood-light it provided, quite forgetting that he had run away and was supposed to be hiding. It was the apples that reminded him. Their presence disturbed him, and he was afraid. He remembered now that he had run away and was leaving home for good.

He thought of the long, dark street, lit up by eerie, orange beams, and the moon slipping away behind the houses and clouds. Here, the moon was round and friendly. Out there on the street, it hid from him slyly. Here, the garden was overrun with rotten apples. Even the moon could not comfort him over that. He was at home nowhere. Neither the street nor the garden wanted him. Each had sent its workers to drive him out.

Suddenly, it was as if a small explosion had taken place in his head. He had been watching and thinking so deeply that he had been completely unaware of sound. Now, with the volume turned up once more, he heard the sounds of the street and houses around him. Shouting and banging doors, people were running into the street. The whole neighborhood seemed to be gathering outdoors. What could they be doing? He listened carefully. A woman was crying and repeating a word over and over again. A man kept on shouting and making the same sound. Now another voice rose high above the rest — a wailing, screaming siren. A police siren. They were looking for him. The whole street was looking for him. Those were his parents whom he had heard crying and shouting. His mother, his father, crying.

But how long could he have been away? Was it long enough for them to notice? It couldn't have been more than half an hour. Well, now he had what he wanted. They had missed him, and they were afraid, but he wished with all his heart that he had not tried to test them. How could he possibly confront them in their anguish? Calmly present himself to them: I ran away, I'm sorry to have caused you so much inconvenience, so much pain, but I'm back now. Should he just creep back among the shadows, slip in through the back door while they were out front, and let them find him sweetly asleep in bed? He could manage it, but he could not bring himself to lie in the face of the full, guileless moon.

Yes, the moon was honest. It hid nothing of itself, because it had nothing to hide, and the light it threw over the garden was bright and beautiful. He took a deep breath. He would have to be brave. This took a different kind of courage. It was not the darkness or the orange beams he had to fear, but facing up to his parents, admitting that he had been thoughtless and cruel. For now that he thought about it, he had to admit to himself that he'd never really intended to run away. He'd wanted to frighten them, punish them. Punish them for their indifference.

But even as he thought this, he knew he was not being truthful. They were not indifferent toward him. They performed a thousand actions that showed they cared. An evil little worm had entered his mind — perhaps the same one that had caused all those apples to rot — and had allowed a momentary impulse, a flash of anger and humiliation, to destroy him.

He got up and stretched. Strange, he was no longer afraid. Calmly, he walked upright out of the garden. A few paces into the street, he was besieged by people. They swamped him, almost crawled over him, but Aaron did not mind. Relief and joy had become almost tangible in the closeness of the crowd. And through it all, he became aware of his mother's embrace and his father's firm hand laid upon him with love. No anger was apparent — perhaps that would come later — only vast, overwhelming love.

Down the street they led him, holding onto him tightly as if afraid he would vanish once more into the night. Down the garden path, to the front door, light, light, light greeted him. The door was wide-open, the lights were burning, there seemed to have been no thought for anything but his safety. Down the hallway they carried him — yes, they were carrying him, like a *chasan* — and they were singing with unsurpassed joy. Not a harsh word, not a flicker of an eyelid betrayed any anger, for Aaron was with them again, and light could once more fill their house. Aaron looked at the faces of his parents, his sisters, his brother, so full of concern and care. He thought of the moon, the rotten apples, his loneliness; yes, above all, the loneliness of the past half-hour. He walked back down the hall to the understairs cupboard.

Quietly, he shut the door and padded off to bed.

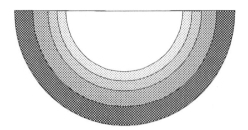

The Decision

Libby Lazewnik

Monday evening started out much the same as any other in the Shapiro home. Fifteen-year-old Gila, and Hindy, almost thirteen, were doing their homework in companionable silence at the double desk in their bedroom.

The girls had the same long, brown hair caught up in ponytails, and the same light brown eyes. Each had a pencil in her hand and a stack of textbooks and papers before her. But both sisters were finding it hard to concentrate. There was just so much to look forward to!

For Hindy, it was tomorrow night's big party at her friend Aviva Katz's house. Aviva had been planning this super-duper bas mitzvah party for ages — a scrumptious birthday supper (she wouldn't leak even a hint as to what was being served) for twenty classmates in her spacious basement.

Aviva was the youngest girl in the class and the very last to be bas mitzvah, so hers would be the last big party for a long time — but what a party! Hindy glanced at her wristwatch and tried not to squirm in happy anticipation. In

If you want to read about LIBBY LAZEWNIK, turn to page 49.

just twenty-two hours, the fun would begin. She honestly didn't know how she would last till then!

Gila's head was filled with visions of her new school play.

Without much hope, she had auditioned for a part — and to her vast surprise, she'd gotten it! Not the lead, to be sure, but a very respectable part nonetheless. The play would be performed for ladies only at a community-center auditorium, with all proceeds going to charity. And opening night was in just one week.

Every afternoon after school, Gila joined the others in rehearsals. How she loved stepping onto the stage — as if into a whole new world — and reciting the lines she'd so carefully memorized. She loved the music and the songs and the parts that made her laugh and the parts that made her cry. She loved acting. From the minute she awoke in the morning she looked forward to rehearsals. They were the highlight of her day.

Until now, the cast had rehearsed in school. Starting tomorrow, however, rehearsals were scheduled for the evenings instead of the afternoons, and they would take place in the auditorium. There would be a real stage, a real curtain that went up and down, and bright, hot spotlights shining on the performers. Gila would speak her lines to rows and rows of empty seats and imagine them filled with rapt, admiring audiences. She shivered in eager delight.

Hindy and Gila's mother could be heard in the background, getting the three youngest Shapiros off to bed. Yitzi and Binyamin, the two middle boys, were still awake and playing downstairs until their bedtime. All was proceeding as usual. A peaceful evening.

Then Ma tapped on the door of the girls' room and walked in. Within sixty seconds, their peace was utterly shattered.

"I'm on my way out to my course now," Ma said, pulling on her coat as she talked. "The little ones are in bed — just peek in on them in a little while to make sure they're asleep — and the boys need their usual firm reminder to go to bed in half an hour."

"Sure, Ma. No problem," Gila said cheerfully.

Hindy nodded in agreement. Ma's Monday- and Thursday-night course was old news by now. They could handle the house just fine in her absence.

"Thanks, girls." Ma half-turned toward the door. Then turned back abruptly. "Oh, by the way, I don't know if I mentioned that your father and I are invited out to a *chasunah* tomorrow night. We'll need one of you to babysit."

As her daughters stared at her in stunned silence, Ma glanced at her watch again. "Oops, I'm running a little late. Bye, now!"

"M-Ma?" Hindy blurted desperately. "W-which one of us do you need?"

"Oh, either of you will do. You girls decide. I know — flip a coin!" And with that, Ma blew them a kiss and was gone.

Hindy and Gila exchanged a quick glance.

Hindy spoke first. "Well, *I* can't stay home, that's for sure. Tomorrow night's Aviva's big bas mitzvah party. Ma must've forgotten the date — I told her about it weeks ago. I guess you'll babysit, Gila."

"No way!" Gila was as surprised as Hindy by the vehemence of her reply. "I have play practice tomorrow night in the community center. The play's just a week away, and Mrs. Friedman said we have to be there."

"B-but — Gila, you can't go out tomorrow night!" Hindy wailed. "I *have* to go to Aviva's party! I've been looking forward to it for such a long time. Everyone'll be there!"

Gila folded her arms across her chest and set her face

in stubborn lines. "I feel bad for you, Hindy, but I still can't miss my rehearsal."

How could she explain to her younger sister the magic of acting — of standing beneath the footlights and speaking lines that belonged to another person — of living, for an hour or two, a completely different life? She didn't want to miss even a minute of it! And besides, Mrs. Friedman *had* insisted that each and every girl be there tomorrow night.

Gila shook her head. "It's very important to me, Hindy. I'm sorry."

But Hindy was not in an understanding mood. "How selfish you are! I can't believe this is my sister Gila Shapiro speaking!"

Gila sat bolt upright. "Me, selfish? What about you? Who does the babysitting around here nine times out of ten? I do! Well, now it's your turn!"

The sisters glared at each other for a long moment. Then they stiffly turned their backs on each other and pretended to return to their homework.

"We'll see," Hindy muttered. "We still have till tomorrow night to decide.

"Yeah," Gila echoed grimly. "We'll see."

Neither girl slept very well that night.

Gila tossed and turned in her bed, trying in vain to banish the thoughts that wouldn't let her sleep. At first she felt self-righteous: I deserve to go out — I have to go out — I will go out! It's Hindy's turn to babysit!

After a while, though, she started remembering. She remembered her own excitement about bas mitzvah parties when she was Hindy's age. How Gila and her friends used to look forward to each one! They'd discuss them endlessly both beforehand and afterwards. And a dinner party was really

special. It'd really be hard on Hindy to be the only one to miss
it. The last party of the year, too...

As for Hindy, she lay face-down on her side of the room,
trying to muffle her sobs in her damp pillow. It wasn't fair!
Gila had never acted this way before. It was being in that
dumb play that was doing it. Gila was becoming arrogant,
that's what. She didn't care about anyone anymore. I won't
miss Aviva's party! Hindy thought with renewed resolution.
I don't care what Gila says. I won't!

Then, as Hindy grew drowsier, Gila's words came back
to haunt her. *Who does the babysitting around here nine times
out of ten?* Nine times out of ten... Though Hindy tried to
recapture her indignation, she had to admit that her sister
was right. Gila never minded staying home to babysit while
Hindy whiled away the evening at a friend's house. Gila had
never minded until now. This play must really mean a lot to
her.

Tuesday morning dawned gray and cheerless, which
suited the sisters' mood just fine. They avoided each other at
breakfast. In silence they went about their preparations for
school and helped their younger sisters and brothers get
ready for their day.

Hindy snatched a moment to speak to her mother privately.

"Ma, I said some nasty things to Gila last night. I didn't
really feel like staying home to babysit, and neither did she.
But," Hindy drew a long breath, "I-I guess I will stay. After
all, Gila has play practice, and besides, she's usually the one
who babysits for you. It's only fair that I do it this time."

Ma studied her daughter's strained smile. "That's very
nice of you, dear," Ma said. "Thank you."

"Uh — Ma, one more thing. Could *you* tell her? I don't

really feel like talking about it to Gila right now." Hindy was afraid that if she did, she wouldn't be able to hold back her tears.

Ma nodded, suppressing the questions on the tip of her tongue. Hindy was obviously not prepared to volunteer any more information.

A minute later, Gila walked in.

"Ma? Could I talk to you for a second?"

Slowly, a smile dawned in Ma's eyes. "Of course, Gila," she answered gently. "What's on your mind"

She had an uncanny feeling she knew exactly what her eldest daughter was about to say.

"Well, how do I look?" Ma presented herself for inspection in her new dress.

"Gorgeous, Ma!" Gila pronounced.

"Hindy? What do you think?"

"Oh, it's stunning," Hindy said. "I love the color especially."

"So do I," nodded her mother with a smile. Then she glanced at her watch — a slender, gold timepiece this time, not her practical, everyday one. "We'll be leaving in about a quarter of an hour, I'd say. Daddy just came home, and he's still showering." She glanced casually at her daughters. "If you girls are ready by then, we can give you a lift."

Hindy and Gila stared at their mother. "A lift? To where?"

"Why, to Aviva's house, of course," Ma told Hindy. "And Gila, don't you have rehearsal tonight?"

"I'm babysitting for you, Ma — remember?" Gila said quickly.

Hindy's face reddened. "Oh, no. *I* am."

Gila's face was the picture of amazement. "Hey, what's going on here?"

Hindy was no less puzzled. "Ma, I told you I'd stay home tonight, remember?"

Ma smiled serenely. "Yes, dear, you did. And so did Gila."

"Sh-she did?"

"Yes. And I want you both to know that Daddy and I are extremely proud of how you've handled this."

Gladness welled up in Hindy's heart. She glanced at Gila and saw the same feeling reflected in her sister's broad smile. "But who'll babysit tonight, Ma?" she asked.

"Oh, I did something unusual — I hired a babysitter. She should be here any minute now."

"Who is she?" Gila asked curiously.

"Estie Katz — Aviva's big sister." Ma grinned. "With twenty of Aviva's friends invading her home tonight, do you blame her for wanting to get out?"

Hindy and Gila looked at each other and giggled. Ma clapped her hands briskly. "You'll have to hurry if you want that lift, girls!"

The sisters joyously jumped out of their seats.

At that moment, the doorbell sounded from below. Ma threw a last, satisfied glance at her eagerly preparing daughters, then flew downstairs to answer.

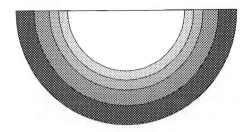

The Birthday Present

Tamar Harkohav-Kamins

Hadassah Miller sat at the head of the long table and gazed around the huge living room. The two walls at her side were gaily decorated with bright streamers, while all around her blue and pink balloons happily waved their greetings. The chairs surrounding the table wore pink ribbons with big bows hanging down, and in front of each chair was a colorful place card. The table was filled with assorted goodies — everything from potato chips and pretzels to cookies and candies. And in the center of it all, sitting on a fancy platter, was a beautiful cake, the words "HAPPY BIRTHDAY HADASSAH" peeking out from between its layers of pink roses. As if this weren't enough, all around the cake, chocolate happy faces smiled up at Hadassah.

But Hadassah was not smiling back. The curly-haired

TAMAR HARKOHAV-KAMINS moved from Montreal to Jerusalem with her family at the age of thirteen. She graduated from Michlalah — Jerusalem College for Women.

Tamar has been writing stories and poetry since she was eight, when she decided to become a writer. Her recent books include several in the *B.Y. Times Kid Sisters* series, published by Targum Press. She is working on additional stories for children and adults.

eleven-year-old was far from happy. In fact, looking around at all the beautiful decorations and tasty food made her so upset, she just wanted to put down her head and cry.

"It's not fair!" she shouted out loud. "It's just not fair!" she repeated, this time pounding on the laden table and sending a stack of plastic cups tumbling.

But no one responded to Hadassah's cry. The empty house was silent.

Hadassah couldn't help thinking that it was probably just as well. If her little brother Chezky had been home, they'd surely be fighting, whereas if her big sister Malkie had been there, she'd definitely be bossing her around as usual. Hudi and Yoni didn't really count. They were rarely home anyway, so they probably wouldn't have been around now either. It was her parents Hadassah wanted to see. Had they been home, it would have all been different.

She sighed. It had been planned out so carefully exactly for this reason. Plans at the Miller house always seemed to go astray at the last moment. But Hadassah had been determined that this time it wouldn't happen, and she'd even taken special precautions to make sure of it.

The food and decorations had been bought ahead of time. After that, her mother had gone with her to buy a new dress for the occasion. And then all that was left was to give out the invitations. She remembered how, the week before, she had brought them to school to deliver to her friends. She hadn't mentioned to any of them that she was planning a party, just in case something went wrong. But now, everything was ready, and she knew it would work out.

"What's this?" her best friend, Zahavi, asked as Hadassah handed her the pink envelope.

"Why don't you open it?" Hadassah replied teasingly.

Zahavi eagerly tore open the envelope. "A party!" she squealed. "You're having a birthday party! Oh, that's great! When is it? What time? Will it be in your house?"

"It's all written down, Zahavi."

"I know, but I don't have the patience to read it now. Just tell me."

Hadassah smiled. "It's going to be in my house, and it's next Sunday at 3:30."

"Next Sunday! Wow, that's soon! Will you be ready by then?"

"Oh, don't worry about that," Hadassah told her, full of pride and confidence. "Everything's done already. This is gonna be one super party!"

The two girls chattered on together as Zahavi helped her give out the rest of the invitations. Nothing could spoil this party now!

How wrong she had been! Hadassah put her head down on the table so she wouldn't have to see the lavish spread in front of her. She didn't want to remember all the plans that had faded away. Why now? Why couldn't her mother have waited just a little? If only...if only...

Hadassah heard the front door slam. Someone was home. It was about time! She quickly lifted her head and tried to wipe away her angry tears, but before she got very far, she heard her name being called.

"Hadassah, are you here?"

Hadassah recognized her sister's voice. Oh great, just what I need, she thought. Malkie was only fourteen, but she always made sure Hadassah didn't forget the three-year gap between them.

"I'm in the living room!" Hadassah shouted back.

Malkie danced into the room. Her eyes quickly took in the scene before her, but she was too excited for it to make a real impression.

"Well, guess!" she said.

"Guess what?" Hadassah answered glumly.

"You know what! Don't be so dumb. Guess!"

But Hadassah felt like being stubborn. "I don't know what you're talking about," she answered.

"Oh, come on, you're no fun. I'll give you a hint. I just came from the hospital."

"So what?"

Malkie was fed up. "You're impossible. You're being a spoiled baby! Just for that, I won't tell you anything!" With that, she spun around and left the room.

It took only a few minutes for Hadassah's curiosity to get the better of her. She followed her sister into the kitchen.

"I bet it's another boy," Hadassah guessed.

"Oh, so now you want to know," Malkie teased. "Well, it's not a boy."

"Okay, then, it's a girl."

Malkie shook her short, black curls. "No, not a girl either."

"What?" Hadassah didn't understand. "Not a girl and not a boy?"

As she paused to think, worry look crossed her forehead. Here she had been considering only herself without a thought for her mother. Had something gone wrong?

Malkie started laughing. "It's twins, silly! Not one girl — two!"

Hadassah smiled. "Really?" For a moment, a grin lit up her face. But only for a moment. Then other thoughts started to creep into her head: Twins. They'll get all the attention now. I'll never have my party. Everybody will be too busy with them. In fact, I'll bet I'll never have a birthday party again. Everyone will always be trying to make special parties for the cute little twins. They'll forget all about me! Oh, why did they have to be born on my birthday?

Malkie was still talking, but Hadassah was so miserable, she barely heard her.

"...anyway, Ima's fine now. They were a little worried 'cause the babies came so early. But they're okay. That's what Abba said. I didn't see them or Ima. Abba said maybe I can go tomorrow. Maybe you can come, too."

But Hadassah shook her head. "I have more important things to do. Besides, I'll have plenty of time to see them once they come home. They'll probably be crying all the time."

"Have it your way," Malkie answered.

"I will!" Hadassah shouted. She ran into her room and slammed the door behind her.

Malkie stared at the closed door for a few seconds. Then she walked into the living room and looked at the beautifully set table. She reached her hand into the biggest bowl of potato chips and absentmindedly started munching, a thoughtful expression on her face. Malkie had an idea...

When Hadassah came home from school the next morning, she was still in a bad mood. The whole day had been just terrible. She had expected sympathy from her friends. After all, her birthday party, which should have been so special, had been canceled. But instead, all she got were countless congratulations. Her teachers kept coming over to ask how her mother and the babies were doing, and each time she had to answer, "*Baruch Hashem*, fine, thank you," and pretend to smile. She was getting so sick of it. Even her best friend had deserted her. All day, Zahavi could talk about nothing but the twins.

"Gee, you're so lucky," she said to Hadassah during recess. "Twin sisters! What a great birthday present."

"Well, you can have them," is what Hadassah had wanted to answer. But of course, she couldn't say that. No one would understand that kind of remark — especially not Zahavi. She had only brothers and would have traded places with Hadassah any day. As it was, her friend pestered her all the way home from school.

"When are you going to visit them?" Zahavi asked.

"I don't know," Hadassah answered bluntly.

"Well, can I come with you when you go? I'm dying to see those little babies."

"I may not go at all," Hadassah replied, knowing that she had no intention whatsoever of going.

But Zahavi persisted. "Then will you call me when your mother comes home with them, so I can come over to visit?"

"We'll see. My mother may not feel like visitors."

Zahavi had to accept that. "Oh well. I guess I'll get to see them eventually."

"I'm sure you'll have your chance soon," Hadassah answered.

Everyone will, she thought to herself. Hadassah groaned inside. Here she was getting sick of the twins when they hadn't even come home yet. What would happen once they were crying in their room all the time?

Their room! A thought struck Hadassah. Where would the twins sleep? For the first ten years of her life, Hadassah had shared a room with Malkie. Last year, when her big brothers had gone away to yeshivah, Malkie had moved into their room, and Hadassah had finally gotten a room of her own. Would that be taken away from her now?

Hadassah turned to Zahavi, who was still chattering away about the babies. "I gotta go, Zahavi. My mother needs help."

"But your mother isn't even back from the hospital yet.

How could she need your help?"

Hadassah had given the first excuse that had popped into her head. Now she was confused for a moment. "I don't know," she answered. "She just does..."

And then, as she ran down the street, she shouted over her shoulder, "...for when she comes home!"

Minutes later, she was racing up the steps to her house, two at a time. Breathlessly, she pushed open the door.

"Oh, hi, Hadassah," came a voice from the living room.

"Yoni! What are you doing home!"

"What's the matter?" Yoni kidded her. "Don't you want to see your big brother?" He changed his tone. "I asked my *rebbeim* for permission to leave the yeshivah. I thought Ima might need help. Hudi said he would see if he can get off, too. He might be home tomorrow. Anyway, I wanted to see the twins. It's not every day that you get two baby sisters at once!"

"That's for sure," Hadassah muttered. But before her brother could comment, she added, "Where's Malkie?"

"I think she's in your room."

"In my room!"

"Yeah, she's..."

Hadassah wasn't listening anymore. She had to see if she had been right. She ran to her room and stopped at the door, stunned. Malkie was moving all her things to one side, as if to make space for...two cribs!

"Oh, hi, Hadassah. How was school?" Malkie asked. Then she added nonchalantly, "How do you like the idea of sharing your room again?"

"I don't!" Hadassah shouted. "This is a free country, isn't it? Don't people get asked anymore?"

"Oh, calm down, Hadassah. It won't be for long."

"Oh, no? What do you consider 'not long'?" Hadassah

countered. "Two years? Five years? Ten? I'll probably be sharing this room until I'm an old lady!" She stared at Malkie, who was laughing hysterically. "I don't know what's so funny. You wouldn't be laughing if it were you! What's more, I don't understand why it has to be me at all. I'm already suffering enough."

Hadassah's words sent Malkie into fresh gales of laughter. "You are such a silly girl! You honestly think Ima's going to move the babies into your room?"

"Well, she is, isn't she?"

"Of course not!" Malkie chuckled. "When they come home, they'll be sleeping in Ima and Abba's room at first, as we all did when we were babies."

"So what's this?" Hadassah asked. "Why are you moving all my things? Who's sharing my room?"

"I am," Malkie stated. "Hey, don't be so happy," she said dryly, noticing the grumpy look on Hadassah's face. "I'm not thrilled either. But it's only for a couple of days, until the boys leave."

"Oh, is that it?" Hadassah was relieved. A few days with Malkie would not be easy, but she could handle it. "I should have realized when I saw Yoni. Phew! And I thought..."

"Well, it wouldn't have been that bad having the twins in here," Malkie said. "I'm sure you'd love it."

"Speak for yourself. They can move into your room. I hate them!"

"Hate them? But you've never even met them."

"I don't care. I hate them already."

"But how can you? They're your sisters, and they're so cute!"

"How do you know?" Hadassah asked.

"How do you think?" Malkie's eyes twinkled. "I went to visit them today."

"Well, good for you."

"You really should see them; they're adorable. Tiny little bundles with teeny hands and feet. Ima said she'd love it if you came to visit them tomorrow."

"Well, I can't," Hadassah quickly answered. "I'm very busy tomorrow. I've got a lot of work to do."

"But Ima said she'd really like to see you. How about if you just go to visit her and don't even see the babies?"

"I told you, I can't!" Hadassah repeated. "I'll see Ima when she gets home. Now just leave me alone."

"Gee whiz. Yes, sir!" Malkie shouted, promptly marching herself out of the room.

Malkie was waiting up for her father when he came home from the hospital late that night.

"How's Ima?" was her first question.

"She's fine, and so are the babies. And how are all my other children doing?"

"We're fine, Abba — at least mostly," Malkie began. "Yoni came home from yeshivah, and he's back in his old room. He says Hudi will probably be home tomorrow. But Hadassah isn't doing too great. She's really mad at the babies for ruining her birthday party. If not for that, I'm sure she'd love them, too. I tried to convince her to visit tomorrow, but she refused."

"Did you tell her Ima especially asked for her?"

Malkie nodded. "But it didn't help. What are we going to do? She's got to go to the hospital."

"Well..." Mr. Miller thought for a minute. "How about if Ima asks her personally? What if Hadassah receives a call from her tomorrow after school? Do you think that would work?"

"I don't know," she said. "But it's better than nothing. I

guess we may as well try it."

"Good," Mr. Miller said. "Then it's set. I'll tell Ima our plans in the morning. Now, how about if you go to sleep, so you'll be nice and fresh for Ima tomorrow?"

Malkie kissed her father goodnight. Then she went to bed in the room she had shared with Hadassah for years. Thoughts danced through Malkie's head as she stared at her sleeping sister. Tomorrow would definitely be an interesting day.

Hadassah hadn't thought it would even be a good day, never mind interesting. She really hadn't wanted to go to school that morning. She knew what it would be like — exactly like the day before, with everyone inquiring, commenting and congratulating. She was sick of it. If anyone asks me one more question about the twins, I'll scream, she thought to herself as she walked to school.

But surprisingly, her dreaded expectations proved untrue. No one mentioned a word about the twins, not even Zahavi.

Why have they stopped asking me? Hadassah wondered throughout the day. Finally, after her last class, she asked Zahavi.

"I guess it's nothing special anymore," Zahavi answered. "Maybe people have just lost interest. After all, there's a limit to how crazy you can get about twins."

"I guess so," Hadassah said, though she wasn't convinced. But it didn't matter. She was glad everyone had stopped badgering her with questions all day. Maybe now life would get back to normal.

"Hey, Zahavi, do you want to come over and do homework together?"

"Sorry, but I can't," Zahavi replied. "I've arranged to go somewhere with Shira and Esti. In fact, I'm already late. I'd better hurry. See you tomorrow." With a quick wave, Zahavi hurried off towards her house.

I wonder why they didn't ask me, too, Hadassah thought as she watched her friend disappear down the street. Oh well, it doesn't matter; I guess they had their reasons.

Hadassah walked slowly down the street until she reached her house. She trudged up the stairs and pushed at the door. But it didn't open.

"Anyone home?" she shouted as she knocked on the door. But there was no answer. "Great!" Hadassah muttered and sat down on the top step to wait. Hopefully, someone would come home soon.

Suddenly, she jumped up and started searching in her schoolbag. "Got it!" she shouted as she triumphantly pulled out the house key. She had forgotten she even had it.

The house was silent. "Well, I guess I'm the only one here," she said aloud. "I wonder where everyone is. Maybe someone left a note on the fridge." But the refrigerator held nothing save a shopping list and an old receipt.

Hadassah took out her math book and sat down to do some homework. But she couldn't keep her mind on it. She was too disturbed about where everyone had disappeared to. They're probably all at the hospital with the sweet babies, she guessed. But they should have at least left me a note.

Suddenly the phone rang. That must be Abba, Hadassah thought as she got up to answer it.

"Hello?"

"Hadassah dear, how are you?"

"Ima!"

It felt so good to hear her mother's voice again. She had been so busy thinking about herself that she hadn't realized how much she had missed her mother.

"I'm fine, Ima, but how are you and — " she forced the

words out of her mouth, not believing she was saying them " — the twins?"

"I'm doing very well, Hadassah, but I miss you so much. The twins are very sweet. I'm sure they'd love to meet their special big sister." Mrs. Miller paused. "Hadassah, why don't you come over? Then we can talk about what's bothering you."

Hadassah considered the idea. It would be good to talk to Ima again. But Hadassah really didn't want to see the twins. Maybe, though, it would help to talk to her mother about this. She would understand. She always did.

"Okay, Ima, I'll come over right now."

"That's my girl."

One twenty-minute bus ride later, Hadassah found herself riding the hospital elevator up to the seventh floor.

"May I help you, young lady?" a nurse at the front desk asked her.

"I'm here to visit my mother, Mrs. Miller. She's waiting for me."

"Oh, you must be her little girl. She talks about you all the time. You haven't been here to visit her yet, have you?"

"No, this is the first time. I was, um, busy."

"Yes, well, go along now, she's waiting for you. She's in room 509, down the hall and to the left. But don't make too much noise because..."

Hadassah barely heard her. She was already down the hall, standing outside room 509. Should she go in? Would the twins be there, too? It seemed quiet, but... She took a deep breath and walked in.

Her mother was fast asleep.

Hadassah quickly turned around and tiptoed out of the room. What should she do now? Go home? But she wanted to talk to her mother. That was why the girl had come.

Well, she couldn't just stand here in the hall. That nurse might see her and tell her to leave or something. Maybe it was rest hour now, and Ima had forgotten to tell her.

I guess I'll just wander around, Hadassah thought. Most of the doors she passed were shut, but when she walked by an open one, she was always greeted by happy voices raised in conversation. Sometimes, she heard the low wail of a baby mixed in with the talking, and she wondered where in this hospital her twin sisters were. But only for a moment. Then she would remind herself that since she really didn't care, what did it matter?

Finally, she reached the end of the long hall. To the right stood a closed door. She thought a moment, then pushed the door open...and gasped.

Through a window, Hasdassah saw row after row of tiny cradles, each bearing a name tag. Some cradles were empty, but most held little bundles.

She looked closer. She had forgotten what newborns looked like. When her brother Chezky had been born, she'd been only four-and-a-half. She barely remembered what he had looked like, except that he was very red and cried a lot. But these babies, they were so sweet...

She started as she felt a hand on her shoulder and spun around. It was the nurse from the front desk.

"I'm sorry," Hadassah mumbled, embarrassed. "I know I probably..."

"Yes, you're Mrs. Miller's little one, aren't you. I expect you've come to bring her the babies..."

"Actually...," Hadassah began.

"Well, you're just in time. I think they're ready for their feeding. Follow me, please."

Hadassah walked behind the nurse until she reached the door of the glass-enclosed room. "You wait here now," the nurse said as she entered the room. It took only a few minutes for her to come back wheeling a small carriage.

"Here, this shouldn't be too difficult. Now go straight to your mother; she's waiting."

Hadassah stood entranced by the carriage and its little parcels. She felt all her bad feelings melt away. These were the little babies she had hated? They were so tiny, so innocent, so adorable.

She bent closer to get a better look at them. One was just waking up, her eyes flickering. The other wasn't far behind. Her arms and legs were squirming. Just like I stretch before I get out of bed, Hadassah thought. She reached out to touch their soft skin.

"I see you've found them," came a voice from behind her. "Ima!"

"Shh, Hadassah. This is a hospital, remember?"

"Oh, Ima, it's so good to see you again! And the babies — I don't know how I thought I could hate them. Even if they made me miss my party, it wasn't their fault. Zahavi was right. They're a great birthday present, and I wouldn't trade them for anything!"

Hadassah gave her mother a big hug. "Thank you, Ima." They stood smiling at each other.

"Well, let's not stand here all day. Come to my room, and tell me what's going on with your life."

They made their way to Mrs. Miller's room, where they sat and talked, noshing on the chocolate other visitors had brought.

It was good to talk to Ima again. In fact, Hadassah probably could have continued forever had she not looked out the window and noticed the sun going down.

"I'd better leave, Ima. I don't want to go home in the dark."

"You're right, Hadassah. I'd also prefer if you left while it's still light outside. Come, I'll go downstairs with you."

"Will they let you?" Hadassah asked.

"Of course. This isn't a prison. Besides, I'm not sick. But we'll have to leave the babies at the nursery on the way down."

At the nursery, Hadassah stared at her new sisters. "Goodbye, babies," she said, bending down to kiss each one. "I'll see you when you come home."

Two minutes later, she stood in the elevator with her mother as it hurtled downwards. "When will you be coming home, Ima?" Hadassah asked as the doors opened at the ground floor.

"In a day or two," her *ima* replied as they started towards the main lobby. "And you know, Hadassah, we still owe you a party. How would you like us to make you another one soon?"

Hadassah's eyes sparkled. "That would be great! I'd like that a lot." She tried to push open the double doors to the lobby, but they seemed stuck. "That's strange," she said, turning to her mother. "The doors weren't even shut before."

"Maybe they close them in the evening," Mrs. Miller suggested. "Why don't I help you?"

Before Hadassah could reply, Mrs. Miller pulled a key out of her pocket and proceeded to unlock the door.

Hadassah stared at her. "Where did you...?"

"SURPRISE!!!"

Hadassah gazed around the large hall. Once more, she beheld a room full of bright streamers, pink and blue balloons, and every treat imaginable. This time, however, the room was filled with people. Cheerful, smiling people instead of one lonely girl annoyed at her birthday celebration being canceled. Zahavi and Shira and Esti were all dressed in their party finest along with Hadassah's other friends. And there was her father with Hudi and Yoni and Chezky. Malkie was there, too, along with Bubby. Even the nurse from upstairs had joined in the merriment.

There were just two people missing. Eyes shining, Hadassah turned to her mother.

"Ima, may I go up and get the babies?"

"You'll have to ask the nurse upstairs, dear. But do you think it's wise? Do you really want someone else to be the center of attention at your party? Now is your time to be special."

Hadassah grinned at her mother, but as the girl rode up to the seventh floor, she realized she didn't entirely agree with her. Maybe it was Hadassah's time to be special, but the kids in her family were special all the time.

Besides, it was the twins' birthday, too. Shouldn't they also be downstairs celebrating?

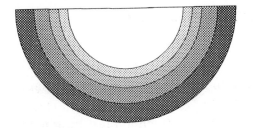

Kibbud Av

Debby Garfunkel

I'm really into mitzvos, that's just the way I am.
I look for every chance to do a good deed when I can.
So when I spied the date last week and saw there "Father's
    Day,"
"It's *kibbud av!*" I yelled and started scheming right away.

I planned a day of sheer delight with Abba's favorite joys.
We'd get up bright and early to go and buy some toys,
Then skip down to the nearby park and rollerskate till
    breakfast.
We'd share a mushroom pizza, feeling bold and rather reck-
    less.

We'd say an after-*brachah*, then head over to the mall
And buy some nifty earrings...oy, my dad would have a ball!
We'd have to stop for ice cream, making sure it had a
    hechsher.
(I'd ask for chocolate éclairs, too, but fear I'd get a lecture!)

If you want to read about DEBBY GARFUNKEL, turn to page 305.
    "*Kibbud Av*" is based on a true, messy Father's Day incident.

We'd prowl down to the zoo to lunch with hippos, bears, and
    apes,
Then whirl a frisbee round the beach while munching mas-
    sive grapes.
We'd hurry home for dinner and tell Mum about our day,
Then pop popcorn to end off in a warm and crunchy way.

Well, that was how I planned it, but it never did come true.
The day before my grand surprise, my *abba* caught the flu!
His nose was blocked, his breathing sounded just like he was
    panting.
With one quick look I diagnosed there'd be no gallivanting.

I went to bed that night and tossed and turned and turned
    and tossed.
It made me sad to think that one great mitzvah would be lost.
And then at dawn I sat upright, a new plan now instead...
I'd make my dad a super-duper breakfast feast in bed!

I crept down to the kitchen, full of fabulous ideas.
I took down all the cookbooks I'd ignored my whole ten years.
I baked and fried, I stirred and whipped, I sautéed and
    frappéed.
I dreamt I was the chef of some exclusive French café.

By 8 A.M. the meal was made — oh my, did it look gorgeous.
I must admit I noshed so much I felt a little nauseous!
I set the tray and made sure that the coffee cup was filled.
I couldn't wait to see Dad's face so proud and pleased and
    thrilled.

With bated breath I knocked and when my mum opened the
    door,
My pup Shimshon raced through my legs and knocked me to
    the floor!

AND THERE WAS ICE CREAM ON THE CARPET, THERE
    WAS FRENCH TOAST ON THE WALL.
THERE WERE PANCAKES TOPPED WITH MAPLE
    SYRUP OOZING DOWN THE HALL.
THERE WERE PEANUT BUTTER CLUSTERS SCAT-
    TERED ALL ACROSS THE BED.
AND SAD TO SAY, THE CHOCOLATE BLINTZES FELL
    ON ABBA'S HEAD!

THERE WAS MILKSHAKE ON THE MIRROR, THERE
    WERE LATKES ON THE LAMP.
AND CHEESECAKE SQUASHED AGAINST THE QUILT
    I MADE FOR MUM AT CAMP.
THERE WAS KUGEL ON THE DRESSER, EVEN OAT-
    MEAL ON THE CEILING.
You probably can tell this feast was somewhat unappealing.

Well, how I felt that moment there is no need to relate.
I just wanted to vanish, to dissolve, evaporate.
I felt like hiding underneath that gooey mess of mousse.
I'd never in my whole life felt like such a silly goose!

I lifted up my head and met my folks' astonished faces.
I'm sure with doggy Shimshon I would gladly have switched
    places.
I stammered an apology but couldn't say much more.
Instead a great big tear welled up and splashed down to the
    floor.

"Come here, my sweet," my *abba* said. "Come give me a big
    hug."
My *ima* sighed, "That's life," and off she went to clean the
    rug.
"You mean you guys aren't mad?" I sputtered, reaching for
    the broom.
"I must have splattered half the kitchen right across your
    room!"

"Well, first, it's not your fault that nudnick Shimshon knocked
    you down.
(Here, let me wipe that glob of kugel off your dressing gown.)
What truly is important is you tried your very best.
That breakfast looks amazing, even though it's one big mess!

"You know it's not results that are the point of what we do.
It's mostly getting started that concerns a thinking Jew.
So armed with good *kavanah*, plus a dose of energy,
We forge ahead and let Hashem decide on what will be."

My *abba* was so touched by all the effort I'd employed.
He hardly even noticed that his room I'd just destroyed!
And as I helped my *ima* clean the chaos round the bed,
She said it was the most delicious feast she'd never had!

So I still love doing mitzvos, but if one now goes awry,
I know Hashem asks only that it is my best I try.
And next year when this day rolls round, I'm sure that I will
    look
To fulfill my task of *kibbud av*...I'll buy my *av* a book!

YOUNG AUTHORS

Readers' Contest

Leah Klein

Dear Readers,

Here I am, cup of coffee on my desk, lonesome for my friends — those special girls on the staff of the *B.Y. Times*, the official newspaper of Bais Yaakov of Bloomfield. No problem. A few jots on my yellow legal pad, a bit of tap-tapping on my computer keyboard, and poof! Here they are:

Shani Baum, dynamic founding editor of the *B.Y. Times*. Can she ever really let go of her former position and influence and let the new staffers thrash out their own ideas — and make their own mistakes?

Chani Kaufman, current editor. Peace-loving and growing in confidence with each issue. But any way you slice it, it isn't easy to measure up to her self-assured predecessor.

Raizy Segal, brilliant and shy former assistant editor. She spent a rough but rewarding year overcoming her shyness and allowing her literary talent to speak for itself.

LEAH KLEIN created all your favorite characters in Targum Press's popular series *The B.Y. Times* and *The B.Y. Times Kid Sisters*. She is working on more great books for your reading pleasure.

Jen Farber, new assistant editor and newcomer to Bais Yaakov of Bloomfield as well as to *Yiddishkeit*. Will she ever completely make the transition from public school to Bais Yaakov?

Nechama Orenstein, distribution manager. Fun-loving and athletic, Nechama is fiery-haired, fiery-tempered, and always good for a laugh.

Ilana Silver, distribution assistant. The laid-back, informal Californian impresses all with her cool, confident handling of the *Times'* new computer, Dusty.

Batya Ben-Levi, business manager. An only child, Israeli-born Batya finds her protective, nurturing nature put to the test when she and her deaf cousin survive a Scud missile attack during the Gulf War. So why does she have such a hard time winning the trust of Davey, her family's six-year-old foster child?

Penina "Pinky" Chinn, graphic artist; and Chaya Rochel "Chinky" Chinn, former business manager and present student-council president. For all their freewheeling camaraderie, these inimitable, identical twins occasionally have their differences, like when both long to represent their school at a convention, but only one may attend.

Judging from your letters from all over the world, the *B.Y. Times* girls are as much your friends as mine. And when Targum Press invited you all to send in your own *B.Y. Times* stories, you proved to be authors and graphic artists of sophistication and excellence. Plots galore crammed the Targum Press mailbox: Pinky and Chinky's babysitting disasters, Raizy's free trip to Israel, a daring rescue when one of the *Times* girls gets kidnapped, and the most popular plot of all — Batya's mother having a baby. I wish we could publish them all! But since we can't, here are some choice samples written about your friends and and mine.

Enjoy!

P.S. I've just reread my letter, and I realized that it may be a bit confusing for those few of you who have never read the *B.Y. Times* books. But over a dozen of them are already available — what in the world are you waiting for?

P.P.S. To answer a much-asked question: you pronounce the "ch" in Chinky like Charley, not Chaya! Keep those letters coming!

Shevi's Party Problem

Nechama Weiss, age 9

Monsey, New York

MANY PEOPLE WERE walking around Ben-Levi's Pizza Shop. Batya Ben-Levi and her friends were lucky to have found a place to eat inside, since a lot of people were still waiting outside. She was eating with Nechama Orenstein, Chinky and Pinky Chinn, and other seventh-graders. The Chinn twins' bas mitzvah party was coming up, and so was Pesach, and that's what they were talking about.

"We've got Pesach cleaning to finish up *and* a bas mitzvah to plan," said Pinky.

Chinky nodded in agreement. "You wouldn't believe all the things that go into one party. Caterers, color schemes, flowers..."

"Outfits, entertainment, menus..." her sister continued.

"And all for one silly celebration," Chinky ended with a grin.

"Silly little celebration?" Nechama repeated indignantly. "Your bas mitzvah happens to be very important! Besides," she giggled, "everybody loves a party."

Shevi Lichtenstein totally disagreed. "Maybe most people do, but not me," she mumbled.

Slowly she followed her friends out of the pizza shop. They all talked about the Chinns' party. All, that is, except Shevi. When they reached the corner of Oak Street and Central Avenue, Shevi parted from the group and went her own way.

She had no destination in mind, but she just walked. She didn't want to walk together with the others, because they were talking about a party. Suddenly, she realized it was getting quite late, so she turned back and headed home.

When she reached her house, she said a quick hello to her mother and went upstairs to her room. Sometimes she felt lonely because she didn't share her room with anybody, but now she was glad. She took out her beloved diary and started writing.

April 2, 1991
Dear Diary,

I have so much to write. I'll leave everything for tomorrow, but I'll just write about one thing — parties. I always enjoyed parties until after my eleventh birthday party. I invited the whole class, and it was to be super-special. My mother said she prepared a surprise and never told me what it was. Two kids showed up! It turned out to be a total flop. From then on I resented parties. Now what do I do if all everyone talks about is Chinky and Pinky's bas mitzvah party?

The next day, when Shevi got home, her mother told her a letter had come for her in the mail. After Shevi looked at it, her joyful smile became a big frown.

"What is it?" Mrs. Lichtenstein asked.

"Oh, it's just an invitation to a bas mitzvah party in one week."

Before her mother could ask any more questions, Shevi rushed into her room and locked the door. She was about to tear up the invitation, but instead she stuffed it into one of her drawers.

The frown on her face lasted through school. During the last recess of the day, Chinky approached Shevi.

"You don't look too happy," she said. "What's wrong?"

"Nothing's wrong," Shevi answered.

"Come on, tell me," Chinky coaxed.

Suddenly, the whole story of the party that flopped came pouring out.

"...and in the end, two people came, and we had a horrible time," finished Shevi sadly.

"So because of that you don't want to come to my party? Don't be silly! I feel bad that only two people came, but that's no reason to hold a grudge against parties."

"No," Shevi said tearfully, "you don't understand."

As Shevi lay in bed that night, she thought about what Chinky had said. It made sense. It really did. So what if her party wasn't a success? That was the past. It happened half a year ago.

A few days later, Shevi was enjoying herself immensely at the Chinns' bas mitzvah party.

The Helping Twin
Brenna Leah Radcliffe, age 13
Bais Yaakov of Toronto

CHINKY SAT DOWN at her desk, trying to do her homework. School was certainly not easy now. But since when was school supposed to be easy? Pinky probably knew the material. Chinky called to Pinky, "Pinky, oh, Pinky! Can you come here for a second?"

Pinky came running up the stairs. "What do you want?" she asked. "Do you know that grade six is protesting? They want to be included in next week's Shabbaton. I just spoke to Shani, and she told me. Anyways, what do you want?" she asked again.

"I want to know, Penina Chinn, why I'm slaving over this math homework, and you're talking to Shani. After all, I will probably be the one who has to take care of the problem, you know," Chinky exclaimed.

"Well, let me tell you, Miss Chinn, that you aren't the only person in this house who has homework. Just because you get pulled out of class all day and don't know the work, that doesn't mean that I can't speak on the phone," Pinky retorted.

"Listen, Pinky," Chinky said, "I don't want to fight. I just want to know if you can help me."

"Well," said Pinky, "I don't want to fight either. But I want to make it clear right now: I'm not going to help you all year just because you are president of the student council. Do you understand?" Pinky asked.

Chinky glared at Pinky. "I understand perfectly, dear sister. When you need my help, I'll do the same."

Pinky's eyelashes fluttered. She pleaded, "Chinks, it's just that I don't think it's fair to me that because you are president, I have to do all your work. I'm not jealous of you. But I don't like to be taken advantage of." She looked at Chinky and then continued. "Really, Chinks, you know I help you a lot, and we study together, but I think that fair is fair, and you should do your share of your homework. Okay?"

"Fine," Chinky grunted. Then she walked away. "Really," she thought, "teachers could be more understanding.

Being president is a big job. And now I have to take care of these sixth-graders as well. Don't they understand that they have to wait their turn? I guess they don't," Chinky muttered.

Pinky stood where Chinky had left her. It hurt not to be able to help her sister. But for Chinky's own good, it would be better not to help her. She hoped that Chinky wasn't too upset with her. Pinky hated when they argued or disagreed. She went down to the basement, where her drawing board and a bag of caramels awaited her. Drawing, art, and caramels always made her feel better.

Pinky began drawing a beautiful picture of herself and Chinky. They were standing against a background of trees, flowers, the sky, and the sunset. They had their arms around each other's shoulders. When she finished drawing, she began painting it. It looked stunning when it was finished. She backed the picture on black construction paper.

She crept upstairs with the picture. Chinky was nowhere to be seen. She propped the picture up against their desks. She went downstairs.

When Chinky came up to her room later and saw the picture, she let out a gasp of surprise. "Pinky, it's beautiful!"

Pinky came running up the stairs, "You really think so?"

Chinky said, "Uh-huh! You got your point across. I really should do the work myself. You're right. I'm just so busy with everything. Adding homework on top of all that seemed impossible!"

"Don't worry about it," Pinky exclaimed. "You're being a great president. I wanted to help you, but for your own good I thought it would be better not to. All hard feelings gone."

"Yup," agreed Chinky. "Why don't we go get ice cream?"

The two of them walked down the street, arms locked, faces smiling. Peace was restored.

The Mysterious Caramels

Chedva Braun, age 12
Monsey, New York

NINETY-NINE CENTS, one dollar twenty-nine, eighty-nine cents; Pinky's groceries were endless. The cashier, a woman nearly in her seventies, was quickly loading bag after bag. Suddenly Pinky remembered — caramels, her favorite snack. She quickly skipped over to the candy rack and grabbed the last bag of Lieber's caramels. Hastily, she handed it over to the woman.

The woman's face lit up. She had a wide smile across her face. She winked. She slowly put the caramels into the bag.

Pinky felt adventure in the atmosphere as she headed home.

"Anyone home?" Pinky called as she entered. Ghan, the Chinns' maid, greeted Pinky happily and helped her take in the packages.

"Tonight I made you your favorite supper!" said Ghan excitedly. "Vegetable soup, French fries, and spaghetti!"

"Great," thought Pinky hungrily. "A delicious dinner plus my caramels for dessert!"

Chinky, Pinky's beloved twin, had gone out to collect ads; she was business manager of the *B.Y. Times*.[*] So today she came in a bit late.

"I got four more ads today!" she called as she entered, out of breath.

Seeing one of her favorite suppers (this was one Pinky and Chinky agreed on), she quickly sat down and began to eat.

"We have to start working on the next *B.Y. Times*," said Chinky.

---

[*]This story takes place before Chinky was elected student-council president.

"I've already sketched the picture for the cover," said Pinky. She was graphics editor for the newspaper.

The conversation continued on.

Suddenly, Pinky started fidgeting in her seat. Her face was bright red, and she was nearly choking.

"Are you all right?" asked Ghan and Chinky simultaneously.

"It's just that..." Pinky quickly spit out the caramel she was chewing. She couldn't go on. "It's just that it seems like there's something unusual in this caramel!" she finally managed to say.

Pinky carefully examined the caramel.

"Come! Look what I found in here!"

In a flash, Ghan and Chinky were at her side. There was a thin strip of wax paper stuck inside the caramel. Blurred words were written on it in blue ink.

"What does it say?" asked Chinky, bursting with curiosity.

"I can make out an *H*, and here's *L*, *P*, and *M*."

"It says, 'HELP ME,' " cried Ghan.

"Somebody needs help!"

Somebody needs help? Who?

That's what they had to find out.

As Pinky ate her caramels, she discovered slips of paper with different sayings, such as "I'M LONELY" or "COME VISIT ME!"

What was going on?

That night, the twins lay in bed, deep in thought.

"Could it be Rivky? She always sits alone at recess, reading books. Is she the one desperate for help?" thought Pinky.

"Could it be Svetlana, the newly arrived Russian pupil in the second grade? She's always eating her lunch alone, and tears always seem to be on their way behind her thick glasses. Is she the one desperate for that love?" thought Chinky.

Who could it be? And how did she get the message into caramels?

"And we still can't figure out who this mysterious person in need is!" ended Pinky as she told the tale to Shani, a close friend and the editor on their hardworking newspaper staff.[*]

Shani hesitated a moment and then jumped up.

"I know! There's a girl, Adina, in the fifth grade, whose father owns the grocery. Maybe she feels out of place and needs more friends. She could have easily put those papers in!"

The perfect solution!

The next day in school, Shani and the twins decided to spy on her. They watched her during recess. They watched her during lunch. They even peeked into her classroom to see how she was doing.

At one point they saw her munching on Lieber's caramels.

"Definitely!" was Pinky's reaction.

"Finally solved!" cried Chinky.

"But we can't be sure!" added Shani.

They couldn't be sure. Adina seemed to be so bubbly, so popular among her classmates. Why would she have written those notes?

One day, as they were watching Adina, she came over to them and asked uncomfortably, "Why are you staring at me? What's wrong? Is it my dress, my hair, or my shoes?"

"Uh, uh...I'm sorry," replied Pinky and quickly walked away.

They couldn't be sure.

---

*This is before Chani's time!

The next time Mrs. Chinn came home with a pack of caramels, Pinky quickly ripped the pack open and bit into one. This time she was shocked.

The note read: "IF YOU REALLY CARE, MEET ME AT BLOOM-FIELD PARK SUNDAY AFTERNOON AT THREE O'CLOCK."

"If I really care? What a question!" thought Pinky.

She ran upstairs to Chinky and showed her the note. Wow! Here was their chance to find out about this lonely, mysterious person! They quickly phoned Shani and told her the news. They would go together to the park on Sunday afternoon.

Sunday finally arrived. The hours went by slowly. One o'clock, two o'clock; it was almost time. With anticipation, they anxiously ran down to Bloomfield Park. They had to wait a few minutes until she finally arrived.

She wore that same gray wig she wore every day. She had the same lonely, blue eyes and that same brown dress she wore every day.

The cashier of the grocery store. They had never thought of that. And then Pinky remembered the strange faces the woman had made when Pinky bought the caramels.

"My girls," she began, "I tank you so much for coming. I really sorry if I caused you too much trouble. But I needed you. You want to hear my story?"

"Sure!" they chorused together.

"Fifteen years ago, my husband and I arrived from Vienna. We knew no one here and hoped for some friends. But things didn't work out.

"Everybody was so cruel. No one wanted to give my husband a job so he can earn a living. We had to live in a old hovel and eat scraps we find in garbage. I could only hope for things to improve.

"But they didn't. Things only got worse. A year later, my husband died, leaving me a poor, old widow who never had children. So I did my best.

"There were nine years of hunger, poverty, and loneliness. But then came a man from Russia with no family who was willing to marry me. But we were childless. My husband managed to get a job sorting out books in a bookstore. But then last year my husband passed away. I had nothing left.

"I felt worthless. I wanted to kill myself. But then I had good luck. I was able to be cashier in a grocery store. So I went. But I still had no friends and lived in a tumbledown apartment. So secretly, I put papers in caramels, which I knew children love. And you good children did come to see and care for me.

"I hope you understand. I felt so lonely. I needed someone to tell my story to."

There was not a dry eye among them. They all felt terrible for this woman. They had to do something for her.

*　　　*　　　*

Things changed for this old woman in Bloomfield. Every Shabbos she has four visitors (Batya joined them) who come to cheer her up.

They make her feel more comfortable in their community and always make sure she has support.

*　　　*　　　*

"See?" said Pinky. "I always knew it was worth buying caramels. Not only are they delicious, they bring you to adventures and lead you to many good deeds!"

And everyone had a good, hearty laugh.

Discovery

Malka Chaya and Rivka Yitta Leider, ages 10 and 11
Yeshiva of Spring Valley
Monsey, New York

BATYA FELT a pang of conscience as she sat snugly on the sofa in the living room, a cup of orange juice in her hands. Lately, she had forgotten to visit "Savta" downstairs. Savta was the Ben-Levis' tenant, who lived on the lower floor. She was a bit on the heavy side, with wire-rimmed glasses that always slipped down her nose and a wrinkly face always wreathed in smiles. She looked so grandmotherly that Batya began calling her Savta.

Batya knew this would be an ideal time to visit Savta. Quickly gulping down her cup of orange juice, she shouted to her mother what she was planning to do and flew down the stairs.

Batya knocked gently on the door, and Savta opened it so wide that the hinges almost broke off.

"Hallo! Hallo!" Savta croaked. "And where have you been so long?"

Batya stepped into the doorway and, with an embarrassed smile, proceeded to give an excuse.

"Vell, vell, mine kindt, how are you feeling?"

"Fine. How are you managing?" Batya replied.

"Oh! You came just at de right time. I need you to help me pack up," Savta announced.

Batya's face darkened. "Where are you going?" she asked apprehensively.

"I am going to Israel to live vit mine daughter."

"Really?" Batya sputtered. "Why? When? How?"

"Vell," the old lady took her time saying, "I got a call from mine daughter. She vants me to come and live vit her. So I said yes. I am going in vun veek by airplane on El Al flight 747 at seven o'clock at night."

Batya sighed. She really enjoyed the company of this old lady, who always had a good story to tell and a delicious snack, too. She swallowed hard and sighed again.

"Can you please pack dees shirts and skirts for me?"

Batya came back to the present with a start.

"Okay." She pretended to be cheerful.

Next week at supper, Batya chewed mechanically at her food. Savta was leaving that night. The thought made her stomach hurt.

"Batya, you seem preoccupied. What is the matter?" Mrs. Ben-Levi asked with concern.

"Savta told me she's going to live with her daughter in Israel."

"And you're upset about that?" Mrs. Ben-Levi asked gently.

"Sort of."

Mr. Ben-Levi put in, "Look on the bright side. You have plenty of other old people to visit in the nursing home. And when did you say Savta's flight is leaving?"

"I think she said seven o'clock tonight," Batya mumbled, toying with her plate distractedly.

"You know what?" Mr. Ben-Levi said with a glance at his wife. "Ima can drive you to the airport to see Savta off."

Batya looked up, excited. "You really would?"

Mr. Ben-Levi jutted up her chin until they met face to face. "Cheered up?"

"Of course!" Batya exclaimed. "I've got some homework that's due tomorrow! I'd better get to it."

With that, Batya said *birkas hamazon* and scrambled out to do her homework.

Problem Solved

"You mean you enjoy history?" Penina (Pinky) Chinn raised an eyebrow at the lunch break.

"Yes, I mean, really, why not? What's wrong with it, anyways?" Chaya Rochel (Chinky) Chinn shrugged her shoulders and bit into the hotdog sandwich she was holding.

Pinky and Chinky were identical twins. But though they may have been alike externally, internally they were very different.

Chinky was simple and down-to-earth and above average in school studies. Pinky inherited artistic abilities and preferred to doodle in her notebooks rather than write words or numbers. At times, she really felt like being anywhere instead of in an eighth-grade classroom — when she was learning history.

Pinky hated history. She couldn't care less about the world wars and what caused them. What did it have to do with her?

"But history is so boring!" Pinky exclaimed. "Sometimes I fall asleep in history, because it's so dull."

Just as Chinky was about to reply, the bell rang, signalling the end of lunch and the beginning of history for the eighth graders.

Pinky was determined to show her teacher that she despised the lesson she taught.

Pinky thoughtfully sat down in her seat. The teacher was droning on and on about Hitler...Japan...concentration camps... Pinky didn't hear anything. She took out a book from her briefcase, sneaked it into her desk, and began reading.

"Penina," the teacher asked, "tell me, what was the first country Hitler conquered?"

Absorbed in the book she was reading, Pinky hardly heard her.

"Penina." The teacher made slow, measured steps to Pinky's desk.

This time, Pinky did hear. She turned red, completely red, and stared straight ahead.

Slowly, the teacher took the book away and gazed at Pinky with icy eyes.

"From here I understand that you don't find history very interesting. The worst part of it is that you don't even try. I'm convinced that if you put a little effort in, you'd find it interesting." She stopped speaking for a minute and stared at Pinky frostily.

"At home I want you to write this entire chapter."

"For when?" Pinky asked hesitantly.

"For tomorrow," the teacher said without missing a beat. "As for that book, I want a note signed from your mother that she heard what happened today. If you do that, you'll get the book back."

Pinky gulped and felt tears stinging in her hazel eyes. Sixteen pages! How would she ever manage such a large amount! And to tell her mother about it? How could she? How...?

After an endless, long day, Pinky was not in the best of moods at all. It had taken her precisely seventy-seven minutes to complete those murderous sixteen pages, and her hand ached. Now one burden was thrown off, but there was still the prospect of telling her mother about the whole mess she had gotten into.

Eyes downcast, feet dragging, Pinky shuffled down the stairs to her mother in the kitchen.

"Mommy," Pinky began solemnly, studying her fingernails, "there's something I have to tell you." Pinky kept shifting her weight from one foot to the other nervously.

"Hi there, Pinky!" Mrs. Chinn called cheerily from the

black and white oven, baking *challos*. She waved a flour-cov-
ered hand. "Why the long face?"

"Well, I-I didn't pay attention in history. I was reading
a-a book hidden in my desk. So the teacher took away the
book and told me I could only get it back if you write a note
that you know what happened."

Pinky looked up from her nails to her mother's face,
trying to discern her reaction. There was a disappointed look.

"I truly hope that this never happens again. I'll write the
note later and give it to you."

And that was it!

Pinky raced outside to Chinky, who was raking the mass
of leaves that fell from the trees onto the lawn.

The twins' eyes locked for an instant. In one of those
peaceful, precious moments, without words, they understood
each other.

The Reunion

"What time is it, Ima?" Batya asked, fidgeting impatiently in the back of the Ben-Levi car.

Ima winked at Savta before answering. "It is now exactly 4:53, and we're almost there. In fact, I see a sign over
there reading 'AIRPORT ZONE.' " She waved the second finger
of her left hand to a sign protruding about a block away.

Indeed, soon enough, she turned into a humongous
parking lot. At the entrance, which had just enough space for
one vehicle to pass through, she grabbed a ticket off a blue
and red machine. Driving through the maze of cars in the
cement parking lot, she finally found an ideal place to leave
the car, near the bustling El Al building.

The moment Batya set foot inside, she was overwhelmed
by the commotion around her. She was standing in an open

area about ten yards by ten yards. On her left, there were about four hundred chairs attached to the gray, tiled floor, and all kinds of people of different nationalities were seated on them. In front of her were long lines of people, including Savta, waiting for their passports to be checked.

Batya's gaze returned to the people on the chairs. A group of Arab women with kerchiefs on their heads were talking amiably in Arabic. A few feet away, some black people from deep, deep Africa were heatedly discussing something and gesturing wildly with their hands. Batya gave a little gasp when she saw the kind of clothing they had on them. It was just like she had seen in pictures. They had embroidered, decorated sheets slung around them and tied at the end. They did not have socks on their wide feet, only sandals. On the chair opposite sat a lonely-looking old lady, who was leafing through a magazine distractedly. Somehow, Batya could not get her eyes off her. Something was clicking in her mind, though she could not quite put her finger on it. Well, Batya thought, it would do no harm to go over to her. She looked so lonely.

Mumbling a hasty excuse to her mother, she took long strides towards the lady. Something about this woman struck her as odd. And when the lady raised her arm for a moment, Batya saw a number tattooed on her arm. Immediately, a scene flashed into Batya's mind. She was asking Savta where the tattooed numbers on her arm came from. A faraway look then entered her eyes as she related her experiences in World War II.

"I was a young girl, seventeen years old. I had a younger sister who was just a year younger den me, and ve had a very peaceful life. Den, Hitler came and began rounding up Yidden and either gassing dem or putting dem in slave labor camps. Vone night, everyvone in mine femily was sleeping, and at midnight the dreaded knock on the door happened. The hardhearted S.S. soldiers, dressed in black, took my parents, my sister, and myself away. I don't remember how I managed in dose cattle trains dat brought us to Austria. My parents were on de left line to be gassed. My sister and I were on de right line for slave labor. After dat, ve vere separated into different barracks, and I never heard of my sister again."

At this point, Savta would usually dab at her eyes with the end of her sleeves.

Batya shoved all thoughts aside as she approached the lady. "Hi," Batya said gaily.

The old lady looked up from her magazine. "Who are you? Vy do you come to me? Vat do you have to do·vit an old lady?"

Batya hesitated slightly before answering, "Uh...you seem so lonely."

Immediately, Batya wished to retract her words. Oh no, she though. I botched it! It's not the kind of thing you say! Oh, Batya. Where are your manners?

"Den you don't mind if I tell you a story dat I didn't tell to anybody for many, many years?"

"No, I don't mind," Batya replied and settled down to listen.

"Ve vere a happy family, my parents, my sister, who vas seventeen, and I, who vas sixteen. Den, Hitler came, and took my whole family and myself avay. My parents vere killed. My sister and I vere put in slave labor camps. Ve vere in different barracks. I never saw her again."

The lady heaved a big sigh and dabbed at her eyes just like Savta did. Savta! Their stories were identical. Maybe... Batya's glance wavered from the lady to Savta, but she knew without a doubt.

"Excuse me, but I have to do something urgent. I'll be

right back." Batya skipped over to Savta, leaving a puzzled lady behind.

"Savta," Batya declared with a determined air, "I want you to follow me."

Before Savta had the time to produce a syllable, Batya pulled her over to the old lady. For a moment, they looked at each other, not comprehending the point of the meeting. Then Savta's eyeballs rolled, and she let out an ear-shattering shriek.

"Shayna Miriam!"

"Chaya Liba!"

The two sisters threw themselves on each other's necks and wept with happiness. Batya made a mental calculation. Savta was separated from her sister when she was seventeen. And Savta was now about seventy-three. That meant that the two sisters had not seen each other for fifty-six years! Goodness!

Batya marveled at the way Savta was able to control her tears for so many years!

"Next!" A booming voice belonging to a man behind the counter resounded through the airport.

Savta hurried back to her place and held out her passport and luggage. After a three-minute wait, she was finally through. Grabbing her hand luggage, Savta hurried through the maze of chairs to her sister, to continue their conversation.

All too soon, though, it was time for Savta and her sister to board the airplane. Batya waved goodbye from the ground as the blue and white airplane took off.

As Batya stood with one hand over her eyes to protect them from the rays of the sun, and the other hand waving at the disappearing plane, she felt indescribably joyful at the thought that she, Batya Ben-Levi, had brought two sisters together.

New Resolve

Batya ran to school with the wind. She was anxious to tell her friends what happened at the airport. The first friend she met on her path was Nechama Orenstein. Batya knew that Nechama, with her irresistible sense of humor, would be certain to yell out something like "Great dream, Batya!" and then turn serious.

"Hey, Nechama! Have I got something to tell you! Oh, will you get a kick out of this!"

"Stop keeping me in suspense. Tell me already."

"Okay, I'll tell you, but listen carefully." Batya related the whole sequence of events without omitting a detail.

Nechama was positively impressed. "Gosh! Never heard of such a phenomenal story. Goodness! I'm going to tell the others."

Next to hear the story were the twins, Pinky and Chinky.

"Oh, Nechama," Chinky cut in the middle of Nechama's narration, "you had a fine dream, or you just want to trick us and then make us look like fools, which I am not, considering the fact that I'm student-council president this year."

"You don't believe me? Go ask Batya. She'll tell you if it's true or not." Nechama pretended deep offense.

Chinky and Pinky marched straight to Batya. Pinky, hands on hips, took up the job as spokesman. "Batya, Nechama told us a story that she said you told her, and it sounds impossible! We just don't believe it!"

"It's true, it's true," Batya nodded, smiling.

Batya's story was part of what Pinky was learning in history. If she found Batya's story interesting, then for sure she'd find the history she learned in class interesting. With a jolt, Pinky realized she hadn't even tried to pay attention.

She had felt that history was boring, no matter what the topic.

But it was still the beginning of the year. She had plenty of time to show that she could improve, although she hoped that her teacher would not think she improved because of the punishment that was imposed on her. It was really Batya's story that had made such a change.

"Pinky!" Chinky sounded exasperated. "The bell rang thirty seconds ago! What are you dreaming about?"

"Oh, sorry." Pinky was too embarrassed to answer Chinky's last question and chose to ignore it. "Race you to the class-room!" she shouted.

Both girls ran, their hair flying behind them gaily, as if to announce to the world: We are free of trouble!

Batya's Garden
Chaya Leeba Plotnik, age 10
Hebrew Academy of Cleveland

BATYA BEN-LEVI was a sixth-grader in Bais Yaakov of Bloomfield. She had long, black hair and a dreamy look in her dark, brown eyes.

It was a Thursday afternoon in the month of July. She was riding her bike to the grocery store to buy things for Shabbos.

As she was riding, she passed a house with a very nice garden.

"Do I know who lives here?" Batya wondered. "Oh, yes! Now I remember! This is Mrs. Handler's house. She teaches seventh and eighth grade in Bais Yaakov. Her garden is so pretty!"

That's when a great idea came to her mind. She would make her own garden. Of course, she would get her parents' permission first, but she was sure they would agree.

As she finished the thought, she reached the grocery store. She parked her bike and felt in her pocket for the list and money her mother had given her.

When she entered the store she looked at the list and said to herself, "Ima wrote on the list that I should get gefilte fish, cold cuts..." But she wasn't really thinking about shopping. She was thinking how nice her garden would turn out.

She would plant roses, tulips, daisies, and carnations.

"That's enough for a small garden," she thought, "but now I really must concentrate on this shopping list."

Ten minutes later, she was out of the store and on her way home, eager to tell her mother her new idea.

When Batya got home, she started to tell her mother her news. As she was speaking, Batya helped put away the groceries.

When she was finished, her mother said, "You know, Batyale, that's a terrific idea. *Bli neder*, on Sunday, you can go to the flower shop and buy the seeds."

Batya was so happy.

That week, Shabbos passed quickly for Batya.

When Sunday came, she davened and ate breakfast, and with the money safely in her pocket she was off to the store! She knew exactly which seeds she wanted.

Right when she got home, she started planting the seeds. It was hard work in the hot sun. Finally, she was finished.

Batya took very good care of her garden, and soon the flowers grew. Her garden was beautiful.

When the flowers were fully grown, she would pick some of them and do mitzvos with them.

She would visit sick people and give them flowers to cheer them up, the family would use some for Shabbos, and she would visit lonely people and bring them flowers.

Batya made everyone happy with her garden.

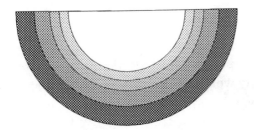

Allowance

Etti Abramcyk

I got allowance once a week,
At first I thought it quite unique,
But once I had my own bills to pay,
I decided to stop the very next day.

I didn't realize, I said to my mom,
That one-two-three my money'd be gone.

A stick of gum used to be fun
Until I had to pay for one.
A piece of candy used to be dandy,
But now the money's lots more handy.

The only way allowance pays
Is if I get a weekly raise!

If you want to read about ETTI ABRAMCYK, turn to page 63.
   She wrote "Allowance" for a school assignment when she was in fourth grade.

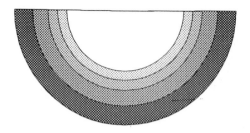

Next Year in Jerusalem

Alisa Rhein

We have to plan this out very carefully," whispered Yaacov. He was in Shmuel Berger's basement. That's where the Haganah always gathered.

"We already have most of it planned," said Shlomo. "The boat is supposed to arrive tomorrow night at 1:45 A.M. Shimon, Yossi, Shmuel, and I will be driving the vans. The rest of you will have to help the people off the boats and hurry them into the vans as quickly as possible."

"We have to be very careful," Yaacov reminded them. "Most of them are not youngsters, and they have suffered terribly."

"Okay, then, it's all set. Everyone knows what to do. Now go home and get a good night's sleep. We will meet here tomorrow at 11:00 P.M."

" 'Next Year in Jerusalem' was part of my sixth-grade English project. My family made *aliyah* when I was entering fifth grade. Until then I had been a student at Hebrew Academy of Long Beach in New York. I like writing, even though all the friends I owe letters to wouldn't believe it." — ALISA RHEIN

The next evening they were all at Shmuel's house on time. By midnight they were at the coast, waiting tensely in the darkness for the boats to arrive. At 1:30 they saw something coming towards them. Quickly the orders were whispered. They were ready.

By the light of the moon, Yaacov could see the fear on the people's faces. He wanted to tell them not to worry, that they were home now, but he had to wait for the signal.

Half an hour later, Shmuel exclaimed, "We made it!" They were safe.

It was starting to get light outside. Yaacov began talking to one of the old men. He seemed so tired and afraid. Yaacov wanted to calm him, to convince him that his dream of coming to Israel had really come true. Yaacov had escaped from Europe several years before, but he still remembered some Yiddish.

"Where are you from?" asked Yaacov.

"From Auschwitz."

"And before that?"

"Before that I had a wonderful family. But the Nazis came, and we had no place to go. They killed my wife and daughter and took my Yankele. I never saw him again. I'm sure he is dead, too. If he had lived, he would be your age now. I look at you, so strong and handsome, and think that's what he would be like, if only..."

"Yankele — that was my name, too. Here they call me Yaacov."

"My name is Moshe. Moshe Rabinovitz."

Yaacov began to tremble. As the tears came down his cheeks, he reached for his father's arms. Now they were both truly home.

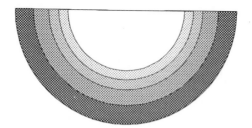

The Couch

Miri Meth

We had just returned from our search and were all sitting down to eat. Mother was serving dinner, Father was reading, and I was trying to think of what to write for my English paper. Brother was reviewing the day's football game and pouting because he couldn't watch the whole game but instead had to come with us on the search. But the search had not gone unrewarded. We had found the couch.

It was a beautiful couch. With its rounded corners and sleek look, it would be perfect in our living room. All we had to do was choose the fabric — which surprisingly was not a simple task. The swatches we had picked all looked nice, but none compared to the amazing, super-extraordinary, champagne-colored Ultrasuede, the Cadillac of fabrics.

"I think we should get it," I said, for I really loved the Ultrasuede.

MIRI METH is a sixteen-year-old junior at Yeshiva of Greater Washington. This is her first published story. She says of "The Couch": "I hope, *be"H*, that our couch will always be filled with guests, friends, family, and happiness."

"I don't," replied my brother. "I hate suede and velvety stuff. They give me the chills!"

"Really?" I said, removing the velvet headband from my head.

"Ak! What are you doing?" screamed Brother. "Get that thing away from me!"

Jabbing the headband in his face, I said, "Ha! Ha! Now I have found your weakness!"

It was three to one. It looked as if we were going to get the Ultrasuede.

"Oooh," I said, "I can't wait to sit on the new couch."

"You're not going to sit on the couch," said Mother.

"What?" shouted Brother and I.

Mother then answered, "The couch will be only for company."

"Why should we spend an extra billion dollars just to *look* at the couch?" asked Brother.

"Maybe we should send it to the American History Museum and have it roped off as a shrine. Forget it, we don't want a new couch," I said.

"This is not a democracy," said Mother.

"And even if it were, we outweigh your vote," said Father.

"We won't argue with that! You guys outweigh us seventy-five to two!" I said, feeling my father's hands slowly closing around my throat.

I cannot believe they are serious, I thought. We are not that kind of family. We go where we please. Anyway, what did we get this extra sixty-dollar lifetime guarantee for? They even have an 800 crisis number just in case you get a stain.

We all started to eat as I whispered into my brother's ear, "I give Mother two weeks of telling us to get off the couch. After that, she'll give up on us!"

The search had come to an end.

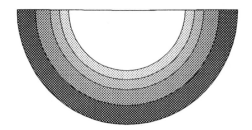

When You Look at Me

Sara Becker

when you look at me
what do you see?
do you see who i am
that i yearn to be free?
do you see that i struggle
i want to be real
but that nobody seems
to understand what i feel
my emotions are stifled
my thoughts can't be said
so i'm confined to a world
within my own head
my thoughts are my friends
because they do not scorn
my heart has been tattered
my pride has been torn
when you look at me
you say "hi" with a smile

The author, who is using a pseudonym, is currently studying in a teachers'
seminary in Jerusalem.

i can see as you sort me
to my place in your file
my type is specific
i'm one of a kind
so you set me aside
all alone in your mind
i'm just somewhat different
so we cannot be friends
because on that sameness
your friendships depend
i don't look just like you
i don't follow the rest
and so in my friendship
you don't want to invest
but did you ever think
that if you'd stop to reach
if you wouldn't hold back
i'd have so much to teach
there are things i could show you
things we could share
but because i am different
you remain unaware
for a person like me
just a bit unconventional
is judged right away
though it's all unintentional
with so much to say
there is no one to hear
the things that i'd share
would just fall on deaf ears
for they're afraid to listen
afraid of the shame
of being with someone

who's not all the same
so i'm left now with no one
in whom i can trust
the pieces of pictures
they now collect dust
the fragments of friendships
are fading away
and i live with my thoughts now
for they will not stray
i put on my show
and i try to pretend
but i'm left with myself
as my own best friend
when you look at me
what do you see?
do you see who i am?
i just want to be me
i must thank you for looking
away through the years
for i've learned whom to trust
when i break down in tears
just one thing i'll tell you
for the chance that you'll hear
the next time you see me
take heed of my fear
and when you look at me
and say "hi" with a smile
be careful where you put me
as you sort out your file

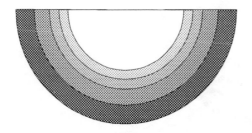

That Big Red Balloon

Batia Elnadav

Time...
That big red balloon.
Your grip loosened,
And now
It's just beyond your reach.
It hangs, suspended —
Taunting and teasing.
You watch it
As it rises
And climbs
Higher and farther
Away.
As it disappears from view,
You wonder —
Where did it go?

If you want to read about BATIA ELNADAV, turn to page 237.

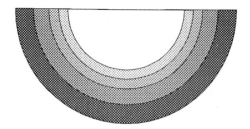

Shosh

Tehila Peterseil

I woke up before dawn on that hot and humid midsummer morning. I was eight years old, and I was late. It was still dark as I groped for a skirt and a top and hurriedly crept down the stairs of my still-sleeping household. I opened the front door and closed it behind me ever so gently. Then, like a shot, I dashed over the hedges and into Shosh's backyard.

I knocked on the old woodshed we used as a base for all our "operations."

"Password!" Shosh barked from inside.

"Operation Sunrise!" I dutifully responded. Then, a bit awkwardly, I whispered, "Captain!"

Hearing the password and her correct rank, Shosh opened the door.

"You're late, Private," she complained, swatting a mosquito off her arm. I followed her into the woodshed and

"I teach in Beit Shemesh, a development town in Israel. I began writing at fourteen and had my first book, *The Secret Files of Lisa Weiss*, published by the time I was sixteen. I live in Jerusalem and am the oldest of nine children (my twin brother is a lot younger — five minutes). I am finishing my second novel." — TEHILA PETERSEIL

noticed she had already brought the crayons and paper.

"My *ima*'s going to kill me," I informed her.

"You'll be back in bed before she wakes up," Shosh assured me. "Just think," she added, "we're the first people up in the whole world."

"How do you know?" I dared to ask.

"I know because I'm nearly ten years old," she reminded me. "Have I ever been wrong?"

Of course she'd never been wrong. If Shosh said something, it had to be true. After all, she was Shosh.

"Now, come on," she commanded, leading me outside. "We have to find a good spot on the lawn to watch the sunrise, and you'd better remember how it looks so you can draw it after."

Shosh selected a spot.

"Lie down!"

"The grass is wet," I complained.

"Lie down!"

Down I went.

"Shosh?"

"What!"

"The mosquitoes were up before us. Do they count?"

"Hush!"

A few minutes later, the first rays of the sun brightened the sky. But I was tired, and it was boring. I decided to sneak a peek at Shosh. She was staring up at the sky in a trance, the most peaceful little smile on her face.

I must have dozed off for a while. When I awoke, the sun was almost completely up. I knew my father and brothers would be up soon, too, getting ready for shul.

I looked at Shosh. Her eyes were still wide-open, and it looked to me like the light of the sun was reflecting off her face. I put my hand on her arm. I felt lucky she had let me watch the sunrise with her.

"It was Hashem's miracle," she sighed.

"In what way?" I asked. I really wanted to know. After all, the sun rose every day, and no one made such a big fuss. But it seemed she didn't even hear me.

When we went back to the woodshed, I kept peeking at Shosh's papers. How could I draw a sunrise if I had slept through it? I didn't dare tell Shosh. What kind of soldier would fall asleep on duty? So I used a lot of yellow and red colors and hoped she wouldn't notice.

She didn't. And I scampered home and into bed just in time to be woken up.

About a week later, summer Little League games were being organized by the shul's youth director, Mr. Levi. This was an "over twelve only" event, but our big sisters let us help them get into shape during practice sessions in our backyards.

Shosh and one of her sisters were the captains, and they chose the sides. Shosh had first pick, and she chose me right away. I felt great. Important. Especially since Shosh was as strong and fast as any of the big girls, and they wanted to be on her team.

Our team was up first. Shosh placed the bat in my hand and whispered, "You can do it!" It sounded like a message from God, a holy mission only I could fulfill. For a moment I actually felt I could do it, but then I remembered my perfect record of never having hit the ball with the bat, a record that didn't escape the notice of any of our sisters.

True to form, I swung three times and never came near the ball.

"That's why you little girls don't have a Little League team," one of Shosh's sisters chided.

I started to cry.

"Don't be a cry-baby!" my sister Yocheved shouted, embarrassed at my babyish behavior.

I cried harder.

Shosh came up behind me and whispered, between clenched teeth, "Stop crying."

I obeyed immediately.

Then she put her arm over my shoulder and, facing the big girls, declared, "We could have our own team if we wanted to."

My sister began to laugh. "You think the shul would ever let you have a team?"

The other girls began to snicker and joke.

They didn't know Shosh like I did. She could do anything she wanted to, anything at all.

"I dare you!" my sister said. "I just dare you."

"You got it!" Shosh answered, a smile on her face.

She would arrange it, and we would do it. That was her way. But I didn't like it one bit.

I was running under the sprinkler with my younger brother and sister, trying hard to cool off from the intense heat, when Shosh suddenly appeared.

"I spoke to Mr. Levi yesterday, and everything is all set. He put a notice on the bulletin board: 'PRETEEN LITTLE LEAGUE STARTS TOMORROW FROM 10:00 TILL 12:00.' I'll pick you up at 9:45. Don't be late."

As quick as she'd appeared she was gone.

The next day we arrived at the shul parking lot way before 10:00.

"We'll wait a few minutes until the others arrive," Shosh told me.

By 10:15 no one else had arrived. Shosh took out the baseball equipment.

"Come on, let's play!" she yelled.

"But there're only the two of us," I explained, "and I can't hit the ball, so that leaves only you."

"When we started the girls' davening section in the youth group, there were only the two of us, too, weren't there?" Shosh countered.

That was true. In the beginning we had half the youth group section to ourselves. (The twenty-odd boys crowded into the other half.) It was great. I sat next to Shosh as she davened. She absolutely awed me with her *kavanah*. I would copy her every move. When she stood, I stood; when she bowed, I bowed; when she cried out, "*Shema Yisrael*," I cried out, too.

After a month, girls started to join in. Soon we had even more kids in our section than the boys had in theirs.

That was Shosh.

Now again, Shosh led me to baseball practice every day. Once I even hit a slow pitch she threw. It went foul, but Shosh ran over to me, cheering and slapping me on the back. She even tried to lift me, but we both fell down laughing. I felt like a real hero.

Then, one morning when she came to pick me up, she said simply, "Today we'll have a team."

I didn't doubt it for a moment, but I felt I had to ask:

"How do you know?"

"I'm nearly ten years old," she reminded me.

Sure enough, six girls were waiting for us when we arrived.

"Where're our prizes?" they asked in unison.

"First we play," Shosh told them, "and then you'll get your prizes."

We played. And played. And played. But Shosh was so much better than everyone else, no matter what sides we chose up, hers always won. After the game, she gave each person a prize. That whole week, she somehow managed to get girls to come and play. But soon, fewer and fewer girls showed up. Exactly one week later, it was just Shosh and I again.

The truth is I sort of liked that.

Fortunately, the Little League season was over. Mr. Levi invited Shosh and me to the awards ceremony. There, Shosh was called upon to give out the girls' Little League awards.

"On behalf of the preteens Little League team...," she announced, beaming at the girls in the front row. She had bribed the other girls to attend the ceremony, promising them each an award their parents would certainly be proud of. "...I would like to thank Mr. Levi for giving us the opportunity to work out and play. The eight girls on the team — " she emphasized the number eight " — will all receive awards for their hard practice sessions. But there is one star player, and we would all like to give her special trophy."

I couldn't believe it when Shosh called me up. My older sisters couldn't believe it either.

I went up and accepted the trophy. I was smiling, and I felt I had somehow entered another world, a wonderful world, the world of Shosh, where everything always worked out and was just perfect.

Best of all, now I would have a trophy just like my big sisters.

"I do have an announcement," Shosh concluded after I was seated. "We girls realize that we are much too mature to hit balls with a stick. That's for people who have enough free time to engage in that kind of activity." She glanced at our sisters, then at Mr. Levi, who was scowling. "So we are retiring from Little League to devote ourselves to more important things."

People didn't know how to react. Some clapped. Others, especially those with athletic children, were not very happy. But Shosh was above it all. She was radiant, and her smile never left her.

That's what I liked about Shosh. Life was always thrilling. Something new was always just around the corner: new forts to build, new playhouses to design, new adventures with fairies and goblins and princesses that seemed to come alive.

So when Shosh burst into my house one evening and said she needed to speak to me "at once," I rushed outside with her, even though we were just about to eat supper.

"Do you know what we're going to do?" Shosh asked, without waiting for an answer. Her face was flushed, almost feverish, and her eyes were bright with a magic that was absolutely contagious. "We're going to fly," she beamed.

"We're going to fly," I echoed, never doubting for a moment.

Flying lessons began the next day. We started with arm-flapping in a stationary position. "You have to learn to flap before you can learn to fly," she lectured. For what seemed like hours, I flapped my arms until she felt I was on the right track.

"First, we'll fly off low things like steps and stones," Shosh explained. "Then we'll advance higher until we can fly off the woodshed roof. Then it will be only a matter of time until we can fly off buildings."

Our flying lessons intensified with every passing day. Shosh constantly prodded me to "flap faster," but no matter how hard I flapped, I couldn't fly from higher than the fourth step in her living room. She, on the other hand, was already flying from the second-floor landing.

"How can you do that?" I marveled.

"I'm nearly ten years old," she reminded me.

Three days before school started, Shosh thought we were ready to fly off the woodshed. By now I had become an expert flapper, but I really didn't feel capable of any major solo flights. Fortunately, Shosh insisted that she fly first.

Shosh was standing on the woodshed roof, her arms stretched out parallel to the ground. That wonderful smile of hers convinced me that if angels could fly, Shosh could, too.

"Here I go," she called down to me. "I'm going to fly." She began flapping her hands up and down, up and down, faster and faster, and then, whoosh, she seemed to glide in the air.

But only for a moment.

Shosh fell to the ground with a terrible thump. I rushed over, crying. Her knees were scraped, and it looked like she might have sprained her arm. When I saw that her nose was bleeding, I cried even harder.

"Stop crying," she scolded me. "It wasn't right this time, but don't worry, we'll get it right next time."

"No, Shosh," I told her, holding back the torrent of tears ready to pour down my face. "There are things that God doesn't want anyone to do...not even you...not even if you're almost ten years old..."

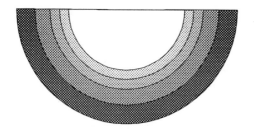

Memories

Breindy Warren

The golden wings of time fly by,
Not always leaving memories that last.
So the person who has witnessed them
Now yearns to go into the past.
To go back to the time and the place
Where a beautiful memory lies,
To see it one last time just before it dies.
To see if it still exists, to be sure it still remains,
To check if it's quite clear and hasn't any stains.
To see if it's just as beautiful as it was
When it was witnessed long ago,
To see it one last time just before letting it go.

"I am fifteen-and-a-half years old and live in the Boro Park section of Brooklyn, where I am in my second year in Bais Yaakov High School. I began writing at the age of ten, shortly after my grandfather passed away. Saddened by his untimely death, I wrote an essay expressing my emotions. I have accumulated a collection of my writings, mostly poems, which I hope to publish.

"'Memories' was written when I was thirteen years old." — BREINDY WARREN